Cultivating Responsible Citizenship

Cultivating Responsible Citizenship
Collective Gardens at the Periphery of Neoliberal Urban Norms

Paul Sherfey

Södertörns högskola

Subject: Ethnology
Research Area: Historical Studies
School of Historical and Contemporary Studies, Baltic
and East European Graduate School

Södertörns högskola
(Södertörn University)
The Library
SE-141 89 Huddinge

www.sh.se/publications

Cover image: Sign at Gemeinschaftsgarten Prachttomate, Berlin, July 2017.
Photo: Paul Sherfey
Cover: Jonathan Robson
Graphic form: Per Lindblom & Jonathan Robson

Södertörn Doctoral Dissertations 227
ISSN 1652–7399

ISBN 978-91-89504-72-1(print)
ISBN 978-91-89504-73-8 (digital)

Abstract

The growing human population is concentrating in urban environments across the globe, leading to urban expansion and densification (OECD, 2020). Consequently, political debates and social movements concerned with urban planning and land use have become ever more relevant. Conflicts over urban space arise where people problematise and challenge dominant land-use rationalities through demonstrations, lobbying, and everyday activism. It follows that one way of critically analysing dominant rationales of urban land use is to examine them in relation to activism and collective action by which these norms are challenged.

Among the many such examples available are what proponents in some countries refer to as *collective gardens,* a subset of community gardens distinguishable by their explicit emphasis on collective management and publicly oriented educational and cultural programming – typically with an expressed intent or mission involving social change and environmental stewardship (see, e.g., Rosol, 2006; Villace, Labajos, Aceituno-Mata et al., 2014). Geographically situated in social environments shaped by capitalism, they can be considered pericapitalist places, "simultaneously inside and outside capitalism" (Tsing, 2015, p. 63) to the extent that their use of urban land and collective forms of social organisation appear inconsistent with the proclivity towards privatisation and a free-market economy characteristic of neoliberal capitalism (cf. Mouffe, 2018). Studying collective gardens in relation to neoliberal capitalism thus has implications for understanding how these places involve political forms of sensemaking, expressing grievances and demands that respond to the dominant political-economic context of contemporary urban life.

Based on this understanding, the aim of this study is to explore discourses about the political significance of collective gardens as places where alternative norms of urban life are developed. What senses of place can be understood to be nurtured in relation to collective gardens? How does this manifest? And what does this convey about citizenship and experiences of urban life in the context of neoliberal capitalism? These questions are investigated through the application of a political discourse framework, supplemented by discursive theories of aesthetics, narratives, and sensemaking to learn about the meanings attributed to collective gardens and how these are constituted in relation to wider social contexts.

The aesthetics of collective gardens are explored through multi-sited research undertaken at gardens across Germany and Sweden to analyse how the materials and design of these gardens reimagine urban space. The study then turns to individual case studies in both nations to explore a range of narratives – first to understand how local history sets up a problem that is solved by the establishment of the garden, and later to analyse how each garden is situated in discourses about contemporary urban development and social life. Through these multiple perspectives on the construction of their meaning and relevance as places of political activity, the study examines how the social critiques being fostered in these places convey a particular ethos of democratic citizenship. Additionally, the complex relationships to responsibility that collective gardens navigate are explored, analysing the duality whereby collectives resist neoliberal capitalist rationalities while also contributing to their objectives.

Keywords: ethnology; urban agriculture; collective action; citizenship; neoliberal capitalism; place; political discourse theory; governmentality; responsibility; gentrification

Sammanfattning
(Summary in Swedish)

En växande befolkning koncentrerar sig alltmer till urbana miljöer världen över, vilket får konsekvenser för såväl tätorternas landareal som deras befolkningstäthet. I kölvattnet av den utvecklingen har både politiska debatter om stadsplanering och markexploatering, och sociala rörelser som mobiliserar kring frågor som rör användning av stadsmiljöer, fått ökad relevans. När medborgare ifrågasätter rådande normer som styr hur det urbana rummet organiseras kan dock konflikter uppstå. En väg mot att bättre förstå vad som står på spel i sådana konflikter är att undersöka kollektiva aktiviteter som på olika sätt utmanar dominerande normer om urbant liv.

Den här avhandlingen närmar sig dessa frågor genom att empiriskt undersöka så kallade *tillsammansodlingar*, det vill säga gemensamma trädgårdar vars tonvikt ligger på kollektiv förvaltning och utåtriktade bildnings- och kulturaktiviteter, vanligtvis med en tydlig inriktning mot samhälls- och miljöfrågor (Rosol, 2006; Villace et.al., 2014). Då dessa i regel är placerade i geografiska och sociala miljöer som i hög grad påverkas av kapitalistiska värden kan de förstås som ett slags perikapitalistiska platser (jfr. Tsing, 2015, p. 63). Deras verksamheter inrymmer både markbruk och social organisering som på olika sätt utmanar och/eller utgör alternativ till nyliberala normer, privat ägande och marknadsekonomi. Genom att studera tillsammansodlingarnas plats i, och relation till, nyliberala städer bidrar avhandlingen med kunskap om hur trädgårdarna kan förstås som en kritik mot den rådande politiska och ekonomiska ordningen samtidigt som de gestaltar möjliga framtida alternativ.

Mot den här bakgrunden syftar avhandlingen till att undersöka diskurser om tillsammansodlingarnas politiska betydelse, samt hur de kan förstås som platser där alternativa normer uttrycks och praktiseras. Utifrån ett teoretiskt ramverk som kombinerar politisk diskursteori och teorier om estetik, narrativitet och meningsskapande besvaras följande frågor: Vilka ”platskänslor” ger trädgårdarna upphov till? Hur uttrycks dessa? Vad förmedlar trädgårdarna om samtida normer om och – konkreta och föreställda – alternativ till samtida medborgarskap i urbana miljöer?

Tillsammansodlingarnas estetik undersöks genom observationer av ett större antal trädgårdar i Sverige och Tyskland, då med analytiskt fokus på hur deras konkreta utformning och användning av material gestaltar alternativa föreställningar om det urbana rummet och dess potential. Därefter undersöks två specifika trädgårdar i Stockholm och Berlin. Dels undersöks trädgårdarnas respektive "platshistorier" och hur dessa beskriver olika problemformuleringar som odlingarna ska bidra till att lösa. Dels undersöks vilka diskurser om det urbana rummet och urbant liv som kringgärdar trädgårdarna på ett mer övergripande plan. I relation till detta diskuteras bland annat hur olika idéer om – och sätt att utöva medborgerligt ansvar på – tar sig i uttryck inom ramarna för trädgårdsverksamheterna, på ett sätt som visserligen kan förstås som ett sätt att utöva motstånd mot nyliberala normer men som samtidigt på flera sätt kan sägas uppfylla nyliberala ideal om ansvarstagande. Utifrån detta argumenterar avhandlingen för att trädgårdarna styrs av ett demokratiskt etos, men problematiserar också deras komplexa och till viss del motsägelsefulla relation till nyliberal rationalitet.

Nyckelord: etnologi; stadsodling; kollektiv handling; plats; medborgarskap; ansvar; politisk diskursteori; nyliberal kapitalism; governmentalitet; gentrifiering

Acknowledgements

It's strange to put my own name on this book as it was only possible through the support and inspiration of others. More people than I can possibly count – or thank – have contributed to bringing the pages that follow to fruition.

First among these is my husband, Eric Amory Strader. It's been a journey – across many years, geographies, and emotional states. Thank you for your support and your patience. Though the journey from idea to manuscript was not always a smooth one, as with life, I have been honoured to share each day of it with you.

I am grateful to have had Jenny Gunnarsson Payne and Maria Zackariasson as my supervisors. You each must have read this text (or versions of it) until your heads spun with all the different ideas and lines of enquiry being worked out along the way. Thank you for your time and patience as I worked this project out in my own mind, as well as your understanding when life got in the way in some not insignificant ways. I couldn't have wished for a better pairing of perspectives, and I feel that I've become a better editor because of you both. Thank you for inspiring me to be a better researcher and writer, challenging my interpretations, and suggesting paths to pursue to make the final product the best it could be.

Thank you to my informants at Vintervikens trädgård for the years I was privileged to spend with you. It was a pleasure to collaborate both in research and gardening, to learn from you all about your passions and experiences and discuss what the garden means to you. Thank you for your time and knowledge. My appreciation also extends to informants elsewhere in Sweden and Germany who took to the time to speak about the project in its preliminary stages; though your comments may not have made it into the final text or the scope of the project as it shifted form, the spirit of those conversations lives on through it. Thank you all for the work you do to provide a special sense of place to your communities and for the care you provide to other forms of life.

My colleagues in the Department of Ethnology at Södertörn University have helped keep me grounded and made me feel at home. Writing this from halfway across the world, I still feel the presence of your kindness and support. In addition to my supervisors, thank you to Aleksandra Reczuch,

Ann Runfors, Daniel Bodén, Daniel Gunnarsson, Elisabeth Wollin, Florence Fröhlig, Jenny Ingridsdotter, Kim Silow Kallenberg, Maria Vallström, Petra Österlund, and Regina Skarp. Thank you all for welcoming me and for the opportunity to be your peer.

My sincerest appreciation to the readers who have provided incisive comments, reflections, and recommendations along the way. This includes the early feedback I received from colleagues including Elisabeth Wollin, Florence Fröhlig, Maria Vallström, and Petra Österlund; the reviews of specific chapters at national ethnology retreats by Alf Arvidsson, Evelina Liliequist, Helena Hörnfeldt, Helena Larsson, Ida Hughes Tidlund, Oscar Pripp, and Åsa Andersson; as well as the comprehensive manuscript reviews from Barbro Blehr and Magnus Öhlander. Thank you for the enriching discussions and the insights you provided to help me clarify my arguments and rethink the direction of my analysis when needed.

Through my affiliation with the Centre for Baltic and East European Studies (CBEES), I was provided many opportunities to talk with and learn from other researchers and get to know many wonderful colleagues at Södertörn and elsewhere. I especially want to thank Natalia Durkalec, Philipp Seuferling, Maria Brock, Lovisa Olsson, and Kateryna Zorya for helping CBEES feel like home and for your friendship even once we dispersed across the campus to our respective departments.

As a project funded by *Östersjöstiftelsen* [The Foundation for Baltic and Eastern European Studies], I am thankful for the financial support that made this all possible.

Vancouver, February 2024

Contents

1. Introduction

As the growing human population becomes concentrated in urban environments across the globe, these environments have increased in overall population and population density (OECD, 2020).[1] While these increases have brought with them the territorial expansion of urbanised areas as well as densification and infill of existing urban land, these trends do not go uncontested. Political debates and social movements concerned with urban planning and land use have become ever more pertinent. In this study, collective gardens are explored as one such challenge to urban land use norms, a form of collective action through which urban agriculture perturbs the status quo of contemporary urban development.

While land development policies and collective action may each be local in expression, cities themselves are not self-sustaining political entities; they are situated within networks of international production, services, and investment that governments, businesses, and collective action groups alike must navigate. Normative discourses about spatial use and land value are entangled in global politics and transnational economics, a social context that is often spoke of as a neoliberal capitalist one. As political theorist Chantal Mouffe (2018) argues, this normative discourse involves a conception of society and the individual

> constituted by a set of political-economic practices aimed at imposing the rule of the market – deregulation, privatisation, fiscal austerity – and limiting the role of the state to the protection of private property rights, free markets and free trade. (pp. 11–12)[2]

---

[1] According to The World Bank (2022a, 2022b), rural and urban population estimates in 1960 were 2.01 billion and 1.02 billion, respectively. As of 2020, the urban population had increased 400 percent, to approximately 4.36 billion people; meanwhile, the rural population had only increased by 69 percent, to approximately 3.4 billion. Data from the OECD (2020) shows that this significant increase in urban population has predominantly been accommodated by increased densification, accounting for 50–60% of population growth in cities between 1975 and 2015; the remaining growth is accounted for by territorial expansion of cities and towns becoming cities.

[2] A similar argument is made by economic geographer David Harvey (2005), who describes neoliberal governance as a political and economy rationality that "proposes that human well-being can best be advanced by liberating individual entrepreneurial freedoms and skills within an institutional framework characterised by strong private property rights, free markets, and free trade" (p. 2).

Despite its normative influence on political and economic matters, however, neoliberal capitalism is by no means an absolute condition of society. As Mouffe and co-author Ernesto Laclau (1985) argue, the manner in which society is organised is "far from being the only natural or societal order, [it] is the expression of certain power relations" (p. xvi); consequently, scrutinising the taken for granted nature of "the so-called 'globalised world'" can help to understand contemporary power relations, the premises on which authority is asserted, and the problems inherent in this order (ibid.).

Accordingly, dominant rationales of urban land use do not go uncontested, no matter how pervasive or taken for granted they may be. One way of problematising and scrutinising them is therefore to examine activism and collective action through which they are challenged. At a local level, contestation can manifest in collective mobilisation to preserve public spaces from demolition or privatisation, demonstrating for the rights of homeless people to inhabit public space, as well as advocacy to alter zoning regulations, protests of proposed development projects, and lobbying that occurs to inform budgets and strategic plans for public space and community resources. In addition to these types of action occurring at discrete points in time, collective action can also take longer-term, place-based forms, observable, for instance, when people come together to squat a location or establish new or atypical uses for urban public space.

Among these latter examples are a movement of what are described by proponents in some locations as *collective gardens*, which are the object of this study. As a subset of community gardens, collective gardens are distinguishable by their explicit emphasis on collective management and publicly oriented educational and cultural programming, typically with an expressed intent or mission involving social and environmental change.[3] Looking at collective gardens through the lens of their collectivised food production and land management, they can be seen to contrast with the predominant division of urban space into private and commercial properties and public lands managed directly by government institutions. Due to this anti-normative character, they can be analysed as manifestations of *prefigurative politics*, a concept described by social theorist Carl Boggs (1977) to describe "the embodiment, within the ongoing political practice of a movement, of those forms of social relations, decision-making, culture, and human experience that are the ultimate goal" (p. 100). Furthermore, because

---

[3] See for example: Partageons les Jardins (2017), Rosol (2006), and Villace, Labajos, Aceituno-Mata et al. (2014).

the people who care for these sites can be seen to take a hands-on approach to social change through the activities organised in these gardens, prefigurative politics can be understood as consistent with a democratic conception of citizenship, both emphasising active political practice (cf. Mouffe, 2018).

As collective gardens are geographically and economically situated in social environments shaped by capitalism, they can be considered *pericapitalist* places, "simultaneously inside and outside capitalism" (Tsing, 2015, p. 63).[4] They exist in relation to the activity of the market economy while at the same time cultivating alternative relationships to urban space that resist any pretences to a uniform or homogenous economic system. By doing so, they reflect practices of *commoning*, the creation and maintenance of spaces for common benefit through collective and non-commodified means (Harvey, 2012, pp. 73–74; see also, Colding & Barthel 2013; Eizenberg, 2012; Müller 2012). Understanding collective gardens as pericapitalist in relation to the consumerist tendencies of neoliberal capitalism, the very notion of 'collective' gardens thus alludes to the complex nature of these places; they exist within regimes of private property and social environments that privilege individualism and entrepreneurialism which, at first glance, would not appear to be conducive to collectivism or commoning.

It is within such political and economic relationships that the prefigurative politics of collective gardens can be made sense of, as they constitute the social conditions which these gardens operate in reaction to. Furthermore, the implementation of urban agriculture to achieve social reform is itself not a new phenomenon. Since the establishment of the earliest allotment gardens in industrial towns and cities in the eighteenth century, there has been a tradition of movements which, especially in Europe and North America, have been characterised by an intent to solve social problems with an underlying belief that food cultivation can promote socially desirable norms and values. Just as preceding urban agricultural initiatives developed in relation to normative social values characteristic of the periods in which they developed, how then do collective gardens make sense in relation to the neoliberal capitalist urban contexts in which they are often established?

---

[4] In describing pericapitalist sites thusly, Anna Lowenhaupt Tsing (2015) distinguishes this from non-capitalist, the latter being reserved "for forms of value making outside capitalist logics" (p. 296). I share her understanding that "this is not a classificatory hierarchy but rather a way to explore ambiguity" in relationship to capitalism (ibid.).

Aim and Research Questions

Because I consider them to be an example of urban agriculture as a mechanism for social change, the aim of this study is to explore the political significance of collective gardens. Discourses about what a place represents are articulated through their form and design as well as through language used to speak about them. Consequently, a political discourse framework is applied to study the aesthetics and narratives of these gardens in relation to their broader social contexts, to thereby learn more about the alternative social norms being sought, negotiated, and nurtured in these places. Informed by this understanding, three research questions are explored in this study:

> 1. What sense of place can be understood to be nurtured in relation to collective gardens, and what does this convey about citizenship and experiences of urban life in the context of neoliberal capitalism?

> 2. Looked at aesthetically, how does the material culture of collective gardens situate them in relation to their contemporary urban environments, and what can their aesthetic expression be interpreted to convey about alternative norms of urban life?

> 3. How do narratives about collective gardens constitute them in relation to the historical and contemporary socio-political contexts in which they were established and now operate, and what significance is associated or attributed to these gardens in doing so?

Place-based relationships are discussed in terms of *sense of place* to emphasise interpretive (or sensemaking) practices associated with places. The form a place takes is the product of social interaction, an outcome of the meeting and negotiation of preferences, values, and experiences (Massey, 1991, pp. 28–29). Articulating a sense of place involves interpreting its significance in relation to other places, and as distinct from them (ibid.; see also Feld & Basso, 1996, p. 11). Sense of place, as a concept, thus emphasises how places *make sense* because they are *being made sense of* through varied means of expression that articulate relationships across space and time (Massey, 2005).

While the first question is more overarching in nature, the other two focus on aesthetics and narratives as specific forms of expression through which a sense of place is articulated. As such, investigating the latter two questions provides a foundation upon which to address the first. To answer each, two forms of collective gardens in two national contexts are analysed – *Gemein-*

schaftsgärten and *tillsammansodlingar*, as they are commonly referred to in Germany and Sweden, respectively. The aesthetics of collective gardens are explored through multi-sited research at collective gardens in Germany and Sweden, whereas narratives are explored through a case study in each nation.

The remainder of this chapter outlines the argument for carrying out research in line with these aims and questions. Beginning by situating the phenomenon of collective gardening in historical context, a case is made for researching them as contemporary manifestations of social change and prefigurative politics through the medium of urban agriculture. The project is then discussed as it relates to, and complements, research on activism and community gardening.

Background: Urban Agriculture for Social Progress

Growing food in urban settings is by no means a new phenomenon. Community and collective food cultivation have often been a part of the agricultural practice of many cultures around the world, alongside independent, slave-based, and feudalistic models of agricultural labour (Rivera, et al., 2014). In Europe and North America, however, the specific form of collective gardens studied here are a much more recent phenomenon. Based on mapping undertaken in the course of fieldwork, most had been in existence less than a decade, and very few had reached two decades of operation.

Despite the recentness of this approach to organising urban agriculture, I believe it is informative to see collective gardens in relation to allotment gardens and community gardens as two ubiquitous forms of urban agriculture preceding them. In addition to a two-century tradition of allotment gardening which emerged independently in various cities in Europe before spreading to North America and other parts of the world, collective gardens are an increasingly common form of community gardens. While collective, community, and allotment gardens each may differ in how land use and land management are organised (based on urban gardening research to date), it is possible to discern a genealogical trajectory that unites the three forms of urban gardening. Though historically shifting in terms of what social problems their proponents attempted to mitigate, all have been concerned with problems connected to urban life, premised on rationales that equated food cultivation with social betterment in urban capitalist contexts. Framing collective gardens within this context thus helps to understand their significance in relation to other approaches to urban agriculture as a mechanism for social change or social reform. The motivators of urban agriculture movements – whatever the form – are entwined with the interest of their proponents and what they consider pressing issues of their time.

Allotment Gardens in the Age of Industry

When industrialisation began to fundamentally alter the nature of work and settlement patterns in much of Europe and North America from the mid-eighteenth century onwards, a distancing from food production co-occurred, as predominantly agricultural and handicraft economies rapidly shifted to manufacturing-based ones. Alongside the development of factory towns and increasing urbanisation came the emergence of *allotment gardens*, constituted by "a collective of garden plots that lie adjacent to each other, effectively subdividing a larger piece of land that is dedicated to gardens" (Bellows, 2004, p. 250). From the outset of their establishment, these gardens were expounded as solution for addressing social ills and public health issues attributed to urban life, and at times explicitly promoted as a means of guaranteeing a sedentary workforce in service of industry (ibid.).[5] Alongside industry-driven initiatives, allotments also developed as philanthropic endeavours, with local rulers, poor relief societies, church leaders, and others awarding parcels of municipal or church land to impoverished citizens. These *poor gardens*, as they were sometimes called, were intended to address pressing hunger and food security issues in the city, providing the poor and labourers – who could not otherwise meet their nutritional needs through their wages – with access to arable land (Buchan, 1769, p. 144; Flavell, 2003, pp. 97, 103).

A commonality between many of these philanthropic allotment gardens was their proponents' interest in promoting specific social dynamics within the family. There was an assumption, or intent, that agricultural labour could rehabilitate those on the margins of society, making them more 'respectable' by teaching morals, conditioning obedience, and developing a sense of autonomy, self-confidence and pride (Acker, 1907; Baratay, 1997, p. 64). It was not uncommon for such gardens to be espoused as alternatives to financial help, argued according to a belief that access to land would help the

---

[5] Some of the earliest examples of parcel or allotment gardens in Europe emerged in England and what is now Germany. Often leased by noblemen to craftspeople and workers at a low rate for household use, they quickly spread among manufacturing towns, with worker health being attributed to the exercise and healthy diet they were seen to provide (see e.g., Buchan, 1769; Flavell, 2003). By the middle of the nineteenth century, it was not uncommon for industrialists and railway companies in many countries to provide *workers gardens* as an income supplement and means of ensuring a sedentary workforce (see, e.g., Bellows, 2004, p. 250; Keshavarz & Bell, 2016, pp. 15–16).

poor to take care of themselves (Schäfer-Biermann, Westermann, Vahle, & Pott, 2016). Additionally, a number of initiatives – such as *Schrebergärten* in Germany and *jardins ouvriers* in France – were developed with the express intent to provide healthy physical activity as a matter of social order, especially, but not exclusively, for the working poor (L'œuvre des jardins ouvriers, 1898; Lancry, 1899; Liesemer, 2019; Lothane, 1992)[6]. Similar *relief gardens* emerged in the United States during the Great Depression, which in addition to providing poor relief through self-provisioning, were also envisioned as places where new immigrants and established communities could interact, the latter helping the former to learn the "American way" (Eizenberg, 2013, p. 17; Villace, Labajos, Aceituno-Mata, Morales, & Pardo de Santayana, 2014, p. 56). While many disappeared from cities in the United States after the Second World War, allotment gardens persisted in much of Europe, increasingly functioning as recreational spaces as living conditions improved in the post-war decades (Boulianne, 2001, p. 66).

Regardless of the form taken or intentions associated with them, each type of allotment was articulated with values and concerns circulating in public discourse, promoting a form of urban agriculture as a solution to problems in urban industrial societies. Rather than being attributed any single type of benefit, values of moral discipline, social organisation, and patriotism often manifested in conjunction with concerns of labour rights, public health, and food security. As allotments shifted from church, government, or philan-thropist-led projects towards union-driven and self-organised initiatives with their own national associations, they also became settings where emerging organisational trends were implemented, not least models of collective management (Bergquist, 1996). Increasingly managed as voluntary associations, allotments and their national interest groups came to operate according to syndicalist and other democratic decision-making approaches, contemporaneous with a global trend of self-organising among trade and

---

[6] The focus on social dynamics within (predominantly lower class) families in the creation of *jardins ouvriers* and similar gardens elsewhere was built upon a tradition of *colonies agricoles* [agricultural colonies], emerging in France the 1830s, themselves preceded by similar initiatives dating at least as far back as the 1760s in France and neighbouring countries. *Colonies agricoles* had a specific focus on reforming the youth of the French underclass, starting with delinquent youth and eventually expanding to include orphans, homeless children and those sent away by their parents. These agricultural penitentiaries were a result of government-funded research of the American penitentiary system, conducted by Alexis de Tocqueville and Gustave Beaumont. Tocqueville was himself a founding member of one of France's first agricultural penitentiaries, his studies informing the coercive behavioural technologies used to cultivate a particular discipline and work ethic (see Foucault, 2007, p. 234; Tocqueville & Beaumont, 1833).

labour unions in the late nineteenth and early twentieth centuries (Nilsen, 2014).

Community Gardens in the Post-Industrial City

As cities in the United States, Canada, and much of Europe began to de-industrialise in the final decades of the twentieth century, new forms of urban gardening began to emerge. As with allotments, these too were promoted as solutions to contemporaneous social issues, also sharing a belief in the potential of agricultural practice to mitigate or solve certain negative effects of urban life. They differed, however, in the social concerns at issue, and thus the changes being sought via their establishment.

Rather than family allotments focused on food security, poor relief, social order, or recreation, these newer forms of urban agriculture were characterised by a shift towards collective activity among the community of gardeners cultivating these sites. In many cases, gardeners began to organise activities in addition to gardening, occasionally even engaging non-gardening publics. Known in English as *community gardens*, these gardens are characterised by their mixture of individual plots with collective management of common areas where "certain plots, trees, or fruit bushes that produce something available to all who participate in the garden" (Bellows, 2004, p. 250; Lawson, 2005, p. 3).

A common characteristic among early community gardens was that they tended to come about through the collective initiative of community residents, as opposed to the initiative of a local politician, religious leader, or organisation. In many cases, these groups first obtained land through squatting or guerrilla gardening, and only later worked with local leaders and non-profit organisations to negotiate use agreements and leases (Eizenberg, 2013, pp. 18–19). Many cities across the world have since developed protocols and policies for identifying and approving requests for groups to develop community gardens, reducing the proliferation of garden squats. Whatever the process through which they came about, community gardens involved a departure from both the philanthropic impetus of eighteenth and nineteenth century allotment gardens and the labour, public health, and patriotic impulses that increasingly characterised the allotment movement from the late nineteenth to the mid-twentieth century.

An emphasis on local food and local community emerged as central values from the outset. The earliest example of a community garden of this type is often credited to Liz Christy, who, along with several other local activists, formed a garden in New York City in 1973 as a response to the recession then causing hardship among poorer residents who were already living in conditions of urban decay with reduced access to communal green spaces. Within five years, the group of Green Guerrillas who formed out of that garden had worked with local residents to develop similar gardens in many of the poorest and most blighted areas of the city, as well as working with the city to negotiate leases and institute a city agency for overseeing and promoting community gardens (Eizenberg, 2013, p. 16). Their actions imagined future alternatives to normative values and uses of urban land at the time, reclaiming unused land to use productively for social and nutritional benefit (p. 19).

This practice spread in the 1970s and 1980s throughout North America and Western Europe, taking on momentum elsewhere in the world in the 1990s and 2000s (see, e.g., Argaillot, 2014; Barron, 2017; Gómez Rodríguez, 2014; Kanosvamhira & Tevera, 2023; Nettle, 2010), often referencing earlier initiatives as inspiration. Like the allotment movement, proponents of community gardens advocated for them in relation to healthy eating, recreation, and connection to the earth; but they also emphasised discourses about local food production and sustainability, presenting them as a response to the increased reliance of many countries on globalised, resource intensive food chains (Turner, Henryks, & Pearson, 2011). Inspired specifically by examples from the United States and later the United Kingdom, many community gardens elsewhere began to articulate goals pertaining to social cohesion, community building, and local revitalisation (Rosol, 2010, p. 209). In the *Gemeinschaftsgärten* of German-speaking Europe, a more specific social focus emerged in the development of *Interkulturelle Gärten* [intercultural gardens], formed with the express intent of supporting refugees and immigrants to develop local social networks with more established residents and engage in mutual cultural exchange through the common 'language' of food cultivation (Appel, Grebe, & Spitthöver, 2011, pp. 37–38; Zwanzig, 2012). While initially driven by community residents, many local governments and religious and non-profit organisations began to establish or promote community gardens, just as had been done with allotment gardens.

Although a departure from allotment gardens in the specific intents their initiators proposed, community gardens nonetheless continued a tradition (at least in Europe and the Americas) of promoting urban agriculture as a solution to social problems, premised on a belief that food cultivation could promote socially desirable behaviours. The difference between these two garden forms, as surmisable from research on each, could be observed in the problems they were believed to solve through their respective approaches to urban agriculture and the values thus privileged and nurtured in these places. Allotment initiatives were typically promoted for their potential to alter individual behaviours seen as problematic, or to improve personal circumstances that affected one's ability to contribute to industrial production (see, e.g., Bellows, 2004; Liesemer, 2019; L'œuvre des jardins ouvriers, 1898). By contrast, community gardens typically developed with a mission to promote ideals of interpersonal and place-based relationships that were seen to be weakened by neoliberal political and economic policies in post-industrial cities (see Cumbers, Shaw, Crossan, & McMaster, 2017; DelSesto, 2015; Tornaghi & Van Dyck, 2015; del Viso, Fernández Casadevante, & Morán, 2017; Follmann & Viehoff, 2015).

Drawing inspiration from traditional forms of urban agriculture and ecological, social, and global justice movements to different degrees, community gardens have continued to spread around the world in recent decades. In doing so, their forms and imperatives have differed according to the local settings in which they take root. Since the early 2000s, newer forms of community gardens have emerged in many countries, characterised by an increasingly public orientation, in contrast to a focus on developing a community amongst only participating gardeners. Many sites are characterised by collective cultivation, as well as hosting collective action initiatives, community events, and political education (see Partageons les Jardins, 2017; Rosol, 2006). Rather than a focus on certain social groups – such as the poor, workers, industrial labourers – or family cohesion, these gardens have been promoted as venues from which to reorient urban social life as well as relationships to land and food (Cumbers, Shaw, Crossan, & McMaster, 2017; D'Andréa & Tozzi , 2014; del Viso, Fernández Casadevante, & Morán, 2017; Gregory, Leslie, & Drinkwater, 2016; Kingsley & Townsend, 2006; Mousselin & Scheromm, 2015; Turner, Henryks, & Pearson, 2011). It is this more recent subset of community gardens where the attention of this study is directed.

Collective Gardens: Defining the Object of Study

Because I am interested in *collective* gardens as a subset of *community* gardens, clarification on the definitions of each term in relation to one another is warranted. As mentioned earlier, the term community garden – at least in the English language – can in fact encompass a wide range of actual forms, at its most basic being "neighbourhood gardens in which individuals have their own plots yet share in the garden's overall management" (Lawson, 2005, p. 3). However, as Turner et al. (2011) note, and much existing research exemplifies, the term community garden is used as an emic (that is, 'insider's') term that encompasses a wide range of forms, practices, and intentions – a fact which is seldom discussed critically within the literature (p. 490). Distinguished from traditional allotment gardens by an increased emphasis on collective management and common use – as opposed to private plots designated for individual households – community gardens have generally been initiated with collective, organic gardening as a unifying activity. However, there are different means by which land is appropriated, arguments for why it is done, approaches taken and types of activities available in addition to gardening.

The community nature of these gardens is thus often in the shared responsibility for maintenance of common areas by the community of gardeners, with planter boxes or sections of land otherwise assigned to individuals or families for their own use; at times, 'community' simply reflects their location within a community, on community land. While open to visitors, the events that occur are usually organised by and provided for the benefit of those who actively maintain the garden. Because of this ambiguity, comparative studies, and even the research that many case studies work from, apply a common name to what are, in fact, a wide range of garden forms with different organisational structures and ways of working. This seems to go unproblematised in many studies – except in a handful of cases where researchers are specifically evaluating how different community garden arrangements work (see Boulianne, 2001; del Viso, Fernández Casadevante, & Morán, 2017; Mousselin & Scheromm, 2015; Rosol, 2006). In other words, there is not always an awareness that different findings or outcomes correlate with different starting points, garden forms, or objects of study. For these reasons, a more specific definition was needed that could be consistently applied to describe comparable gardens before identifying sites for fieldwork.

While I encountered a similar ambiguity in German research of *Gemeinschaftsgärten* [community or fellowship gardens], Marit Rosol's (2006) research was an exception. In order to make more generalisable findings, she specified a subset of *Gemeinschaftsgärten* as her object of study: "Open spaces, which are characterised by their use for gardening, communal care of the area, and an orientation towards a general public" (p. 2; my translation). Contrasting with the majority of community gardens, these gardens put more emphasis on communal care and engagement with the public – not just the community of gardeners sharing the space. Parallel with this distinction, regional and national garden networks in France made use of a typology, differentiating types and forms of community gardens by how they were organised and managed. Whereas the most basic form of community gardens in France were the *jardins familiers* [family gardens] due to the mixture of family parcels with common space, sites comparable to those in Rosol's study were referred to as *jardins partagés* [shared gardens], the name itself emphasising how they were used and oriented:

> Gardens designed, managed, and animated collectively with the aim of developing local social ties through social, cultural, and educational activities, and being accessible to the public. (Partageons les Jardins, 2017; my translation) [7]

What was emphasised by Rosol, and conveyed in the description of *jardins partagés*, was the existence of a subset of community gardens for which collective management and public access were explicitly emphasised. Such gardens were oriented towards a wider public, not contained to actively participating gardeners. By organising activities such as collective food production, informal education, guerrilla gardening, participatory design, and cultural entertainment, they often convened a larger public to explore alternative ways to organise and experience everyday life.

In a study carried out by Villace, Labajos, Aceituno-Mata et al. (2014), they explicitly refer to the gardens they researched in Madrid – overall quite similar to *jardins partagés* and the *Gemeinschaftsgärten* at the centre of Rosol's study – as *huertos urbanos colectivos* [urban collective gardens], motivating this choice based on a key distinction with community gardens:

> The term 'collective' is used instead of 'community' because in several cases they are not being initiated by an institution, but rather by a free association of citizens with common interests who make decisions jointly, although the allocation of what is produced and of tasks undertaken are not carried out in a communal manner. (p. 62; my translation)

Because of the emphasis in this description on collective action and collective impact in how participants work, organise, and engage a wider public in their activities, I have opted to utilise the term *collective gardens* as an English translation for the form of gardens being explored here. In refining a definition for the purposes of this study, however, I draw upon the descriptions of

---

[7] Partageons les Jardins is a regional network of *jardins partagés* covering the administrative region of Occitanie [Occitania] in southwestern France. The description is a distillation of a more comprehensive description provided in the charter of the national organisation to which the regional network is a signatory. Compare with Le Jardin dans Tous Ses États (2012).

jardins partagés and the variety of *Gemeinschaftsgärten* studied by Rosol as complementary examples of this genre of garden. In doing so, my intent is to encompass the commonality of the three under a term which can be applied to other, similar gardens. Consequently, for the purposes of this study, *a collective garden is a garden designed, managed, and animated collectively, and with an orientation towards the general public through social, cultural, and educational activities.*

Previous Research

Community Gardens and Allotments

As discussed earlier, research on community gardens works from an often-unproblematised use of the term that does not account for the wide variance in what the name describes. Nonetheless, as a related – and arguably derivative – form of urban gardening, there is value in considering collective gardens in relation to research on community gardens. Many community gardens share some of the features according to which collective gardens are being defined in this study. Whatever the constraints or limitations of comparison may be, community gardens demonstrate that there continue to be social and political intents and implications for urban agriculture. Furthermore, as I consider collective gardens to be a derivative form of community gardens, my findings in this study may have relevance or applicability within the broader field of community gardening research.

The scope of research on community gardens is diverse, exploring a wide variety of approaches and interests, and doing so from an impressive range of disciplinary perspectives – most associated with the human, social, and natural sciences, but also some in the fields of public health, architecture, and even law. [8] In the past twenty years alone, two key trends that emphasise the political potential of these gardens have been discernible in research – explicit in the positioning of some studies, implied in others where research results included policy recommendations.

The first of these trends, noticeable from the late 1990s encompasses a body of evaluative research on community gardens and similar forms of urban agricultural practice, prioritising investigations of the social, environmental, and public health impacts of engagement in these initiatives. Studies

---

[8] Because this is a review of research to date, and the majority of research discusses community gardens in general (not collective gardens specifically), I have chosen to retain usage of the term community garden for purposes of this review. For examples of studies which reflect what I term collective gardens, see Rosol (2006), Villace et al. (2014), Follmann and Viehoff (2015).

from around the globe have suggested strong correlations between engagement in community gardens and improved *trust, inclusion and empowerment of marginalised communities* (Armstrong, 2000; Boulianne, 2001; Cumbers, Shaw, Crossan, & McMaster, 2017; Halweil & Nierenberg, 2006; Kingsley & Townsend, 2006; Lööw, 2010; Wakefield, Yeudall, Taron, Reynolds, & Skinner, 2007); *physical and psychological health* (Grahn & Stigsdotter, 2003; Halweil & Nierenberg, 2006; Kaplan & Kaplan, 2005); and *economic sustainability and food security* (Feenstra, McGrew, & Campbell, 1999; Koc, MacRae, Mougeot, & Welsh, 1999; Monroe-Santos, 1998; Mougeot, 2005; Smit, Ratta, & Nasr, 1996; van Veenhuizen, 2006). More recent studies in this vein have moved from case-making research to analyse organisational structures and factors that affect garden sustainability, impact, and longevity (Boulianne, 2001; Firth, Maye, & Pearson, 2011; Mousselin & Scheromm, 2015).

From about 2010 onwards, another trend in research is apparent, particularly within sociology, human geography, and affiliated disciplines. This trend can also be described as one of evaluative research, but with a focus on evaluating the extent to which these gardens realise theoretical concepts. Compared with the more implicit political treatment of earlier research, researchers have increasingly applied a more explicitly political view of community gardens – in some cases referring to them in terms of *political gardening* – through a focus on the political struggles faced by participants, political antagonisms with city government or landholders, or the experimentation with spatial use and social structures observed to take place (Certomà & Tornaghi, 2015; Follmann & Viehoff, 2015; Tornaghi & Van Dyck, 2015). In this more explicitly political approach, researchers have used community gardens and similar political gardening forms as case studies to explore whether, how, and to what extent they operate as manifestations of concepts such as *the right to the city* (Linn, 1999; Müller, 2012; Purcell & Tyman, 2015), *urban commons* (Eizenberg, 2012; 2013; Follmann & Viehoff, 2015), *urban citizenship* (DelSesto, 2015; Demailly, 2014), and *autonomous geographies* (Chatterton & Pickerill, 2010), and through these also make recommendations for government policy to support them (Beilin & Hunter, 2011; Bonow & Normark, 2016, 2018; Colding & Barthel, 2013; Rosol, 2006). Across these studies, one can discern a common interest in exploring how community gardens "[question] the laws and social norms of society and a creative desire to constitute non-capitalist, collective forms of politics, identity, and citizenship" (Pickerill & Chatterton, 2006, p. 1).

Broadly speaking, these varied lines of enquiry can be interpreted as evaluative or case-making research. As with the proponents of community and allotment gardens, researchers too have promoted them as, or assessed them in terms of, solving pressing social issues or fulfilling vital social needs. While they often do give voice to participants through ethnographic research, this project complements and builds upon the wide body of knowledge and disciplinary perspectives of existing research with an ethnological study, engaging intentionally with the material environment of gardens and their political significance as constituted aesthetically and narratively by those involved with them. Because I approach collective gardens as places of prefigurative politics, it is consistent with the political approach of contemporary research in the field, using theoretical concepts to the extent they facilitate an *exploration* rather than *evaluation*. I consider this an appropriate addition to existing research on urban agriculture, as it contributes a discourse analysis of collective gardens to address *how* they are collectively constituted and attributed significance through material and linguistic means.

A significant influence on this study has been Magnus Bergquist's (1996) archival research into the history of the allotment gardening movement in the Swedish city of Gothenburg. Like others who have researched allotments (see Baratay, 1997; Bellows, 2004; Flavell, 2003), his dissertation explores how people seek to realise social change through a specific form of urban agriculture. Bergquist's particular contribution, relevant to this study, is that he expands beyond concerns of social reform to analyse the aesthetics and organisational models of allotments as reflective of utopian discourses. Among other things, he examines how these gardens were articulated within competing discourses of the ideal city life and the relationship between individual and society during periods of social change that saw Swedish cities industrialise and modernise, thus influencing aesthetic and ethical judgements made about them (Bergquist, 1996, pp. 278–282). From this, Bergquist engages with antagonisms involving rationalisation, the division of labour, and power relations that circulated in municipal and association politics. As he argues, the allotment associations he studied simultaneously reproduced the existing social order while also orienting themselves towards developing a new one. In light of this, his findings can be seen as compatible with the prefigurative political potential of urban agriculture argued for here, underscoring the complex relationship between political activity, aesthetics, and the social visions they are premised upon, through which alternative forms of social relations become embodied within the ongoing political practice of collectives working for social change (Boggs, 1977, p. 100).

Environmental Humanities

Because this study addresses how people make sense of collective gardens, as places constituted in relation to their physical and social environments, ethnographic research in the environmental humanities has provided inspiration and ontological considerations for material collection and analysis. Studying the interplay between humans and their environment, research of an environmental humanistic character takes up the cultural construction of knowledge and how this is entangled with interactions with other species and representations, values, and beliefs about responsibility towards the physical world (Rose et al., 2012). Given such a broad scope, research in this tradition can involve interspecies relationships, as seen in studies on interspecies kinship (Baker, 2022; Desai & Smith, 2018; Haraway, 2016), the role of land based pedagogies and learning from plants to develop ecological consciousness (Kimmerer, 2003, 2013; Poe, LeCompte, McLain, & Hurley, 2014; Ruck & Mannion, 2021; Simpson, 2014), or the ways in which contemporary human relationships to other species can be shaped by cultural narratives and historical relationships (see e.g., Ekström & Kaijser, 2018; Moore & Kosut, 2014; Saltzman, Sjöholm, & Gunnarsson, 2016; Sherfey, 2020; Sumner, Law, & Cini, 2018).

Among the latter trend in environmental humanities research, Anna Lowenhaupt Tsing's (2015) research with mushroom foragers in the forests of Oregon, Finnish Sápmi, and Japan is especially pertinent to this study. Investigating cultural, ecological, and economic practices surrounding Matsutake mushrooms, Tsing provides insight into the interaction of non-capitalist accumulation and capitalist extraction as they pertain to ecosystems and collaborative survival. Through her analysis of global commodity chains and the post-industrial ecology through which these mushrooms flourish, Tsing makes a compelling argument for the porosity and interdependency of what are often viewed as distinct economic systems. This is relevant to the study of collective gardens as political projects insofar as they can be considered to reflect a tension with the land privatisation characteristic of neoliberal capitalist cityscapes.

In addition to this line of research concerned with interspecies relationships, research focused on how people relate to and make sense of their physical environment is also pertinent here. Studies of this nature often focus on relationships to place and the cultural norms that shape values, perceptions, and behaviours in relation to places, but also more general relationships towards nature and the environment. Common themes within this area of research include the roles of narratives and discourses in shaping people's perception and behaviour in relation to climate change (see Brüggermann & Rödder, 2020; Jones & Song, 2014; Renouf, 2020; Ryghaug, Sørensen, & Næss, 2011), as well as green lifestyle practices and their relation to perceptions and beliefs about individual responsibility regarding sustainability and consumption (see Dobernig & Stagl, 2015; Marshall, 2016; Miller, 2001). Beyond those related to environmental change and environmental impact, however, are more general studies on sensemaking related to one's local environment that enquire into narratives by which places are deemed unsafe or undesirable (see Högdahl, 2007; Sherfey, 2011), and how changes to the built environment and ways of life in a given place impact local attachment and identification (see Agnidakis, 2013; Cashman, 2006; Koskinen-Koivisto, 2016).

The interpretive framework for this study is most in line with these latter studies, focused on the intersection of physical environment and narratives in sensemaking. Among examples of research on this theme, Keith Basso's (1996a, 1996b) research done on placenames, undertaken in collaboration with members of the *Dził Łigai Si'án N'dee* [White Mountain Apache] community at *Dishchii' Bikoh* [Cibecue, Arizona], is especially salient to my own aim and research questions. Exploring how informants understood stories told about places to play a part in the acquisition of wisdom, his research, and the theory of *'igoyą́'i* [wisdom] his informants shared with him, provide important reflections on the cultural construction of sensemaking, whereby observation and experience of one's physical environment, and stories that help make these experiences intelligible, are instructive for how to live well in the world. I believe that studying collective gardens according to such a perspective underscores the relevance of storytelling as an interpretive practice, by which people make sense of their environment and experiences, and in associating stories with specific places, these stories too come to shape how people experience those places (see also Koskinen-Koivisto, 2016).

Collective Action and Social Movements

As I am looking at collective gardening in terms of prefigurative politics, with a specific focus on the narratives and aesthetics used to situate them in relation to dominant discourses of urban life in the context of neoliberal capitalism, inspiration is also drawn from prior research reflective of the 'cultural turn' in social movement research. In speaking of culture, the term is used here to refer to tangible (material objects) and intangible (knowledge, practices, and skills) expressions of values, behaviours, and experiences within a group; because culture is social, and societies are not static, cultural expressions may be shared, contested, and mobilised as resources (Geertz, 1973; Hall, 1997; Yúdice, 2003). Accordingly, the role of culture in motivating, manifesting, and giving meaning to political activity has been a popular area of study among ethnologists and ethnographic researchers with an interest in social movements and collective action. Whether examining the politics of lifestyle and consumption choices (de Moor, Marien, & Hooghe, 2017), or how people work to nurture specific types of relationships with other people and other species (Head, Atchison, Phillips, & Buckingham, 2014; Stephenson-Abetz, 2012; Zembylas, 2013), a common feature of such research is an engagement with the political potential of cultural practices when they depart from normative expectations. Through study of "political aspects, dimensions and implications" of everyday practices in a particular cultural context, it is possible to observe how dominant values are problematised through challenges to the status quo (Blehr, 2001, p. 9; my translation). Consequently, ethnological research of narratives and aesthetics in collective action has also informed this study's methodological and theoretical focus.

Where narratives are concerned, ethnographies of social movements have often explored how they can be employed to constitute, sustain, and redefine collective identities within groups through appeals to a sense of collective suffering, grievance, or demand (see Blehr, 1999; Escoffier, 2023; Nieto López, 2010). An especially relevant example here is Maria Zackariasson's (2006) study of Swedish and Norwegian youth involvement in the global justice movement. Through her analysis of organisational identity politics, Zackariasson makes a compelling case for considering the meeting and decision-making practices of a social movement organisation as a site of internal activism, wherein narratives about power, gender, and media relations are negotiated in the process of evolving the democratic identity of local associations. Francesca Polletta (2002) takes up a similar analytical focus in her study of participatory democracy, particularly the work of the Student Nonviolent Coordinating Committee (SNCC) during the American Civil Rights Movement, exploring how meeting, volunteer, and training protocols played important roles in peoples' commitment to sustaining the movement (p. 65). She also analyses how the personal narratives of movement members seemed to influence their stances in periods where competing visions about the mission and methods of the movement caused internal tensions, whereby individual narratives articulated and transformed the identity of the civil rights movement and the authority of different people and interest within it (p. 104).

The role of narratives in social movements is a recurring theme in Polletta's (1998a) research, not least how sharing stories can sustain collective identity amongst movement participants, and how they can also contribute to public visibility and raising awareness (p. 143). In making her case for the study of narratives in social movements, she demonstrates how they can be used to call forth feelings of suffering or abuse, as well as optimism that collective action can make a difference (p. 140). Based on this, Polletta asserts that "movements in which the goal is self-transformation as much as political reform may see personal story-telling *as* activism" (p. 154; emphasis in original). In addition to collective narratives, a number of researchers have also explored the activism that can occur through sharing personal narratives, whether dialogue between mothers and daughters as a form of feminist empowerment and heteronormative social critique (Stephenson-Abetz, 2012), the sharing of personal stories by LGBT individuals as acts of political visibility (Vivienne & Burgess, 2012), or complaint processes as a means of addressing workplace harassment and inequality within institutional settings (Ahmed, 2018).

This approach to narratives is relevant to this study insofar as collective gardens can be interpreted as manifestations of collective action. Among other things, analysing narratives can offer insight into the reasoning that motivates collectives and how collective histories told to account for the political and social values they advocate. Approaching narratives in this manner, they can illuminate how the past and present of collective gardens are configured and woven together to promote a certain vision of the future. Like Polletta (1998a), Stephenson-Abetz (2012), Vivienne and Burgess (2012) and Ahmed (2018), I apply this perspective to my analysis of personal histories as a potential site of activism as a means of gaining insight into the values, worldviews, and perspectives that informants seek to convey through the selection, configuration, and interpretation of events in a causal sequence.

As for exploring the relationship between movement aesthetics and changing values of its political role, inspiration is derived from Scandinavian ethnological research dealing with the politicisation of aesthetic styles, genres, and movements as a critical component of collective identity in social movements. Barbro Klein's (2001) study of the *hemslöjdsrörelsen* [a movement promoting Swedish handicraft traditions] demonstrates how aesthetic values become a source of political tensions when dominant social values and relationships to the concept of 'tradition' change. For her part, Jenny

Gunnarsson Payne investigates the role of DIY media in constituting communities, whether producing norm-breaking film and television to articulate a more inclusive queer community (2013) or producing feminist fanzines as part of efforts to promote a shared sense of sisterhood (2006). In a similar vein, Norwegian ethnologist Connie Reksten-Kapstad (2001) analyses the role of political aesthetics in norm-breaking and norm creation through her study of collective action in connection to a proposed gas-fired power plant in western Norway. Among other things, she explores how the tent encampment established by activists occupying the site manifested a sense of place that stood in material opposition to the planned power plant. Through her analysis, Reksten-Kapstad offers insights on the expression of political discourses in material culture and the sense of place this evokes. Doing so, I understand her study of place-based collective action to address prefigurative politics – though she herself does not use this term – as her study emphasises how emotions are invoked, and public support garnered, by presenting visitors with a living example of an alternative social vision.

As I explore collective action in the current day, this study aligns most closely with a contemporary interest within the field that is concerned with how people break and foster norms withing activist groups and communities and the role of political aesthetics in these cultural practices. It complements and contributes to this trend in research through an explicit focus on the aesthetics of collective action, in addition to its political and ethical dimensions, as an entry point into the place-based activism being studied. At the same time, I draw upon research emphasising the role of narratives and discourses in framing and motivating collective action (see Griggs & Howarth, 2004, 2008; Polletta, 1998a), as well as research which explores organisational structures and decision-making processes as political experiments through which counter-normative or anti-establishment critiques manifest and alternatives are developed (see Polanska, 2018; Polanska & Piotrowski, 2015; Polletta, 2002; Yates, 2015; Zackariasson, 2006).

Overview of the Thesis

Having now situated collective gardens within the context of urban agriculture, social reform, and activism, the following two chapters outline the theoretical and methodological approaches through which collective gardens were analysed. In Chapter 2, collective gardens are contextualised in relation to prefigurative politics and political discourse theory, which together informed my overarching analytical approach. Through these two perspectives, I discuss relevant theories of aesthetics and narratives that aid in understanding the political significance of collective gardens as something constituted by people rhetorically and relationally, through linguistic and non-linguistic means.

Chapter 3 then takes up the methodologies that informed the fieldwork process and provides an overview of the empirical material collected through this approach. In addition to describing the process of multi-sited site visits and the selection and fieldwork undertaken with two cases studies, the chapter also addresses how pre-existing materials and those created in the process of fieldwork involved different possibilities and constraints, depending on how they were produced and by whom. Finally, I outline the ethical considerations involved in this research, and how interviews, photography, fieldnotes, and digital research were shaped and analysed due to this.

From there, I turn to the phenomenon of collective gardens themselves. Chapter 4 is the first of four empirical chapters, in which I describe the process of locating collective gardens in geographical space and analyse the aesthetics encountered in visits to them. Through this, common aesthetic characteristics of German *Gemeinschaftsgärten* and Swedish *tillsammans-odlingar*, are explored, analysing their locations, layouts, and material cultures to begin to understand the significance they conveyed through these elements. This is done by approaching aesthetics discursively, exploring gardens in relation to other places to examine how they reimagine urban space through the materials and designs by which they are constructed.

In Chapter 5, the focus narrows in from a broad sample of collective gardens to analyse the two case studies – Prinzessinnengarten in Berlin and Vintervikens trädgård in Stockholm. Founding narratives that account for the establishment of these gardens are explored to understand how the history of each garden is recounted in a manner that portrays them as solving social problems. Among other things, the sense of place being conveyed relative to both gardens is explored through temporal juxtapositions of local conditions and events, and how these details articulate historical grievances and social critiques against which the gardens are attributed value and meaning.

The focus on narratives continues in Chapter 6, with the emphasis moving from historical to contemporary ones. With Prinzessinnengarten as the case study explored in this chapter, I analyse how discourses of global and local political economy are expressed in narratives about the quality of life in Berlin, grounded in different rationales of land use and land value. In addition to narratives produced by the social enterprise, I also examine local government discourses concerning Prinzessinnengarten, *Gemeinschafts-gärten*, and urban agriculture more broadly, problematising the attribution of any single discursive position on the part of Berlin's government. Examining how various narratives constitute the relationship between the garden and the city, I also explore how these discourses help to interpret the expressions of solidarity and resistance that characterise the garden's material culture.

Chapter 7 addresses concerns about land, work, and social life, with Vintervikens trädgård as the case study in focus. Interviews, board meetings and participant observation at working days are analysed to explore discourses about the association's organisational model and approach to voluntary work. Antagonistic portrayals of the cityscape, internal factions, and working life are each examined in turn. Through these, an understanding is developed about the significance of the garden as a counterpoint to normative relationships to work and social life. Additionally, the chapter addresses concerns expressed about Vinterviken's future and social significance, analysing portrayals of the garden as threatened and how competing positions about its organisational model relied on different interpretations of professionalisation and obligation.

The final chapter offers a concluding discussion, revisiting prior research and my theoretical and methodological positions as pertinent to my analysis. Reflecting on the potential of aesthetics and narratives for social commentary and prefigurative politics, I consider how each is called upon to express a sense of place that reconfigures time and space to constitute alternative social and environmental relationships. Finally, the nature of collective gardens as diverging from the status quo while also being constituted through it is addressed, nuancing the implications of this for social change.

2. Investigating Collective Gardens: Discursive Theories of Politics, Narratives, and Aesthetics

Understanding collective gardens as manifestations of prefigurative politics presupposes a certain understanding about the nature of the social world and places as products thereof. Places involve the meeting of different social relationships and understandings of the world and, as a result, characterising a sense of place about collective gardens requires interpreting them within social contexts that extend beyond the sites themselves (see Massey, 1991, 2005). It follows, therefore, that the political significance of a place is part of this sensemaking practice. This has consequences for how to study and interpret collective gardens as social phenomenon.

Drawing on a range of linguistic and non-linguistic materials, analysis of the social significance of collective gardens was informed by a tradition of political discourse theory developed by Ernesto Laclau and Chantal Mouffe (1985, 1987). Invaluable as an overarching influence, applying their framework resulted in a theoretical approach that synthesises concepts related to prefigurative politics, narratives, and aesthetics developed by multiple theorists working from complementary understandings of discourse – Keith Basso (1996a, 1996b), James Clifford (2001, 2005), Mikel Dufrenne (1953, 1973, 1983), Michel Foucault (1982, 1988, 2007, 2008), Doreen Massey (1991, 2005), Francesca Polletta (1998a, 1998b, 2002, 2006), and Luke Yates (2015). Additional concepts have been proposed as relevant to interpret the design and construction of collective gardens in terms of the aesthetic discourses they manifest in relation to their immediate environments.

In addition to motivating why political discourse theory provides an apt framework for interpreting the data collected for this study, a selection of concepts of relevance to my analysis are discussed in this chapter. The theories of sensemaking and expression put forth by the authors included here offer insight into prefigurative politics as a spatial phenomenon. Providing an interpretive framework through which to analyse the political construction of places, the concepts discussed help to understand how aesthetic and narrative choices come to manifest alternatives to normative rationales of urban space and social organisation.

Prefigurative Politics

As explained in the prior chapter, the collective gardens studied here are actively oriented towards a broad public in their operations and the activities planned and hosted within them. In addition to these features, their statutes, descriptions, and other media often make explicit reference to being places for creation, experimentation, and alternative ways of living in the city. Because of this, I posit such gardens can be studied as manifestations of *prefigurative politics*, offering present-day attempts at utopian social relations, in contrast to simply imagining or longing for alternatives at an indeterminate point in the future.

First used by Carl Boggs (1977) to describe the embodiment of counter-cultural practices within social movements as a starting point for larger-scale social change, in this study I work from the concept of prefigurative politics as further developed by sociologist Luke Yates (2015). According to Yates, the term refers to political activities which "attempt construction of alternative or utopian social relations in the present" (p. 1). Prefigurative politics, he argues, involves simultaneously experimenting with and creating alternative ways of living and relating to one another alongside actions that seek to solidify and propagate these experiments (p. 2). This isn't to say that prefigurative politics represent a subgroup of political activity or a specific approach to collective action. Rather, it is an element of most – if not all – social movements, emphasising the internal workings of movement organisations and how collective norms and practices are developed and negotiated in relation to broader social goals. Approaching activism on these terms is particularly fitting with the ethnographic nature of this study, as a prefigurative political perspective is consistent with studying informal activism as a spectrum of political activity grounded in cultural practices and cultural production.

Another researcher who makes use of this concept is Francesca Polletta (2002), arguing a compelling case for studying prefigurative politics to learn about the internal practices of social movement groups. As Polletta observes, doing so places an analytical focus on and how political principles are negotiated and put into practice within collectives, both to avoid reproducing social structures they oppose and to develop and refine the alternative values they aim to propagate on a larger societal scale (p. 6). As she argues, the voluntary work, trainings, and meetings through which social movements organise and carry out their work matter to how people are enculturated in the norms and values of a movement, while also being testing grounds for contestation, negotiation, and experimentation. These varied activities provide opportunities for individual convictions and interests to come into contact in the articulation of collective values and decisions made about concrete actions to pursue (pp. 65, 104).

I consider Polletta's research a model example for analysing work and meeting practices as sites of prefigurative politics, not least for understanding the conflicts and negotiation of alternative social relations that this perspective entails. To the extent that collective gardens are collectively managed, they manifest forms of participatory democracy. As she argues, there is "a prefigurative, utopian element to participatory democracy as an organisational process, a sense that building a democratic movement in the here and now would lay the groundwork for a radically egalitarian society" (2002, p. 205). The organisational models and decision-making processes of social movements are thus well suited to study in terms of prefigurative politics, with the potential for analysis correlative to how internal practices and routines manifest counter-normative or anti-establishment critiques.[9]

Furthermore, in referring to the efforts of people who are active at these gardens as prefigurative or utopian, an emphasis is placed on their recognition of the future as open to possibilities. The future is always 'not yet', and as such is 'yet to be determined', and therefore open to being imagined and shaped (see Muñoz, 2009; Ricœur, 1997). Understood thusly, collective gardens can be analysed in contrast to their environments to understand how the knowledge, relationships, and practices being fostered in these gardens reflect alternative social norms.

Political Discourse Theory: Social Life as Political Life

Because of the counter-normative focus of prefigurative politics, political discourse theory provides a central reference point from which the study of collective gardens is being approached. In speaking of *political discourse*, it is important to first clarify what is meant by each of the words constituting this term before addressing political discourse as a *theory*.

As described by Ernesto Laclau and Chantal Mouffe (1985, 1987), the term *discourse* refers to how people collectively constitute meaning as a social practice, with the meaning of something a product of how relationships are

---

articulated between practices, phenomena, objects, or other elements. Importantly, they argue that this is done through linguistic *and* non-linguistic means, the two being interrelated in creating meaning. Language can provide one way of constituting and expressing meaning, but it can also be expressed in the forms given to physical spaces, the materials and imagery selected and presented within them, and the plant and animal life made possible within them. The design of a physical space therefore involves interpretative choices that manifest beliefs and values concerning spatial and social organisation. Accordingly, I analyse how collective gardens are discursively articulated through both narratives and aesthetics to express alternative visions of contemporary urban life.

In speaking of *political*, I work from Laclau and Mouffe's (1985) description of the term "as having the status of *an ontology of the social*" (p. xiv; emphasis in original).[10] In other words, society is by its very nature political; life among and in relation to others is pluralistic, discursive, and subject to irreducible antagonisms as people bring to bear different experiences and understandings of society and its ideal organisation (see, e.g., Mouffe, 2005, p. 12). Considered in this light, prefigurative politics can be understood to involve active engagement with the political nature of social life, as opposed to passive acceptance of sedimented institutional structures. Such active engagement is reflected in the negotiation of social norms within collectives and social movement organisations through their work and decision-making practices, rationalities of land use, and strategies for interacting with political institutions, among other examples (see, e.g., Bergquist, 1996; Polletta, 2002; Zackariasson, 2006). As a collective enterprise, I therefore consider prefigurative politics to involve fostering a *political ethos*, as it reflects an amalgamation of ideals, beliefs, and attitudes about the organisation of society, not least its inherently political nature (see, e.g., Mouffe, 2005, pp. 8–9; cf. Gunnarsson Payne, 2006, p. 51).

Such an interpretation of the nature of social life has implications for thinking about activism. Accepting that antagonism is a constitutive element of political life and social organisation, a consequence of this logic is that mobilisation behind one cause implies mobilising against other ones. As Mouffe (2005) notes "[m]obilization requires politicization, but politicization cannot exist without the production of conflictual representations of the

---

[10] Similar descriptions are provided by both authors elsewhere. In Laclau (1996a), he discusses the politicisation of society as an acknowledgement of its contingency, with social organisation necessarily instituted through political acts (pp. 49-50). In Mouffe (2005), she offers a description of the political as "the way in which society is instituted" (pp. 8-9).

world, with opposed camps with which people can identify, thereby allowing passions to be mobilized" (p. 24). Political discourse theory is thus appropriate to analyse the political representations of the world articulated in relation to collective gardens through a broad range of activities and expressive forms. The ways in which relationship between gardens and their surrounding cityscapes are represented can be informative about how people interpret and characterise the nature of urban life in late modern capitalist cities.

Citizenship

As Mouffe's concept of the political emphasises, the organization of social life is not a technical question but a political one that "involve[s] decisions which require us to make a choice between conflicting alternatives" regarding what visions of society to believe in and how to act in a manner that help to pursue their realisation (2005, p. 10). Activism, she reasons, is naturally antagonistic, a reaction 'against' something as well as an orientation or investment 'towards' something else believed to be better and worth striving for. Such an understanding of activism can therefore be seen as an enactment of *citizenship*. Contrasting it a liberalist tendency to treat citizenship as a legal status with associated rights and responsibilities, Mouffe (2018) asserts that

> in the democratic tradition, however, citizenship is conceived of as active involvement in the political community, as acting as part of 'we', in accordance with a certain conception of the general interest. (p. 65)

Whether discussed in terms of activism or citizenship, for the purpose of this study engagement in political life is understood to involve making sense of, navigating, and contesting various discourses about living in the world. The collective experiences of society being articulated and expressed through collective gardens, and how experience is given coherence, can reveal social tensions, grievances, and desires. To analyse what collective gardens prefigure in relation to these, it is salient to investigate what about these places is considered to serve a general interest, and what the practices and reasoning of collectives and individuals convey about ideal practices of citizenship. I thus analyse their cultural production and cultural expressions in political terms, investigating how these places are made and made sense of through a discourse theoretical analysis of cultural expressions associated with them.

Articulation and Chains of Equivalence

As alluded to already, meaning is relationally constituted, requiring instances of *articulation* where dissimilar elements (things, concepts, people, or values) and their symbolism are linked together to give a sense of order and meaning (Laclau & Mouffe, 1985, p. 85). To explore articulation, I draw on this concept as formulated by Laclau and Mouffe, as further developed by anthropologist James Clifford (2001, 2005), and as applied to the study of places by Doreen Massey (1991, 2005). Exploring collective gardens as places, the meaning they hold for the collectives who care for them can be analysed through how various aspects are articulated to constitute a coherent discourse about the type of place it is or should be and its role vis-à-vis other places. As Doreen Massey (1991) phrases it,

> they can be imagined as articulated moments in networks of social relations and understandings [...] where a large proportion of those relationships, experiences and understandings are constructed on a far larger scale than what we happen to define for that moment as the place itself, whether that be a street, or a region or even a continent. (p. 28)

It is according to this logic that sense of place, as "an understanding of its character" is similarly articulated, being that it "can only be constructed by linking that place to places beyond" (p. 29). Discussing how people develop a sense of place, anthropologist Keith Basso (1996b) argues that discourses about places are one way in which they are made sense of, a social process whereby reflections on places "lead commonly to thoughts of other things – other places, other people, other times, whole networks of associations" (p. 55). How people make sense of places can be studied by engaging with how people express places to be known, how they imagine them, and how they interpret them as meaningful (Feld & Basso, 1996, p. 11). Considered in relation to discourse theory, Basso's and Massey's conceptualisations of place share an understanding of sense of place as emergent via articulatory practices. Applied here, the significance of a collective garden can be understood to be the product of relationships being constituted between it and other places.

A particular result of articulations, *chains of equivalence* are also explored to the extent they facilitate analysis. These refer to instances of articulation where there is an explicit or implied construction of commonality (or equivalence) among different social demands or interests. According to Laclau and Mouffe (1985), it is through experiences of suffering, or the sense of a perceived threat or opportunity for action, that people articulate equivalences to create narratives of common suffering or common interest. Studying chains of equivalence thus provides information about different experiences, interests, and causes that are articulated as sharing values, grievances, or demands (p. 105). From the perspective of collective gardens, this aids in mapping the conceptual field through which their significance is situated within broader discourses of social change, especially how collectives understand their cause in relation to other causes when navigating threats and grievances and motivating collective responses to them.

Disarticulation and Rearticulation

In his treatment of articulation, anthropologist James Clifford (2005) reflects that "even the best established canonical traditions are seen to have been constituted and reconstituted in practice through interdisciplinary articulations and rearticulations" (p. 45). Or, as he discusses elsewhere, "something that's articulated or hooked together [...] can also be unhooked and recombined" (2001, p. 478). In each case, Clifford explores how the defining elements of a category or concept undergo *disarticulation* and *rearticulation*, with sedimented relationships undergoing ruptures and redefinition. Whereas disarticulation concerns instances when taken for granted definitions and identities appear to become decentred and their contingency accentuated (p. 477), analysing rearticulation involves a focus on what features are being selectively appropriated or excluded (2005, p. 25). Applied to my study, both are useful for looking at the construction of meaning through the relationships. As engagement in prefigurative politics implies a desire to change the status quo, and replace it with an alternative one, they are relevant for understanding how this attempted transformation occurs through acts of analogy, rejection, or redefinition, by which normative practices and social values become reconfigured in practice – in this case in the form of the social life and spatial use practices nurtured in collective gardens (ibid, p. 480). As sense of place is constructed in the articulation of relationships between places (Massey, 1991, 2005), disarticulation and rearticulation accentuate how normative relationships to place are contested, negotiated, and reconfigured in practice.

Rationality and Projected Social Rationalities

With regards to antagonism towards sedimented, normative values and practices, I am thus interested in discourses as articulations of *rationality*, normative 'truths' or ways of thinking according to which people arrive at "a reasonable and calculable measure of the extent, modes, and objectives of [...] action" (Foucault, 2008, p. 92). Competing social values circulate in society, and the multiplicity of discourses is premised on people having different perspectives from which experiences are interpreted to be normal, just, or appropriate. Based on this reasoning, I analyse how discourses about collective gardens articulate rationalities in relation to society at large. Rationalities necessarily influence how collective gardens are spoken about, how they are presented, and the beliefs people have about how they should feel and behave in relation to these gardens. Because one of the premises of this study is that collective gardens realise social change through pre-figurative political practice, they can be understood to some degree as constituted through articulations that locate them on the margins of normative social practices. An implication of this is that analysis should attend to the ways in which the peripherality of gardens is imagined in relation to those rationalities ascribed normative status.

Because the cultural production associated with collective gardens involves cultivating alternative norms within these sites in order to propagate them more broadly in the future, it is also relevant to examine gardens in terms of *projected social rationalities*.[11] As Glynos et al. (2014) discuss, such a perspective emphasises that what are being analysed are 'imagined alternative practices' that "have not yet been materialised in concrete practices" (p. 48). This perspective highlights the political nature of such rationalities as they seek to supplant an existing social order.

'Constitutive Outside' and Governmentality

In exploring both rationalities and projected social rationalities, a related consideration is how these become articulated in discourses that concern gardens' *constitutive outside*, a term which Laclau (1990) puts forth as a way of thinking about the reactionary aspect of the construction of a social movement's collective identity. What a social movement stands for or represents is in part defined, or constituted, by the values and practices that are being collectively excluded or rejected (p. 192; see also Laclau, 2006b, pp. 669–671). The articulation of antagonism is rhetorical, Laclau argues, as it

---

[11] Glynos et al. (2014) discuss this in terms of projected social *logics*, with an emphasis thus situated on imagined norms of behaviour to be brought about (p. 48). Opting here for the term projected social *rationalities*, the intent is to emphasise that norms of behaviour (e.g., logics) – current or projected – are premised on norms of reasoning (e.g., rationalities), by which actions are deemed reasonable to pursue.

requires *constitutive exclusion* to define a political cause in contrast to what it is not (2006b, p. 652). Or, as Jenny Gunnarsson Payne (2006) argues, the articulation of a constitutive outside establishes an antagonistic relationship between a social movement and aspects of dominant society, a movement being distinguished by its challenge to the sedimented views that characterise the status quo in society. As such, the significance or identity of a movement is "constantly being produced through the renegotiation of its own boundaries" (ibid., p. 33; my translation). The projected social rationalities by which collectives imagine alternate norms and work towards their realisation cannot be understood without also enquiring into what is being rejected as part of these visions.

This concept is especially relevant to my position, as stated in the introduction, that collective gardens can be considered as pericapitalist spaces, "simultaneously inside and outside capitalism" (Tsing, 2015, p. 63). Though they can be understood to experiment with and explore alternatives to the conditions of contemporary urban life under neoliberal capitalism, they are nonetheless situated – geographically, politically, and economically – in urban, neoliberal capitalist environments. In other words, they can be considered *peri*capitalist because they manifest physically within urban market economies, constituted ideologically by their critiques and challenges to their urban contexts. While the concept of a constitutive outside or constitutive exclusion helps to interpret collective gardens in pericapitalist terms, it remains to be studied and analysed what aspects of neoliberal capitalism are being called upon by individuals and collectives to constitute the outside or ideological boundaries of these gardens.

There is a particular aspect of neoliberal capitalism, however, that is of clear analytical relevance from the outset. As a defining characteristic of neoliberal political economy, it is pertinent to investigate how collective gardens are made sense of in relation to *governmentality*. As described by Foucault (2007, 2008), this refers to a 'governmental rationality', a *'rationality'* by which people come to regulate, or *'govern'*, their behaviours in a manner conducive to being effectively governed; it reflects a condition of being 'governed at a distance' as people come to regulate their own behavi-ours without the need for government coercion or force (see also Foucault, 1982, p. 208). Analysis of prefigurative politics, and consequently citizenship, in relation to governmentality involves exploring how individuals and collectives

> … question over and over what is postulated as self-evident, to disturb
> people's mental habits, the way they do and think things, to dissipate what is
> familiar and accepted, to re-examine rules and institutions and on the basis
> of this reproblematisation … to participate in the formation of a political will.
> (Foucault, 1988, p. 265)

Because the qualities of collectivism and commoning associated with collective gardens appear to be in direct contrast to neoliberal rationalities of individualism and privatisation, they can be analysed as sites of social critique. Doing so through the perspective of governmentality thereby raises questions about how these places are being made sense of in relation to behaviours and practices conditioned by the norms of neoliberal capitalism and neoliberal governance under which they operate.

Analysing Narratives and Aesthetics as Discursive Forms

Stories, and the events and other details that comprise them, are always located somewhere. As Basso (1996a) argues, how we talk about places reveals why they matter and their significance to us. Places are significant, he submits, precisely because our lives are interconnected with them (p. 70). Furthermore, recounting a story mediates how places and events are interpreted and understood by the story's audience, the act of narrating actively constituting and reproducing the significance of a place in relationship to events, people, and setting (Basso, 1996b). This is as true of places where we live and work as it is of those we dream about, read about, and tell stories about without ever visiting. Just as Basso believes that we can know places in a landscape through how they are talked about and the values, views, and wisdom associated with them, this study is predicated on an understanding that we can know what a collective garden means through how they are talked about, especially in relation to other places. This includes the ways in which collective gardens are articulated in chains of equivalence with places deemed similar, complementary, or otherwise related; it also includes instances when other places are juxtaposed to provide a garden's constitutive.

As a means of linguistic expression, narratives are a common form of discourse, and thus one of the primary ways through which the sense of place of collective gardens, as deemed significant by their advocates, can be studied. The discursive nature of narratives, through which people create meaning from their experiences and communicate particular ways of perceiving social reality, is especially evident in narratives used to motivate activism and collective action (see, e.g., Errejón & Mouffe, 2016; Griggs & Howarth, 2004,

2008). Considering narratives in the context of prefigurative political practice, I therefore work from an understanding consistent with Polletta et al. (2021) by which storytelling, as a discursive practice, "sets the terms for its own evaluation and how it constitutes speakers and audiences, doing both in ways that foreclose alternatives" (p. 71). In other words, a story projects a particular perception of reality, along with cues that condition the relationship between speaker and audience.

As Polletta argues elsewhere, narratives are important in accounting for mobilisation because it is through individual and group narratives that people come to identify with a cause and have the capacity "to make sense of unfamiliar events, to engage as they explain, and to sustain identity during periods of rapid change" (1998a, p. 143). Narratives offer a sense of meaning and coherence to events and activities as part of an unfolding chronological process. Conveying a selection of events as a coherent, interrelated sequence, they explain how and why people mobilise by projecting a collective identity that gives order to various events and engages individuals at the same time.[12]

To imagine a possible future, and to grow and proliferate practices and values, movement participants and organisers use narratives to reach and influence the public, and to account for and frame setbacks in a manner that helps to move past those events. They provide an interpretation of events that retroactively explains the past in a way that motivates current day actions and choices, while also making the case for a particular vision of the future (Polletta, 1998a, p. 140; cf. Yates, 2015). As Polletta (1998b) maintains, "the story's end is consequential; it is not only outcome but moral of the events which precede it" (p. 423). The significance of a story emerges from the configuration of events, including chains of equivalence through which disparate events and experiences are articulated as analogous to convey a compelling moral.

Narratives of mobilisation thus necessarily articulate social issues that collective action is represented to address. Carol Bacchi (2012) discusses this in terms of problem representation, maintaining that "policies and policy proposals contain implicit representations of what is considered to be the 'problem'" and that "what one proposes to do about something reveals what

---

[12] It is because of their potential for influencing people and garnering support that digital and news media and communications play such an important role in the success of collective action in contemporary society (Melucci, 1996), influencing cultural values, beliefs, and behaviours (Bolin, 2012, p. 5). In this way, it is valuable to study both activist media practices and media coverage of collective action movements and initiatives; looked at together, both are relevant for understanding how groups influence media coverage and how narratives work to suffuse public opinion.

one thinks is problematic" (p. 21). Though Bacchi advocates for the application of this perspective specifically for policy analysis, it is arguably relevant well beyond this, not least for how narratives of collective action are interpreted. Government policies and proposals rationalise a course of action that retroactively constructs the problem which they are presented to solve. Narratives of collective action must also, like policies and proposals, present themselves as solving social problems to motivate the course of action taken, and thus rely on the construction of problems for their narrative impact. It is therefore pertinent to analyse narratives of collective gardens, and the social changes attributed to them, for the solutions they are represented as bringing about *and* the nature of the problems they are being premised upon. Asking "what's the problem represented to be?" (Bacchi, 2009, p. xii), it attunes analysis to the rationalities and articulatory practices that make it possible to interpret a problem and thereby propose a reasonable solution.

Considering Basso's and Polletta's respective positions on narratives alongside Bacchi's approach to problem representation, it can be argued that the significance attributed to collective gardens is interpretable through narratives insofar as they portray gardens as resolving social problems. Looking at narratives in terms of problem formulations can offer insight into perceptions of social norms and how gardens are constituted in relation to the causes and conditions that collectives articulate as influential to the establishment of their gardens. Collective histories and other storytelling practices are a central focus of this study because they provide a means through which relevant events and actions are located within an unfolding process, providing people with ways to make sense of their past and present, and through these, to imagine and prefigure alternative possibilities for society. The stories and histories that are told, and how the people within them are portrayed seek to arouse aggrievement alongside optimism that collective action can induce change (see Polletta, 1998a, p. 140).

Much like narratives involve ordering events and relationships between characters, so too does the built environment manifest different ways of physically ordering space and objects within it, and the relationships between places or between objects. The appropriation and use of a site, and intervention into its material constitution (such as when constructing a garden where one previously was not) necessarily involves the cultivation of a particular aesthetic, whereby materials are selected and organised according to certain rationalities or intentions. Whether explicitly or not, something is expressed aesthetically, and through this the significance of a place materialises. Whether a collective garden or another use of urban land, discourses are aesthetically represented in the built environment, transmitting values, tastes, and beliefs about the most appropriate environment to create.

Mindful that political discourse theory posits that non-linguistic expression is interrelated with linguistic expression in constituting meaning, a specific contribution of this study is the exploration of discourses as expressed aesthetically as well as linguistically. Although working from a phenomenological theory of perception, Mikel Dufrenne (1983) offers a useful way of conceptualising non-linguistic elements of discourse in terms of "learning to read" aesthetic expressions (p. 209). As he contends, the ability to make sense of aesthetics and interpret what is being conveyed requires the observer to perceive an object as both an 'object in space' and an 'object amid other objects' (Dufrenne, 1973, pp. 135–155). For the purposes of this study, the aesthetics of collective gardens are analysed in terms of what I call their *aesthetic vocabulary*, the totality of materials and images through which meaning is expressed visually and thereby 'readable'. Where a prototypical aesthetic manifests across garden sites, it is discussed in terms of *aesthetic genre*. An aesthetic genre can be considered to express a political ethos for garden collectives and movements to the extent that it reflects characteristic ideals and beliefs about the material constitution of space and how it is used, moved through, and made sense of (see Gunnarsson Payne, 2006).

According to my interpretation of Dufrenne's conceptualisation of aesthetic expression, surmising the potential significance of collective gardens – by observing their aesthetic vocabularies and the genres such features reference – requires analysis of their visual and material presentation in relationship to other places. Another way to think about this is that aesthetic objects are interpretable through the development of an aesthetic literacy, whereby the significance of one object – in this case a collective garden – is constituted through how it relates to others. In a similar spirit, Connie Reksten-Kapstad (2001) argues that how a place is constituted through its material culture creates meaning while also communicating to observers how they should interpret and experience that place. Reflecting on her assertion in dialogue with Dufrenne's discursive conceptualisation of aesthetic expression, 'learning to read' the aesthetic expression of a place is possible through the totality of many aesthetic elements by which an observer develops their aesthetic literacy.

With collective gardens as the type of place in question, their material culture involves aesthetic choices and exclusions to constitute a sense of place, readable in how the material elements of these places are articulated in relation to their surroundings. This means that their aesthetics can be analysed discursively to the extent that (1) they are materially constructed by collectives with certain intentions in mind *and* (2) those collectives establish a type of place and make choices about its material constitution as a form of critical engagement with their social environment. Collective gardens are situated within aesthetic discourses informing how places should be constituted and can thus be seen to manifest rationalities about the social function of places. Knowable in relation to other places, the aesthetics of collective gardens can offer a complementary empirical source to narratives, each conveying a sense of the significance of these places through different expressive means.

3. Methodological Framework: Constructing an Ethnographic Bricolage

Studying the significance of collective gardens as expressed through discourse became possible through a bricolage approach to research that combined a range of methods and material types, undertaking data collection and analysis iteratively (see Ehn & Löfgren, 2012, p. 18; Hallqvist, 2022, p. 21). Such a retroductive research approach meant making intuitive judgements as to the significance of materials and provisional conjectures, thereby approaching theory and hypothesis construction as reflexive processes (Glynos & Howarth, 2007; Howarth, 2005, p. 337).[13] Just as fieldwork and analysis develop iteratively in response to one another according to such an approach, revisited and refined as appropriate, so too follow the contents of the empirical archive and the theories by which empirical materials are interpreted and analysed. As a study of the phenomenon of collective gardens, this ultimately resulted in a multi-sited ethnographic approach, employing digital and visual ethnography to begin to make sense of collective gardens as types of places, before selecting a pair of case studies for more focused research and analysis.

Multi-Sited Ethnography: Discerning Trends

Because they have emerged as a subset of a broader, transnational community gardening movement over the last two decades, collective gardens have necessarily taken different forms in different communities. I was therefore interested in the relevance of local context to what could be observed – what transcended borders, what changed in a new context, and what might have influenced this at the local level? With these questions in mind, the multi-sited ethnographic approach to qualitative research promoted by George Marcus (1995) was a source of inspiration, emphasising "observation and participation that cross-cut dichotomies such as 'the local' and the 'global'" (p. 95). In fact, this project could be understood as an exercise in 'following

---

[13] A retroductive approach is similar in many ways to an abductive approach. As I work here within a tradition of political discourse analysis, I have opted for the term more commonly used in that research tradition.

the movement' which in Marcus' formulations blend together both 'following the thing' (in this case a phenomenon) and 'following the story' by seeing the sites of inspiration that influence the narratives at other sites (pp. 106–109). Following the movement, and the meanings ascribed to it by the collectives who maintained these gardens, could provide points of comparison at the local level as well as across geopolitical boundaries.

A transnational multi-sited approach was deemed appropriate as a more localised focus ignored the relevance of geographically distributed relationships and influences. Even a cursory review of garden websites and social media accounts reveals that the inspiration for many were attributed to initiatives in other parts of the world, and that it is not uncommon for collective gardens to be part of networks that promote partnership and learning across borders. For instance, in its digital materials and archival interviews with its founders, Prinzessinnengarten – one of the two case studies – made frequent reference to urban agriculture in Cuba as the source of its inspiration. In materials pertaining to gardens such as Ogród Powszechny in Warsaw (Teatr Powszechny, 2016) and Trädgården på spåret in Stockholm (Cornell, 2012; Söderpalm, 2016), they in turn made explicit reference to Prinzessinnengarten as the prototype for the type of place they hoped to create. As Chris Lorenz (1999) discusses, a comparison across national contexts dismantles the assumption that what arises within a nation "must have national causes" (p. 28) or must be understood as locally exceptional (p. 36). Different social and political contexts can inform normative relationships to collective action and thus collective gardening, even if they may at first glance appear the same. It should not be assumed, therefore, that what is permissible, prioritised, or actually done by people involved at gardens will be the same in every location, no matter how similar they may seem. A transnational analysis thus highlights the 'taken for granted' and the 'unaccounted for' when different national constructions are applied to local realities (Damsholt, 2008).

Locating Gardens, Identifying Patterns

Potential fieldwork sites were first identified through internet searches in the winter and spring of 2018. This digital research was documented through a combination of fieldnotes, screen shots, and printouts of salient digital documents amounting to approximately twenty (20) pages of fieldnotes and forty-five (45) pages of primary source text. Because the operational definition of collective gardens being used emphasised sites that exhibited an active public orientation in their programming, the existence of some form of digital presence, as one of many means by which to reach a wide public, was a relevant criterion for identifying potential sites. Furthermore, it was important to investigate different national contexts to explore collective gardens in relation to various local contexts.

This mapping work focused on four nations – Germany, Sweden, France, and Poland – where many collective gardens had their own websites and social media accounts and were therefore relatively easy to locate. In both France and Germany, this research was facilitated by the existence of organisations that worked at a national level to promote collective gardens and similar models. In France, the national association of *jardins partagés*[14], Le Jardins dans Tous Ses États [The Garden in All Its Forms], provided links to regional organisations that were members of the network, whose websites then provided maps and lists of member gardens. In Germany, *Gemein-schaftsgärten*[15] were first identified via a national map available through anstiftung, a Munich-based foundation providing research, capacity building, and technical support for *Gemeinschaftsgärten* and other civil society initiatives (anstiftung, 2022).[16] There were no comparable national actors in Poland or Sweden, where *ogrody społeczne*[17] and *tillsammansodlingar*[18] were identified through searches of news articles, social media accounts, and websites with these terms (and related variants) used as keywords.[19]

It was quickly observed that a majority of French and Polish gardens had more irregular calendars of public activities, and comparatively constrained access to the site when events were not taking place, making participant observation a challenge. By comparison, many of those in Sweden and Germany were accessible at any time, or at least eight (8) to twelve (12) hours daily, with exceptions made for winter months. They were also much more likely to have a calendar of regular events beyond gardening days, providing more opportunities to experience the garden as a human-inhabited space. A

---

[14] As discussed in Chapter 1, this is the term used to describe collective gardens in France.

[15] The German term for community gardens, as discussed in Chapter 1.

[16] Primarily operating in German-speaking Europe, anstiftung's mandate is to promote sustainability through civil society practices such as commoning, do-it-yourself, and sustainable regionalisation. *Gemeinschaftsgärten* are a core focus area within this work.

[17] The most common term in Polish for referring to community gardens.

[18] One of several terms for community gardens in Sweden, it translates literally as 'together farms', emphasising the social nature of the approach to urban agriculture.

[19] In Sweden, websites for local networks in Malmö and Gothenburg featured interactive maps, helping to locate sites in those two cities. An official network did not exist in Stockholm, however, though an informal network between several initiatives maintained a Facebook page where news articles, photos, and videos from their gardens were occasionally shared (Stadsodling Stockholm, n.d.).

significant number of gardens in both countries had an *active* digital presence, with regularly updated websites and Facebook accounts. This meant there was more empirical material to work with before even visiting sites in person.

In addition to these commonalities between the two national contexts, there were also three aspects in which they differed, and thus were of particular interest to explore alongside one another: (1) the relative scale of the movement, (2) the average age of gardens at the time my study began, and (3) the forms of networks and partnerships apparent amongst gardens and between gardens and local government. As concerns the first, there was a significant difference in the number of gardens identified in each country. Based on the national clearinghouse curated by anstiftung, there were around four hundred (400) sites at the time I began my research (anstiftung, 2018). Searching for sites in Sweden, which was by no means exhaustive, resulted in the identification of approximately fifty (50) *tillsammansodlingar* across the country, the majority of these being in the country's three largest cities (Stockholm, Gothenburg, and Malmö).

This was likely related to the second contrast – the different 'ages' of the movement in the two countries. Many German *Gemeinschaftsgärten* date back to the early 1980s, whereas Swedish *tillsammansodlingar* were a relatively new phenomenon, with almost all the latter seeming to have been established no more than five years prior to the start of my project. The final difference between the two countries concerned the relatively formalised networks of gardens in two Swedish cities – and the municipal support for them – in contrast to what appeared to be more informal networks in Germany. For this combination of reasons, I selected Germany and Sweden as national contexts in which to undertake fieldwork. This involved reviewing garden websites and social media pages, documenting observations thematically in my fieldnotes, and observing trends and themes in the events organised at each site.

Whereas in Germany there was the near universal use of the term *Gemeinschaftsgärten* to describe collective gardens and similar types of sites, there was no consistent term used to describe or name collective gardens in Sweden, neither among gardens themselves nor among those writing about them. Starting with a translation from the German name, the search began by using *gemenskapsträdgård* [fellowship garden] and *gemenskapsodling* [fellowship farming] as initial search terms, finding only a few gardens described thusly. Other common terms included (1) *stadsodling,* translatable as 'city farming' and thus emphasising the location of the activity; (2) *kollektiv-*

odling, which spoke to the 'collective' nature of how they were managed; and (3) *medborgarodling*, or 'citizen farming', which underscored the political aspect of civic engagement. Ultimately, the term *tillsammansodling* was selected for describing Swedish collective gardens, being the term most frequently encountered. The first half of this compound word, *tillsammans* [together], also seemed to best encapsulate the idea behind collective gardens as bringing people together in a social and spatial sense, sustained by the collective efforts of people working together. In such a manner, this term arguably encompasses the varied social and political significances privileged in other terms for describing such places.

Visiting, Visualising, and Making Sense of Collective Gardens

Because a retroductive approach was opted for to study collective gardens, it was necessary to 'get to know' them through visits to actual gardens. Following upon an initial phase of digital research to map potential sites, fieldwork thus proceeded to visual ethnography in and around collective gardens. As an outsider to collective gardens, to gain awareness and move beyond my own interpretative background and biases, I needed to familiarise myself with their material construction. This facilitated a new background of experience – an aesthetic sensibilisation – through which to interpret observations and determine which paths of enquiry to further pursue. Additionally, I sought to interrogate my own sensory experiences and responses to the gardens via stimuli that prompted bodily reactions and features interpreted to be salient for knowing something about the sites visited (see Pink, 2009, 2013).

This visual and sensory material was collected for my empirical archive through twenty-six (26) site visits in Sweden and thirty-four (34) in Germany over an eighteen-month period (between March 2018 and October 2019). During this time, I familiarised myself with the environment within and around collective gardens. This included sites in a range of environments – urban core and periphery, suburban cities, and small towns – in different regions of each country to ascertain if any trends emerged within and between regions or types of city spaces. Observations included fieldnotes and a sizeable archive of over four thousand (4,000) photographs. Salient features were noted through both visual and linguistic means, and qualitative details of each garden were registered in a spreadsheet to identify trends regarding site type, planting method, planting materials, built structures, and exterior visibility.

In noting trends during visits and upon comparison of photographs and spreadsheet data, particular focus was placed on aesthetic features – observable in building materials, garden layouts, and signs and banners – as well as behavioural observation of ongoing activities. Observable demographics of those present within each garden were also noted. Exploring the material culture articulated in collective gardens, as well as the more holistic sensory experience of being within them, it was possible to discern recurrent themes, characteristics, and circulating discourses that warranted further investigation. Observations were also made of the physical environment beyond the gardens, taking note of features in their surrounding communities for comparative purposes.

This last point is particularly important to emphasise, as I believe there is a methodological benefit to discussing the interpretive process required to analyse aesthetically expressed discourses. As Sarah Pink (2013) discusses by way of sociologist Elizabeth Chaplin, visual representations are "not simply a mode of recording data or illustrating text, but a medium through which new knowledge and critiques may be created" (p. 25; cf. Chaplin, 1994, p. 16). This suggests the need to look at aesthetics in context for them to become readable as signifying something (see, e.g., Dufrenne, 1973, pp. 135–155). As this applies to collective gardens, their curated aesthetics can be understood to reflect how normative social values are interpreted and related to, thus opening the potential to gain insight into the backgrounds against which these political orientations emerge and come to the fore. Socio-political context can be expressed and critiqued through aesthetics means (see Gunnarsson Payne 2006; Reksten-Kapstad 2001). Interpreting such critiques with collective gardens requires studying them in relation to their surroundings to develop the contextual frame of reference prerequisite to understand and recognise aesthetic vocabularies and genres, and thereby understand the values they articulate. My presence as a researcher is thus more pronounced in the analysis of aesthetic materials undertaken in Chapter 3, with an explicit methodological point in discussing the process of aesthetic interpretation.

Collective Gardens in Digital Discourse

While digital research was first used as a means of locating and mapping suitable locations for site visits, digital ethnography of a subset of gardens involved more detailed engagement in their digital presence as a follow-up to site visits. As an approach to research, digital ethnography looks at social media practices and the use of digital technologies as used by people to interpret, negotiate, and mediate their social environment (Pink, et al., 2016). Exploring websites and social media accounts for dozens of collective gardens as an ongoing activity between autumn 2018 and late summer 2019, it enabled "an understanding of social media practices as part of, and producing, place […] inextricable from both the materiality of being online and the offline encounters that are intertwined in its narratives" (Postill & Pink, 2012, p. 127). In other words, the digital media practices of collective gardens were one of many ways in which the sense of place of these gardens was being constructed, with digital technologies used as one of many resources to articulate and communicate an understanding of place. Paired with observations in and around gardens, digital ethnography offered points of comparison and critical reflection from which to identify salient discourses for characterising these gardens. Among other things, analysing social media and websites helped to put in relief themes, activities, initiatives, and partnerships through which individual locations were attributed significance within broader networks of social relations (cf. Massey, 1991, 2005).

The selection of sites for this portion of the research process was made based on a combination of factors. This included the extent to which people were present and active during the first phase of fieldwork. Whether or not garden location, design, and signage invited a broad public, or seemed oriented to a closed group of participants, was also considered. This involved noting the open hours, signage, ease of locating, and active presence of people, as well as observing the extent of site maintenance. Analysis of activity calendars – either physical calendars posted at sites or uploaded to social media accounts and websites – was also a factor in making this determination, as these provided evidence of regular schedules of events beyond gardening maintenance days.

This digital ethnography involved a more intentional exploration of the public messaging of collectives and framing of the concerned gardens in public discourse. Alongside review of social media accounts (as far back as they went, which on average was 2015 but could be as far back as 2010), webpages and related digital documents were also reviewed, as well as news reports about sites and interviews with participants and other stakeholders. Where websites and social media were concerned, it was not only posts and blog activity, but also the range of events advertised and event partners throughout their history, including changes over time that could be noted in these. These materials provided curated resources for mapping the discourses in which collective gardens were being articulated and how they were positioned therein. In reading these materials, I was able to observe and note the chains of equivalence whereby they were articulated with other social and political causes implied to be analogous (see e.g., Laclau & Mouffe, 1985, p. 110), as well as how they portrayed issues that they were critical of. This approach facilitated learning about the tensions, hopes, concerns, setbacks, and accomplishments that were emphasised as relevant to the values promoted in these gardens.

Case Studies: Prinzessinnengarten & Vintervikens trädgård

Based upon multi-sited mapping and aesthetic analysis, as well as salient themes arising through digital research, two cases were selected for intensive fieldwork – Prinzessinnengarten [Princesses' Garden] in Berlin and Vintervikens trädgård [Vinterviken's Garden] in Stockholm. Apart from Chapter 3, which focuses on the multi-sited ethnography undertaken in the first phase of research, analysis builds primarily on research conducted in relation to these two locations. As Elin Nystrand von Unge (2019) discusses, working with case studies offers "a means for challenging general, accepted truths […] generating ambivalence and ambiguity in the material" (p. 51; my translation). Moving between specific cases and more general points interpreted from them, case studies thus provide a productive conflict, helping to complicate interpretations rather than assume a single case can speak summarily for a wider phenomenon (see also Eriksen, 2014; Passeron & Revel, 2005).

The selection of the two collective gardens as cases studies was arrived at through consideration of a combination of factors: national context, garden size, length of operation, frequency of public events and activities, and their representativeness of broader themes and trends observed during site visits. Selecting two such cases enabled me to "desediment and defamiliarise understandings of phenomena by drawing attention to their contingent peculiarity" (Howarth, 2005, p. 333). It also facilitated comparison, exploring why and how a similar phenomenon might give rise to different values, material forms, and cultural practices. These case studies focused primarily on repeated participant observation at gardening days, events, site descriptions, and interviews.

Established in 1999, Vintervikens trädgård celebrated 20 years of operation during fieldwork. In this sense, Vinterviken was not only unique in its longevity compared with other *tillsammansodlingar* but also an atypical model of collective urban agriculture in Sweden for the time in which it was established.[20] Located in parkland nestled between three neighbourhoods to the south of central Stockholm – Aspudden, Gröndal and Liljeholmen – and a short walk from an inlet of Lake Mälaren, it was a self-described *visningsträdgård* [demonstration garden], operated by a voluntary association which leased the site from the city of Stockholm. As the largest collectively managed, open-to-the-public garden in Stockholm, Vinterviken had a land area of approximately 10,000 square meters (2.5 acres or 1 hectare), and predated other sites I visited in both countries by over a decade.

Founded in 2009, Prinzessinnengarten was located at one corner of a busy roundabout in Kreuzberg, part of the borough of Friedrichshain-Kreuzberg in Berlin. Bordered by streets on two sides, the 6000 square meter garden was located on a corner lot between two buildings. A self-described *Nutzgarten* [market garden] and *Gemeinschaftsgarten* [community garden], it was operated by Nomadisch Grün [Nomadic Green], a social enterprise established to operate the garden. A decade later, during my fieldwork, the social enterprise relocated Prinzessinnengarten to what had first been a satellite location in another borough. In January 2020, the original location became a completely different, self-organised garden, Nachbarschafts- und Inklusionsgarten Moritzplatz [Neighbourhood and Inclusion Garden Moritzplatz]. As I learned anecdotally, many participants followed the social enterprise to its new home, while others stayed behind to develop the new garden with its vastly different organisational model and methods of cultivation.

Considering the unique qualities and circumstances of each, both case studies provided fruitful, though different, bodies of empirical material for analysis. The material and linguistic means through which each gardens' significance was conveyed to the public were complemented, enriched, and challenged by speaking with participants and my own observations of what occurred at each site. As relevant, the two case studies are compared, analysing how different local contexts and constraints influence the varied forms a single type of place can take and the similarities and differences between their prefigurative political activities. The retroductive research approach employed meant that comparison was a result of the process of

---

[20] In mapping collective gardens and reviewing relevant research, comparable gardens existed in France at this time, evidenced by a national association for *jardins partagés* forming two years prior (Partageons les Jardins, 2017), as well as some *Gemeinschaftsgärten* in Germany operating according to a similar approach. Though certainly possible, I found no evidence to suggest comparable models of collective urban agriculture were operating in Sweden contemporaneous with Vinterviken's establishment. Had others been in operation at that time, it appeared they had not persisted until the time in which my research took place, and therefore not readily identifiable through digital searches.

analysis, occurring as salient and empirically possible, rather than being based on predetermined parameters of comparison from the outset. Making use of different combinations of empirical material for each case study, there were limits to the comparison possible. Consequently, I understand each case study to provide different examples of what collective gardens can be and how meaning can be expressed and analysed.

Observation and Participant Observation

Observations at Prinzessinnengarten were limited in scope, taking place in summer 2018 and again in summer 2019, and amounted to approximately twenty-five (25) hours, five (5) of which involved participant observation at events organised on site. Two developments occurring within a two-month period posed a challenge to further onsite observational fieldwork. In December 2019, Prinzessinnengarten relocated to what was once its satellite location. Two months later, the coronavirus (COVID-19) pandemic halted international travel and led to the cancellation of most in-person activities, making follow-up observations at either the new or former site impossible.

By contrast, participant observation was a central component of my case study of Vinterviken – taking place at events, working days, and meetings – to better relate to the experience of being part of a collective garden's community. Taking place primarily between the spring of 2018 and spring of 2019, this took the form of participation in weekly working days with the gardening group, and attendance and volunteering at various events organised by the association. Between 2019 and 2021, I was also able to attend meetings of the association's board for additional insight into how work occurred, particularly discussion and decision-making practices and the scope of influence the board exercised. In total, my fieldnotes account for over one hundred (100) hours of participant observation and comprise the majority of my almost three hundred (300) pages of fieldnotes.

Participant observation facilitated experiential insight into the everyday activity of collectives – the topics people discussed, how work was organised, and the general sense of place that manifested in how people inhabited and used each garden. This served two purposes, both involving the relationship between practical experience of collective gardening and how people make sense of this. Firstly, it allowed me to familiarise myself with everyday practices and the discourses that people made use of to explain, encourage, and make sense of their actions in context (see Tjora, 2006, p. 430). Secondly, it aided me in developing a shared base of experience from which to interpret and nuance the narratives and discourses that later emerged in interviews, complementing retroactive narratives of participation with my own sensory experience of the types of experiences referenced in those narratives.

Participant observation in working days provided insight into how people worked together, and the types of activities undertaken. Informal small talk also helped to highlight common discussion themes and points of contention that arose amongst participants. Meeting attendance provided insight into the organisational tensions and priorities related to the gardens, and how professed ethical values informed decision-making. My presence as a researcher was made aware to other participants, with the only conversations converted into fieldnotes being those with participants who took interest in my project and expressed interest in contributing through informal interviews and conversations about the project.

Empirical Archive

Employing a range of methods for data collection resulted in a range of empirical data, including both linguistic and visual forms of material. Some of these materials were pre-existing, others created as part of the research process. The aggregate of these materials constituted what I, inspired by Howarth (2005), refer to as my *empirical archive*.[21] Sharing his Foucauldian understanding of the possibility to analyse 'all data as text', as well as his acknowledgement of archives as discursively constituted (pp. 335–337; see also Foucault, 1969), I work from an awareness that material collection and presentation are necessarily subjective activities. Empirical materials are influenced by my position as a researcher who has created, collected, and organised the data being analysed to varying degrees (see Davies, 2008, p. 256). Decisions and selection are unavoidable to create a manageable archive from which to articulate coherent and credible interpretations.

Photographs provide an illustrative example of this point. Images created for the purpose of the project were necessarily taken from specific perspectives or points of view, capturing features that were deemed relevant for documentation. Similarly, fieldnotes contain details that were determined to be salient through observation. Even with texts and images created by others, it was necessary to make choices about their inclusion, based on assessment of their relevance to the project's aim and research questions. The consti-

---

[21] Howarth (2005) refers to this as a *documentary archive*. In effect, there is no difference between the two, with the choice of nomenclature being one of personal preference on my part. While all of the materials I collected could be considered documents – whether written texts or images – I opt for the term empirical in order to avoid the conflation of documents with texts in the quotidian, linguistic sense of the term.

tution of my archive thus has implications for what is possible to interpret or know about a given topic (see Foucault, 1991, pp. 59–60) – in this case, collective gardens. As Howarth (2005) argues, this is not a failure for scientific research; rather it demands of researchers that the "principles underpinning these decisions are explicit, consistent and justified" (p. 337). Given the open-ended, qualitative nature of this project, and the retroductive research approach employed, it is especially pertinent to describe and motivate methodological and material choices that developed during fieldwork and analysis. Among other things, this has involved contextualising interpretations being made where appropriate and relevant.

The archive of empirical material collected for this study can most easily be categorised into two broad groupings: *linguistic* data wherein people articulate and communicate values and perceptions of the world (Howarth, 2005, p. 336), and *non-linguistic* data comprising elements of the physical environment and activities observable in that environment (p. 340). Both types are relevant in the case of collective gardens as they constitute different but complementary ways through which people interpret and express the meanings that places have for them. They communicate something about the significance of these places to their advocates in their own sensemaking processes and provide means by which to represent them to a public (p. 336). Linguistic materials can be seen to do so through how places are written and spoken about, as communicated in interviews, conversations, and documents; non-linguistic materials pertaining to collective gardens can be interpreted in terms of how they are designed, decorated, and inhabited, as observable in images, built structures, and behaviours. I share Howarth's position that non-linguistic materials such as observed actions, images, and objects can provide meaningful context to spoken and written linguistic materials, as the understandings, perceptions, and interpretations that people articulate through language necessarily emerge in relation to human existence within material environments.

In addition to a linguistic/non-linguistic distinction, Howarth also distinguishes between reactive and non-reactive materials – a distinction that is relevant for how the variety of empirical data collected and generated should be regarded. Reactive materials, he argues, "presuppose an element of intersubjectivity for their generation", whereas non-reactive ones do not (Howarth, 2005, p. 335–336). The former is most obvious in interviews and participant observation, where my role as a researcher, and my presence in the context or setting being studied, influences what is said and done by others; This demands a degree of reflexivity on my part to account for how my presence affects the data generated. For non-reactive materials such as documents and images, they are pre-existing materials, meaning that I as researcher have not played a part in their generation. Whether or not a researcher influences the generation of materials are influenced by the presence of a researcher, a researcher must nonetheless interpret those materials. This means being cognisant of my own subjective position as a researcher; though not influencing the content of non-reactive materials, they must nonetheless be interpreted and selected for inclusion based on assessment of their salience to the scope of the project.

However, based on analysis of my materials, I would argue that a division into three categories would be more appropriate, with a bifurcation of the concept of reactive materials as provided in Howarth's schema into *reactive-subjective* and *reactive-intersubjective* materials. Whereas Howarth's description is specific to the latter, the former encompasses reactive empirical materials whose perspectives and details are necessarily affected by how I, as a researcher, make sense of these impressions as a means of generating these materials. This is relevant with photographs and observational fieldnotes developed through fieldwork. The creation of these materials required translating sensory experiences of non-reactive data into reactive materials; an observed landscape where my presence was not a factor in generating the landscape as a physical and geographical construct was translated into linguistic and visual materials influenced by my subjectivity.

Non-Reactive Materials

A range of materials were collected that could be considered non-reactive, as my presence as a researcher was not a factor in their generation (see Howarth, 2005, p. 336). Texts within this category offered insights into the official presentations of collective gardens, including how their significance was articulated to external audiences and how this was done in related to broader social discourses. Two of the most common genres analysed in this study are narratives concerning the founding or establishment of collective gardens, and historical background provided to give context about the communities in which the gardens emerged. The sources of these narratives included official documents, social media accounts, and websites. Narratives about collective gardens mediate how they are intended to be understood, actively constituting and reproducing their significance in relation to events, people and setting, (cf. Basso, 1996b). Understanding narratives in discursive terms, their audience should come away with a certain reading of power relations in society. As such, the media and messaging produced about collective gardens can be analysed as a record of collective narratives being articulated and promoted.

Websites and Social Media

Over one hundred fifty (150) websites and social media accounts (primarily Facebook) created and managed by collective gardening groups were reviewed. They provided insight into the official internal narratives of gardens and the how their work was portrayed to the public at large, using digital technologies as a resource to mediate public perceptions (see, e.g., Pink, et al., 2016). Public messaging communicated via these channels articulate the significance of collective gardens, including collective understandings of what they signify and why they matter. Additionally, these media provided official interpretations by collectives about the origins of their gardens. As official histories or founding narratives, they articulate collective beliefs and values, and the conditions of emergence that are considered important to convey to the public and potential participants, underscoring the shared values important to being part of a collective (see, e.g., Lave & Wenger, 1991).

News Media

A variety of news coverage was also reviewed to get a sense of public discourse and events, especially pertaining to 'newsworthy' events at both case study locations. Amounting to eighty (80) news articles – seventy-five (75) print and five (5) video segments – these were printed out for analysis and supplemented with field notes to draw out salient details and narrative themes. Additionally, Prinzessinnengarten's website provided links to hundreds of news articles, constituting its own archive of externally produced media. The choice to provide this resource implied agreement with the garden's portrayal in news media narratives, as the website was used to intentionally curate coverage of Prinzessinnengarten consistent with the values communicated in the garden's official media.

Legal Documents

Research also involved analysis of legal documents, including lease agreements, articles of association, annual reports, and local government reports and proposals of relevance to the gardens in question. In the end, this amounted to sixteen (16) documents pertaining to my two case studies and local legal contexts. This final category of media gave important context regarding the social and political environment surrounding these gardens and the conditions under which they operated, providing knowledge about official discourses and legislation pertaining to urban agriculture and community gardening initiatives such as conditions of use, lease costs, and stated priorities. This enriched analysis of the legal positions of gardens, as both self-defined and as defined by government leaseholders and other stakeholders.

Other Documents

Additional documents included flyers and brochures produced or posted at the gardens – both official and from external sources – providing insight into what was permitted to be posted within the gardens, and therefore deemed to cohere with the values each garden was considered to signify. Documented photographically and in fieldnotes, twenty (20) such documents were analysed, giving a sense of which events were hosted onsite, as well as offsite events that the garden supported through advertising them to their visitors.

Reactive-Subjective Materials

Non-Linguistic: Photographs

Photographs served as a visual survey of materials and spatial organisation within the collective gardens visited (Collier & Collier, 1986). Providing a rich source of material for visual analysis of the gardens even after my visits, these enabled analysis across gardens, calling attention to recurrent themes that were not present in my fieldnotes, or providing an additional level of detail to fieldnotes. Combined with my observations and narration, they also act as a photographic tour of the collective gardening movement, an impressionistic account of the aesthetic experience of visual ethnography (see Pink, 2013, pp. 80–86). This choice was motivated by the potential for comparison between the material construction of different gardens to elicit inferences about them. Photographs were thus a material for ethnographic analysis – a means of conveying to readers the experience of travels to and between collective gardens, bringing them along in the process of interpretation and analysis.

In his study of the allotment movement in the Swedish city of Gothenburg, Magnus Bergquist (1996) maintains that photography provides a type of documentation of the 'message' of gardens in a manner that might be difficult to capture in other types of materials, such as interviews or documents. Whereas Bergquist uses archival photographs in his study, the photographs produced in the course of this study also have what he refers to as a "declarative or missionary goal" (p. 30; my translation), reflecting an interest in giving concrete form to the prefigurative visions being conveyed by sensory and aesthetic means. Photographs are necessarily partial, as I have chosen what it within the frame, and even which photographs are included in this text. This should not be seen as a shortcoming, though it is a constraint. Rather, it can furnish readers with insight into what was observed and how this, alongside observational descriptions, informed my impressions; it can also enable readers to experience their own impressions and aesthetic judgements of what is described herein (Pink, 2013, pp. 167–170). What people feel in connection to gardens, and what these sites mean to them, can be studied by observing and noting their aesthetics and their environment, and analysing these in relation to other types of information. Interpretations of collective gardens were unavoidably influenced by sensory factors and personal experiences. For this reason, the use of photography in analysis, and the inclusion of a selection of images in the text, is done to illustrate the aesthetic experiences described and thus lend transparency to my interpretive process.

Linguistic: Observational Fieldnotes

Although observations are non-linguistic, my fieldnotes constitute linguistic interpretations of them. Observations in and around collective gardens proved invaluable to my analysis, taking place at sixty (60) gardens visited during the initial phase of multi-sited, sensory ethnography. Additional observations were made as part of in-depth fieldwork at the two sites which became my case studies. Fieldwork occurred during a variety of events and during different times of day, days of the week, and times of year. Visitors, volunteers, objects, and activities found in these spaces were noted, attentive to behaviours and body language, design, discussions, and other details. Fieldnotes were taken either during visits or directly following them.

These materials came to comprise approximately three hundred (300) pages of handwritten text, describing how gardens were organised and designed, as well as who visited the space and the uses occurring within them. Observing the materials used for food cultivation and built structures provided an entry point to explore the influences from which gardens drew inspiration, as well as values shaping the physical form and how gardens should look and feel. Heeding Sarah Pink 's (2009) appeal for an increased awareness of sensory subjectivity in ethnographic research, it was important to regularly interrogate my own perceptions and impressions while observing and writing up fieldnotes. This meant being aware of biases that emerged in my reactions and questioning what conditioned these reactions.

Reactive-Intersubjective Material: Interviews

While much of the linguistic material was produced without my presence as a factor, interviews provided a source of empirical data in which my actions had a direct role in the interaction and the content of those discussions. Because I consider a type of place as the focus of my study, and peoples' feeling towards places are influenced by whether or not they are in that place or not in the moment they reflect upon it (see Kusenbach, 2003, p. 474), interviews were conducted within the gardens themselves, to the extent possible, to stimulate responses that are informed by the sensory experience of these spaces and how it is interpreted *in situ*. While formal interviews have been recorded and transcribed, many more informal interviews took place that were not recorded due to the preference of participants. In the case of informal interviews, I therefore draw upon notes taken during the interview – often in the form of specific themes or quotes – and fieldnotes written directly after.

At Vintervikens trädgård, four (4) recorded and transcribed interviews of approximately one hour each, were conducted in-person with participants at Vinterviken; an additional nine (9) informal interviews, ranging from thirty minutes to an hour, were also conducted and summarised in fieldnotes.[22] The latter were primarily with people who preferred to speak during working days rather than setting aside additional time, or who preferred a less formal conversational context. In analysing interviews, I understand there to be an element of self-mediation on the part of interviewees, whereby they position and configure their narratives, "constructed with characters in time and space" in ways that articulate how "the teller wants to be understood, what sense of self they index" (Bamberg & Georgakopoulou, 2008, p. 380). Similarly, I as an interviewer and author must necessarily select out those portions of interviews interpreted to be most salient to my research questions. The presentation of interviews and discussions in this study is therefore necessarily a partial, mediated one. By curating the salience of content to share, both informants and I shape which symbolic and social values should be associated with collective gardens. Given such constraints and challenges, interviews can be analysed for how informants are understood to present and

---

[22] Interviews at Prinzessinnengarten were planned as well. However, because the social enterprise's relocation dispersed those involved at the original site, and the coronavirus pandemic interrupted travel and in-person activities, it was not possible to solicit informants via shared participation in events (as had proven decisive elsewhere). As such, the case study of Prinzessinnengarten relies primarily on digital ethnography and photography, and to a lesser extent observation.

position these values, giving due diligence to arguments that motivate my interpretations and the choice of themes considered salient to discuss.

Research Ethics

As the project involves other people, I have an ethical responsibility to them, as they entrust me with their stories and opinions. This is an interpersonal and legal obligation. Because interviews have touched upon potentially sensitive personal information as defined in 3–4 §§ of *Etikprövningslagen* (the Swedish law concerning ethical review of research), the research project was submitted for approval by *Etikprövningsmyndigheten* [Swedish Ethical Review Authority].[23] Accordingly, all research material has undergone pseudonymisation compliant with Regulation (EU) 2016/679 (2016) – the European Union's General Data Protection Regulation (GDPR) – making informants anonymous to the extent that there is no risk of reidentification without access to additional information that has been securely archived (see also Commission Implementing Decision (EU) 2021/914). Additionally, as interviews touched upon several types of personal information – including race and ethnic origin, political opinions, philosophical convictions, and membership in trade unions – these have been omitted from the text unless absolutely relevant to analysis *and* no risk of potential traceability or identification of an individual is possible based upon details provided.

Furthermore, all potentially identifying information has been withheld. Particular attention has been paid to the description of specific events and situations, especially those involving other people, which run the risk of revealing either the participant's identity or that of others involved in those events as described in the text. This is particularly relevant in my case studies of two collective gardens, as communities with smaller core groups of participants – some of whom have known each other for more than a decade. As such, I omit or alter biographical and situation-specific information as necessary to protect anonymity and personal integrity of participants and others who may be affected by the repercussions of their comments.

To ensure transparency and informed consent, research participants were provided with information on the project at multiple stages and invited to ask questions. First, the purpose of the project was described in my request for interviews. Next, those who expressed interest in participating were provided with a more detailed description of the project, outlining its scope and purpose, the specific relevance of interviews to this, my legal res-

---

[23] Dnr 2020-02733.

ponsibilities as a researcher, and their rights to their personal data and continued participation in the project. This was reiterated verbally on the day of the interview, allowing for additional questions prior to signing an informed consent form. This process of informed consent and open discussion was important for developing a trust-based relationship even in advance of interviews.

In addition to interviews, ethical considerations informed photography, digital research and observational fieldnotes. For instance, an intentional choice was made with images to not show the faces of people present at gardens, so that anyone who did not explicitly consent to being photographed could not be individually identified in photographs. This had implications for the perspectives possible through photography. At times, it involved photographing areas of activity from a respectful distance to at least capture a sense of how space was inhabited; in many cases however, it meant that the images I came away with gave an impression of gardens lacking much human activity. This constraint was supplemented through fieldnotes, which for their part thus focused more on human activity within gardens. At the same time, the ethical choice to respect privacy in my photography also allowed for images to privilege the material and aesthetic character of collective gardens.

Where digital research is concerned, particularly social media sites such as Facebook, I've made the choice not to quote user posts or comments, opting instead to describe the general character of discourse in my fieldnotes. Although a public platform, with the account pages for collective gardens visible to the public, I respect the fact that contributors and commentors have not given explicit consent for their views and beliefs to be published in my text. Additionally, my interest in developing a sense of the themes and character of discourse within collectives did not require specific examples that weren't already communicated by more public means – on websites or in official documents, and materials posted at physical locations.

Going Out into the Gardens

With this methodological framework established, alongside the theoretical framework outlined in the chapter prior, the focus now turns to the analysis of collective gardens made possible by the two. This exploration begins in the next chapter with a broad overview of the visual presentation of German *Gemeinschaftsgärten* and Swedish *tillsammansodlingar* by way of the aesthetic discourses they manifested. This initial phase of fieldwork was fruitful in and of itself, not least for developing an approach to aesthetic research; findings from this more generalised exploration of the phenomenon of collective gardens also aided analysis with the case studies where in-depth research later occurred, providing a broad contextual foundation through which certain generalisable inferences were possible. I now turn to collective gardens – the process of identifying and locating them, impressions of what was observed, and how these impressions were made sense of in relation to their surroundings and – as became apparent – places far beyond.

4. Rearticulating the Aesthetics of Urban Space
"For a City Worth Living In"

In this chapter, I explore the physical environment of the sixty (60) *Gemein-schaftsgärten* and *tillsammansodlingar* visited in Germany and Sweden, analysing the aesthetics of these gardens in relation to one another as well as the built environments in which they were located. This is done by exploring site, layout, and materials in terms of the *aesthetic vocabularies* by which meaning is expressed visually and thereby 'readable' to an observer, and the *aesthetic genres* through which these vocabularies articulate prototypical ways of materialising collective gardens in discourse with their surroundings. As a discourse analysis of gardens as aesthetic forms, I am indebted to Mikel Dufrenne's (1953) theory of aesthetic experience, James Clifford's (2001, 2005) development of disarticulation and rearticulation, and Sarah Pink's (2009, 2013) discourse analytical approach to visual ethnography.

Analysing aesthetics as elements of prefigurative politics emphasises the role of material culture in realising alternative social norms (see e.g., Gunnarsson Payne, 2006, 2013; Reksten-Kapstad, 2001; Yates, 2015). Informed by this understanding, the aesthetics of collective gardens are investigated as expressions of the political ethos being fostered in these places. Places, Doreen Massey (2005) argues, involve "the negotiation of intersecting trajectories; [they are] an arena where negotiation is forced upon us (p.154). Collectively produced through the selection and exclusion of design features, their material cultures manifest as the product of negotiation, their arrangement, design, and use informed by the meeting of multiple interests (cf. Gunnarsson Payne, 2006, p. 51; Mouffe, 2006, pp. 8–9).

As Pink (2009) discusses, the sense of place invoked through material culture articulates a meaning by mobilising a particular way of knowing or interpreting one's social environment (p. 32). As advocated in her approach, observational fieldnotes and photography – here concerning the design and ordering of collective gardens – are utilised to "enable a focus on the sensorality of place" (2013, p. 81). Because the creation of these empirical materials itself involved sensory interpretation and translation, a point is made to discuss how a contextual analytical baseline was created by investigating garden aesthetics in relation to those of the immediate surroundings of these gardens. In doing so, it became possible to understand how aesthetic elements in both countries were being disarticulated from their normative associations, their value being rearticulated through their use as features of collective gardens.

While the process of identifying potential garden sites in both Germany and Sweden was the same, it played out rather differently in practice. Research in *digital* space to identify *Gemeinschaftsgärten* was made expedient by the availability of an interactive map that was quite comprehensive (anstiftung, 2018), but this did not translate into ease of locating those same gardens in *geographical* space, on the ground in German cities. Conversely, a more involved process of locating potential *tillsammansodlingar* via search engines, social media platforms, and municipal websites did not portend a similar challenge when seeking out those gardens during my travels around Sweden. In both cases, the relative ease or challenge appeared to be related to garden aesthetics and, as I explore in this chapter, my ability as an observer to 'read' the sense of place communicated by means of their aesthetic vocabulary. While I observed that *tillsammansodlingar* and *Gemeinschaftsgärten* tended to be situated in built environments that shared certain similarities, the sense of place that they expressed in relation to those environments differed quite significantly.

Gemeinschaftsgärten: Life on the Margins of Capitalist Cities

Moving from online to onsite research in Germany, my fieldwork quickly came to feel like a nationwide scavenger hunt. Treks often involved traversing the far ends of each city visited, as it was common for gardens to be located at the margins where city limits gave way to fields and nature reserves, small slices of land between or alongside train tracks, within apartment communities or in industrial areas in the borderlands between adjoining towns. In Konstanz, one garden was alongside an international border, with the back wall of the garden running along a stream that also demarcated the border between Germany and Switzerland where it separated Konstanz from the Swiss town of Kreuzlingen. Berlin was an exception in this regard, with most gardens located not in the periphery of the city, but rather in the ring of boroughs directly bordering the centremost borough, Mitte. While an address or intersection to navigate towards helped, in many cases wandering was still necessary to find the gardens being sought out. Not all were visible from the street address or intersection provided; many were hidden behind walls, concealed by buildings, or located deep within large parks. Often, they lacked signs, or their signs were posted in the middle of gardens, rather than at their entrances or periphery. Some had limited opening hours, and others required wandering through industrial sites, school grounds, or among apartment blocks to locate them. Still others were on abandoned lots on backstreets, upon what appeared to be the ruins of demolished buildings.

If the gardens weren't hidden away or hadn't restricted access, I nonetheless found myself navigating obstacles to reach many of them. It was common for gardens to be in neighbourhoods that were undergoing surges of new development, with the surrounding streets transformed into labyrinths of scattered sidewalk closures and construction crews. Whether in the centre of Berlin, Nuremberg, and Rostock, or the periphery of Munich and Konstanz, office buildings, hotels, corporate office parks and apartment blocks were rising around me. A mix of glass, steel and concrete grew against older brick structures. However, it wasn't only construction which presented challenges to finding my destinations. In Freiburg, I had to ford a stream when unable to find the one bridge that connected the two sides. And in Spandau, on the western edges of Berlin, I had to quickly leave a garden when a pair of intoxicated men appearing to be in their 50s began to verbally harass me.

In Search of Lost (and Relocated) Thyme

In several cases, after searching a neighbourhood for a quarter of an hour I would determine that a garden had closed or recently moved without having been updated in the interactive map being relied on. Occasionally, it was possible to quickly find where gardens had relocated, accessing their blogs or social media pages on my phone, or chancing upon them in a nearby location only after I had already given up hope of finding them. The causes of their dislocations became clearer by noting trends in what had displaced and replaced them. As observed in my fieldnotes from Munich:

> Emerging from the U-Bahn, I was met by an expansive business compound comprised of older stone buildings set among green lawns and a 20-storey high-rise hotel that appeared to have been only recently completed. Turning down the side street separating these two structures, I looked for several minutes for the garden's address as listed in anstiftung's map. Instead of a garden, I saw blocks of brand-new apartments and condominiums, apartment hotels, a vocational school, and more and more apartments. Some of these structures were still unfinished, as evident from the construction crews still at work in and around them. Even the sidewalk I was walking on, and the street itself, appeared recently paved.

> Pausing for a moment to double-check the address on my phone, I realised that the business compound I had first seen had itself recently expanded into the area where the garden had once been. Behind a security checkpoint and security fencing were several glass and steel buildings, some completed and some still under construction. On flag poles near the security gate, a flag with the company's logo was accompanied by the flags of Bavaria, Germany, and China, suggesting the company was involved in an international partnership. Realising the garden had been displaced, I found the garden's website, where I learnt that they had lost their site at the beginning of the year, and that only a few weeks prior to my visit they had secured a new location on the grounds of a Montessori school 2.5 km away. (fieldnotes, 12 July 2019)

I encountered similar circumstances in Nuremberg, Freiburg im Breisgau, Hamburg, and many parts of Berlin, where entire neighbourhoods were being built or rebuilt at the time. In a number of these, the gardens visited lay just beyond areas of development, causing me to wonder if, or when, redevelopment might reach their locations. Even in areas of parkland, development still managed to displace gardens, as I found in Freiburg im Breisgau:

> Following a street along the edge of a park, the path eventually opening up to an area with several sports fields. Coming to an intersection where two small roads met, I should have found the garden. But it wasn't there. Instead, all I saw were sports fields, trails, and a new sports complex under construction. Looking back at the map on my phone, I guessed that the sports complex had displaced the garden. Returning to the intersection and following a walking path, I found the relocated garden a few minutes later. (fieldnotes, 16 July 2019)

Similar observations to this were made elsewhere as well, in cities such as Rostock, Konstanz, and Berlin. Parkland was being developed, sometimes for public facilities, but most often for condominiums and commercial spaces.

Just as actual property development displaced some gardens, the potential for development apparently weighed upon others, forcing them to reduce in size despite the absence of approved development plans. This was the case at one location in Berlin, where I observed the aftermath of just such a contraction of space. Prachttomate, located on a backstreet in the borough of Neukölln, was in the process of being reduced to half of its original size when visited in the summer of 2017. As learned by speaking with a participant there – or *Gartenaktivistinnen* [a female garden activist] as they referred to themselves in their materials – the work had mostly taken place the prior weekend:

> Looking through the metal grill of the fence, it appeared that the garden was being cleared away – or at least one half of the site was. The half to my right consisted only of concrete and a scattering of wild plants that had grown through its cracks. A fence also appeared to separate the two halves, with a gate joining between, suggesting that they were in fact two separate lots. The half to my left, where the main gate was located, seemed chaotic, as if everything from the other side had been quickly moved into it without time to organise it. Speaking with a *Gartenaktivistinnen* I met once I entered the site, my impression was confirmed to be accurate. A dozen or so volunteers from the local community had quickly cleared the site in a single day, after the owner had informed the gardeners, with little notice, of their intent to begin development of the site. (fieldnotes, 31 July 2018)

Through digital ethnography conducted after my travels in Germany, it appeared that it wasn't only a few gardens which had moved, disappeared, or were threatened with eviction. In reading the histories of gardens as posted on their websites and social media accounts, I learned that many of the gardens visited had moved at least once since their initial establishment. In some cases, social media posts suggested that relocation was imminent, either explicitly calling attention to the need of a new location by a particular date or highlighting a general uncertainty about the future of the land use agreement at their current location. Therefore, if it hadn't already happened, dislocation and relocation appeared to be pending or looming possibilities for many.

The redevelopment observed in most neighbourhoods would understandably impact the potential for gardens to be displaced. It seemed, however, that there was a heightened state of precarity, considering how prevalent relocation was across multiple cities in the span of less than five years. It impressed upon me just how generalised the trend for property development or redevelopment was and how a specific phenomenon of civic engagement and collective action was acutely affected by this trend. *Gemeinschaftsgärten* appeared to exist in a state of precarity, displacement looming in the background, visible in the extensive construction projects taking place at the time of my visits.

Salvage Gardens: Re-used, Re-purposed and Re-articulated Materials

While relocation, dislocation and hidden locations created challenges to locating many *Gemeinschaftsgärten*, certain recurring elements of their aesthetic vocabulary made them more easily recognisable over time. Ultimately, it was their fences, buildings, and planter boxes which provided the aesthetic vocabulary needed to find my way to them. These objects, and the materials they were composed of, provided a background against which plants and people could come together in the gardens. An observable trend in the materials used was what could be described as their aesthetic of post-consumer waste, using reclaimed industrial products such as plastic buckets, wood crates, and steel shipping containers as building and garden construction materials. This material repertoire seemed to have propagated throughout collective gardens and established itself as the *de facto* aesthetic. As noted in fieldnotes from a garden in one of the southerly boroughs of Berlin:

> A variety of reclaimed items had been repurposed as planters – shopping carts were filled with various potted plants, plastic milk crates were filled with soil and had herbs growing from them, and even bathtubs and wooden crates had been transformed into planter boxes. The varied sizes, shapes, and scales of plants – and their containers – gave the feeling of wandering through a wild meadow, but one that had grown from the cracks and remnants of an abandoned building site. It was difficult to discern any specific organizing principle for how and where things were planted. In some ways, it appeared to me as a post-apocalyptic landscape, where a surviving tribe of urbanites had created a thriving oasis from materials, they were able to salvage, gathering shopping carts, bathtubs, plastic milk crates and other post-consumer waste items, using their resourcefulness to support life on an unhospitable ground of concrete and remnants of tile flooring. (fieldnotes, 31 July 2018)

While this fieldnote excerpt was from one of the first sites visited, to some degree it could have also described the majority of *Gemeinschaftsgärten* visited later. The typical building aesthetic observed was constituted from a post-consumer collage of reclaimed wood and plastic. The reclaimed wood – often from pallets used in their intact form and not first deconstructed for raw materials – was lined with plastic and used for planter boxes (refer to figures 1 through 3, page 78). Buildings were often built entirely from reclaimed or repurposed wood, and others used such materials to cover the exteriors of steel shipping containers which were repurposed as cafés or bicycle workshops (refer to figures 4 through 6, page 79). Many sites also used pallets and other pieces of repurposed wood to create unique outdoor furniture – lawn chairs, benches, or planter boxes that doubled as seating. In addition to repurposed wood, plastic milk crates, grain sacks and buckets of various sizes and shapes were used extensively as planting pots (refer to figures 7 through 9, page 80). At a few locations, bathtubs and shopping carts were also given new life as planters, filled with strawberries, herbs, and vegetables.

As alluded to in this description, *Gemeinschaftsgärten* tended to manifest as makeshift spaces, built in piecemeal fashion from whichever materials and resources their makers had access to. Their layouts were rarely neat or orderly, instead offering winding paths, somewhat chaotic in comparison to the order and geometry characteristic of many parks and other public green spaces. Because of the frequency with which the same design features and material repertoires repeated, I argue that the elements of layout, design, and materials articulated a *genre* among *Gemeinschaftsgärten*, a prototypical aesthetic that seemed to have propagated across the country (cf. Gunnarsson Payne, 2006), articulated through a decidedly post-consumer aesthetic vocabulary. Much like literary genres, there was a configuration of details, tropes, and progression through space – comparable with the plot structures in literature through which a story unfolds to readers as they progress through the text.

The prototypical aesthetic of *Gemeinschaftsgärten*, as a genre of gardens, could best be described as a large-scale, collective DIY project. As Jenny Gunnarsson Payne (2006) attests, DIY can be understood as a political aesthetic as it is premised on an anti-elitist ethos that "anyone can do it"; to subscribe to a DIY aesthetic implies an orientation away from professional design in favour of amateur production (pp. 63–66). Manifesting a DIY ethos in this manner, *Gemeinschaftsgärten* could be seen to articulate a counter-normative aesthetic that was itself an element of their significance. This aesthetic genre could be interpreted in counter-normative terms because it manifested different ideas about which materials belonged in a garden and which could be appropriate for food production. In so doing, it made possible an alternative definition of what a garden is, how it can be constructed, and even how it might look.

Figures 1–3: The most common materials for constructing planter boxes in *Gemeinschaftsgärten* was reclaimed wood. In many locations, salvaged pallet boxes constituted the majority of the garden (**Fig. 1**, top). Elsewhere, DIY construction from planks of various sizes, shapes, and colours made for creative solutions (**Fig. 2**, centre), at times resembling abstract art in form (**Fig. 3**, bottom). (*Credit*: Author)

Figures 4–6: A building at Rosenheim, in München, has been constructed from a shipping pallets and other materials (**Fig. 4**, top left). In the background, plants in painted boxes of reclaimed wood are visible, as well as hubcaps and other materials used to deter birds. At Prinzessinnengarten, in Berlin, a building has been constructed from reclaimed wood of various sizes, with a small sign on the exterior explaining how it was built by amateurs as part of a workshop (**Fig. 5**, top right). A similar theme manifests at Himmelbeet, also in Berlin, where pallets have been arranged to form a seating platform, while a shipping container that serves as a café has also been covered in pallets (**Fig. 6**, bottom). (*Credit*: Author)

Figures 7–9: Post-consumer waste repurposed as planters. At Prachttomate (**Fig. 7**, top left) and Prinzessinnengarten (**Fig. 9**, bottom), both in Berlin, plastic milk crates are used to grow cucumbers, kale, and beans. In the background at the former, a greenhouse has been constructed from wood and plastic sheets, all atop the tile floor remaining from a demolished building. In another photo from Prinzessinnengarten (**Fig. 8**, top right), tomatoes are growing in plastic grain sacks. (*Credit*: Author)

Because the DIY aesthetic of *Gemeinschaftsgärten* was made possible through the repurposing of post-consumer waste, these gardens could be characterised as examples of *salvage accumulation,* a term used by Anna Lowenhaupt Tsing (2015) to describe processes by which the remnants of capitalist extraction and industrial production come to produce value without capitalist control (p. 63). Their materials, once used for storing and shipping consumer goods, had been discarded once they no longer contributed to the production of profit through reuse or resale. Through the improvisation of those who built and maintained gardens, grain bags, buckets, and pallets were given new use values – salvaged and repurposed to make agriculture possible about atop concrete and rubble.

Salvage and re-use could thus be argued to involve disarticulation and rearticulation of material use values and life cycles. As Clifford discusses, disarticulation involves an "unmaking" or decentring of taken for granted definitions and identities (2001, p. 477) and a simultaneous process of rearticulation, a "selective, syncretic transformation" (p. 478) whereby identities are redefined "by selectively appropriating and excluding elements that impinge" (2005, p. 25). The numerous bathtubs encountered during fieldwork offer an illustrative example (refer to figure 10, page 84). Their relocation from bathrooms to *Gemeinschaftsgärten,* and their shift in use from bathing to food cultivation by focusing only on the features that made them suitable for garden design – i.e., being a sturdy container with a drain – broadened the value they could be understood to have. They were not considered as being past their useable life simply because they were no longer considered suitable for bathing. By filling them with soil and plants instead of soap and water, an object normally associated with cleanliness and the home became features of public space and the 'dirty' work of gardening.

Using post-consumer materials in garden construction, *Gemeinschaftsgärten* could be observed to manifest alternative rationalities by which to deem these materials useful. Seen in an atypical use context, bathtubs as well as pallet boxes, grain sacks, and other objects were capable of being perceived as something other than post-consumer waste. Disarticulated from a waste context, they were rearticulated within contexts of meaning and use value beyond normative rationalities by which they were designed, used, and disposed of after serving a specific purpose. New ways in which to relate to these objects became possible through their articulation in a new context. The moving of these items from their typical (household or consumer) use contexts – and relationship to other objects in those places – thus made it possible to associate new meanings with them. Relatively fixed idea about the value and appropriate use of those objects were literally and semiotically re-sedimented through gardening.

As such, one reading of an object's value did not discount or deny alternative readings. Both the pragmatic benefits of salvaging materials and the will to repurpose them for new purposes as part of a DIY ethos can be considered reflective of a broader political ethos, as each concern ideals, beliefs, and attitudes about society's relationship to objects and how they are deemed usable and valuable (see Gunnarsson Payne, 2006, p. 51; see also Mouffe, 2006, pp. 8–9). Interpretable as an improvised solution born of precarity or an anti-elitist DIY ethos, the salvaging and repurposing observable in these gardens could be argued to represent a shift away from a normative view of materials as disposable. They were no longer treated as losing their value once they cease to fulfil the purpose for which they were initially produced.

However, the aesthetic genre of *Gemeinschaftsgärten* was not only political because of its DIY gardening ethos and utilisation and repurposing of materials; there was also a spatial aspect that characterised it. The sites on which these gardens were established were typically abandoned properties, located in areas that were undergoing extensive redevelopment, as observed during fieldwork. By continuing to exist in precarity, *Gemeinschaftsgärten* could be argued to represent an aesthetic contrast and inversion of the late modern capitalist rationality of urban space, by which land use decisions are normatively shaped by ideals of privatisation, market economy, and property rights (see, e.g., Foucault, 1988, p. 265; Harvey, 2012; Mouffe, 2018). These gardens visibly disturbed normative patterns and relationships to urban land, unsettling sedimented rationalities of development and design.

Furthermore, making use of abandoned or unutilised plots of land for collective gardens, rather than property development for housing or commercial purposes, means that the land itself can be viewed in terms of salvage. The commoning taking place in these post-industrial sites by means of collective agricultural production could occur specifically because they had been left otherwise vacant due to their lack of value to capitalist production (cf. Tsing, 2015, p. 63). Salvaged garden sites deviated from the neoliberal capitalist rationality of urban development, whereby urban land was normatively treated as a private good, a commodity spoken of in terms of building stock, property values and development potential (see, e.g., Harvey, 2012; Mouffe, 2018). Articulated as a good – or part of an inventory of goods – land is classified and priced according to square feet and zoning permissions, according to which rationality "value can be translated through accounting"

(Tsing, 2015, p. 64), and as such the abandonment of property reflects its removal from inventory as it is perceived to have lost value and is therefore no longer – or not currently – fungible. By rendering abandoned properties into *Gemeinschaftsgärten*, they manifested an observable contrast to the normative rationality by which land value was assessed – i.e., as a commodity whose value was determined by the potential for extraction of exchange value from it.

With both land and materials being rearticulated thusly, the landscape architecture of these gardens could be categorised aesthetically as a language of salvages, and through these two concurrent practices of salvage, the presence of *Gemeinschaftsgärten* could be interpreted as a rearticulation of discourses of both urban land use and garden construction. Materials and plots of land were being disarticulated from taken for granted definitions whereby their significance was determined in terms of exchange value, in favour of a rearticulation whereby their value became reconfigured through redefinition according to broader social and use values (cf. Clifford, 2001, 2005). Constituted from commodities disposed of once their value was extracted, the pericapitalist nature of *Gemeinschaftsgärten* could be observed to the extent that the ethos of salvaging and reuse visible in their aesthetics relied upon capitalist rationalities for their very possibility to be realised.

While I interpreted the significance of their materials in constituting an ethos of adaptability, there could also have been other meanings or symbolism for gardeners who made these choices – for instance, practical considerations of affordability or the ability to resource materials that were easy to transport. Whatever these meanings may have been, they could nonetheless be understood in terms of a particular ethos of recycling, reflective of an anti-waste attitude towards land and materials and which involved salvage and creative reuse and repurposing (see, e.g., Gunnarsson Payne, 2006, p. 51). To better understand the significance of such an ethos, it was necessary to see how different elements of their aesthetic vocabulary articulated with one another.

Figure 10: A not uncommon sight at *Gemeinschaftgärten*, salvaged bathtubs have been repurposed as plant beds. At front, seedlings within smaller pots get their start. At back, mature herb plants are grown directly in the tub. (*Credit:* Author)

Creative Precarity: Alternate and Entangled Economies

Through the DIY practices and recycling ethos observable in the aesthetic vocabulary of *Gemeinschaftsgärten*, their inversion of normative design practices and consumer behaviours also appeared to extend to garden layouts and the uses of built structures. Many of these 'oases' – a term used in the name of many sites, seen on signs or when later looking up their descriptions

– could be likened to small communal settlements or villages which had organically grown in their locations. They did not appear to be the result of comprehensive design plans. Few had a clear centre; instead, layouts suggested diffuse loci of activity. Beyond the building materials themselves, trends were observed in the types of structures erected in gardens and their purposes. It was common to encounter cafés, community kitchens, wood-fired ovens, workshops, and performance stages in these gardens. Equally common were bicycle workshops and flea markets, and dedicated spaces for food, book, and clothing exchange. Judging from the flyers and noticeboards observed, most gardens had regular schedules of music and theatre performances, and many even screened films as part of their summer programming. They were hubs of activity, communities in miniature where people of all ages could eat, exchange, learn, be entertained, or relax.

Gardens may have differed aesthetically from their surroundings, and yet they offered similar resources and services. Although there was rarely a shortage of the services and resources to be found in the surrounding neighbourhoods, there were however distinct differences with how these services and resources were provided in *Gemeinschaftsgärten*. They were collocated within gardens and not compartmentalised into individual commercial spaces as they were beyond the boundaries of these gardens, taking the form of grocery stores and restaurants, bookstores, clothing boutiques, art galleries, performance venues, and movie theatres. In the gardens, food, events, books, clothing, and cultural activities were either free, low-cost, or 'pay-what-you-can' donation-based.

Alongside their prototypical salvage aesthetic, garden architecture and the functions these places served could be seen to articulate a sense of place that was distinctly non-commercial. This was an observable contrast to the broader commercial economy of cities, by which similar goods and services were provided according to the normative capitalist rationality whereby their value was determined as commodities (cf. Foucault, 2008, p. 92; Harvey, 2012). Interpreting this contrast in discursive terms, the resources and services provided in *Gemeinschaftsgärten* could be understood as disarticulated from their normative association as commodities within a capitalist economy, simultaneously rearticulated as common goods through their inclusion in a collective, non-commercial context.

In such a manner, I understood them as manifestations of *urban commoning*. As described by economic geographer David Harvey (2012),

> at the heart of the practice of commoning lies the principle that the relation between the social group and that aspect of the environment being treated as a common shall be both collective and non-commodified – off-limits to the logic of market exchange and market valuations. (p. 73)

Described thusly, Harvey's conceptualisation of urban commoning lends itself to be interpreted as a manifestation of non-capitalist or anti-capitalist practice, involving "an unstable and malleable social relation between a particular self-defined social group and those aspects of its actually existing or yet-to-be-created social and/or physical environment deemed crucial to its life and livelihood" (ibid.). In other words, a sense of place is, at least partially, constructed in the practice of sustaining a garden as a *common*, a shared resource accessible for individual and collective benefit.[24]

Discussing the anti-capitalist character of urban commoning, Harvey specifically identifies community gardening as an example where transactions of personal benefit may occur within a context of common benefit (2012; p. 74).[25] As a subset of community gardens, his argument is thus relevant to *Gemeinschaftsgärten*, where non-commodified social relations were observable in the types of structures present and their use for the provision of collective and non-commodified goods, services, and activities. *Gemeinschaftsgärten* were thus interpretable as places for social and economic rearticulation, privileging de-commercialised relationships to goods, services, and entertainment.

Although turning away from the commercial activity of their surrounding neighbourhoods, and towards collective, non-commercial relationships, the existence, aesthetics, and resources provided in many *Gemeinschaftsgärten* were nonetheless dependent upon the economic system they appeared to operate in contrast to. Though their precarity was connected to an operative rationality of capitalist commercial economics, by which the land they were located on should be developed for financial gain, this same view of land as having an exchange value also provided the possibility for temporary use which *Gemeinschaftsgarten* benefit from. They emerged due to landholders and developers who had opted to wait out the right project or price. The

---

[24] As Dellenbaugh, Kip, Bieniok et al. (2015) discuss, the commons are constituted by shared resources, as well as the institutions that regulate them and the communities that maintain those institutional structures in order to manage and benefit from resources held in common (pp. 13–15).
[25] Though Harvey draws on this example in passing, many researchers have analysed community gardening and similar forms of urban agriculture as specific examples of urban commoning. See, for example, Colding & Barthel (2013), Eizenberg (2012), and Müller (2012).

materials many gardens used were first by-products of consumer capitalism. And as the many examples of gardens along railroad rights-of-way demonstrated, even the movement of people – between home, work, and travel destinations – and goods – between harbours, warehouses, and storefronts – had created areas of land on their margins that were suitable for salvage. Finally, the clothing and book exchanges present at many gardens were also entangled with consumer capitalism, as the items observed were typically industrially produced goods, purchased at some point from retail businesses.

As each example underscores, *Gemeinschaftsgärten* relied on the same commercial economic values and activities that simultaneously threatened their persistence. Because of this, I interpreted them as *pericapitalist* spaces, existing both inside and outside capitalistic relationships – situated near to and in relation to the activity of a market economy (cf. Tsing, 2015, p. 63). Due to their locations and materials, the majority of *Gemeinschaftsgärten* visited were observed to be made possible through capitalism, existing in relation to it, even when prefiguring alternatives. As Tsing (2015) argues, examples of salvage accumulation are evidence of economic diversity and the interdependence of multiple orientations or ways of living (p. 65). Accordingly, *Gemeinschaftsgärten* demonstrate how alternative economies become possible not by escaping the capitalist contexts around them, but through the active rearticulation of relationships to objects and materials and the exclusion of profit and privatisation as the primary rationalities by which to use and value urban land.

Ideologically speaking, *Gemeinschaftsgärten* were situated at the periphery of capitalist rationalities. Conversely, normative ideas of waste, urban land use, and garden aesthetics were being relegated to the periphery of these gardens through the aesthetic choices and building and land use practices they manifested. Much like different species are entangled in webs of interspecies relationships, so too are different species of economy – gift, capitalist, and otherwise. Observing the adaptability of gardens over the course of my research and noticing their growing number despite the precarity of their land tenure, it led me to see them in a similar light. *Gemeinschaftsgärten* reflected the limits of the economic status quo, evidence that no single approach to economic activity – and therefore no single approach to the value of land or packaging and shipping materials – held absolute authority or legitimacy, even if one genre of economic logic was perhaps dominant.

The gardens I visited and learned more about did not seem to be impeded by their precarity. Rather, they appeared to be designed to survive under these circumstances. The materials used to grow food in were not only readily available, due to being post-consumer products; they were also mobile. Much as learned in relation to Prachttomate, the garden in Neukölln which had been reduced to half of its size just prior to my visit, a dozen volunteers could move shopping carts and milk crates on short notice without the need for special equipment or careful digging to transplant earth-bound root systems. With mobile containers, plants did not have to be abandoned because of a garden's relocation. Such resourcefulness demonstrates that a garden can be physically relocated and needn't be considered as a geographically bound, static place.

Aesthetic choices, such as the layout and design of a garden, are not random or without meaning. Whether driven by practical considerations or individual and group tastes or preferences, "a thing is more than what it is, and this more is its significance" (Dufrenne, 1953, p. 477; my translation). The aesthetic of *Gemeinschaftsgärten*, and the material repertoire they relied upon reflected an inventiveness and commitment to survive, whether in the place a garden was originally established or elsewhere if needed. They were built to last by being mobile, rather than being made to last by remaining in place.

Signs of Resistance and Solidarity

In addition to the salvaged materials and uses of land through which *Gemeinschaftsgärten* made use of what was normatively considered outside of the scope of capitalist value, another common feature of their aesthetic vocabulary had a linguistic element to it. Political messages were frequently on display at these gardens, and they tended to set up stark contrasts between what was conveyed as the 'order of the day' and an alternative order that *Gemeinschaftsgärten* were being equivalated with.

I first thought that locations like these were exceptions in their density and variety of political messages, and the antagonistic positions that many of those messages expressed through word choices such as *'versus'* or *'statt'* ['instead of' or 'rather than']. It was only later, in reviewing photos and field-notes and comparing across locations, that the prevalence of such political messaging across most sites became apparent. Slogans, flags, flyers, and manifestos were frequently on prominent display throughout the interior of gardens – hanging high over structures, spray-painted in large letters across walls and fences, or stapled and nailed onto noticeboards or walls. At some gardens, signs were also posted around their exteriors, on fences, gates, or message boards for passers-by to see. Though messages varied, certain themes were recurrent.

For instance, many signs bluntly stated priorities, contrasting the significance of these gardens with what they were seen to stand against (refer to figures 11 through 14, next page). This was visible in one garden in the southeast of Berlin in examples such as "Gemeingut statt Eigentum" [Common good instead of private ownership] and "Tomaten statt Prachtwohnung!" [Tomatoes rather than fancy apartments!], collocated with messages such as "Für eine Lebenswerte Stadt" [For a city worth living in]. Viewed as a totality with other similar signs, these could be interpreted to outline a manifesto for urban commoning, with gardens signifying "a city worth living in" made possible in resistance to land privatisation and luxury property development. Other messages across the country emphasised the potential of solidarity to shape the quality of city life, such as the many "Stadt für Alle" [City for all] signs observed that rallied for inclusive urban design, calls to "Stadt selber machen" [Make the city ourselves], or musing how "Nachbar. scha(f)ft. Stadt." [Neighbour(hood)s make a city] – the latter conveying individual and collective roles in constituting urban life.

By collocating linguistic and visual references to discourses of commoning, civic engagement, and counter-normative urban planning policy, garden aesthetics appeared to articulate chains of equivalence. These varied calls and encouragements towards solidarity and resistance together constituted a collective cultural identity for *Gemeinschaftsgärten* whereby their significance was juxtaposed with normative urban planning practices. *Gemeinschaftsgärten* thus reflected a particular projected social rationality about 'a city worth living in', as the practices within these gardens were associated with imagined practices and norms intended to be materialised in the city at large (cf. Glynos, Speed, & West, 2014, p. 48). This projected rationality was articulated with elements such as urban commoning, grassroots development, and food cultivation, while the threat to this vision was articulated through private ownership and property speculation as obstacles to realising a liveable city.

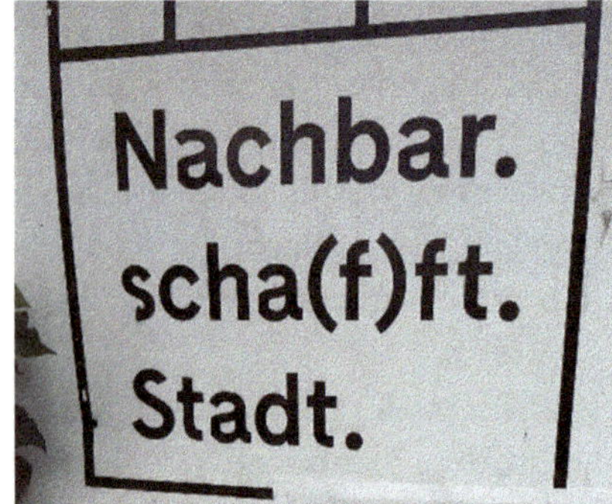

Figures 11–14: Signs posted at Gemeinschaftsgärten could invoke confrontational language, inspired reflection on the nature of urban life, or appeal to a sense of duty and action to realise a just and equitable city. (*Credit:* Author)

Importantly though, their messages could be observed to critique certain rationalities while also proposing solutions – as seen in the presentation of tomatoes (as a metonym for food cultivation) as the solution to luxury housing developments. They did not target individuals or lament the problems they presented for critique. Juxtaposing inspiration and hopeful appeals to grassroots activism alongside statements of defiance and criticism, they presented what was already taking place in these gardens as the solution to the problems also being communicated (cf. Bacchi, 2012). Looked at in this way, a sense of place was being conveyed through an aesthetic vocabulary that explicitly communicated values of resistance and rejection. This was observable not just in political messaging, but even, in retrospect, in the ways by which their material repertoires of salvaged waste provided a stark aesthetic contrast to the many new glass and steel structures being erected in the proximity of *Gemeinschaftsgärten*.

Echoing once again Laclau and Mouffe (1987), identities can be understood as discursively or relationally constituted, and these discourses (or relationships) involve linguistic and extra-linguistic elements in their expression. Consequently, I submit that the signs and banners displayed at sites articulated with the materials used in garden construction as part of their overall aesthetic, thus readable or interpretable in relationship to each other. By the same reasoning, they were also thus interpretable through their articulation of various people, places, concepts, causes, and values being referenced, using both equivalence and negation to constitute the significance of *Gemeinschaftsgärten*. Analogy and contrast offer means by which a group "constitute its own forms of rationality and intelligibility [...] by expelling outside itself any surplus meaning subverting it" (Laclau & Mouffe, 1985, p. 137). The language of signs may have used linguistic means to express socio-political grievances and alliances, and to articulate proposed solutions to the grievances expressed, but considered as a discursive totality these signs were equally dependent upon the imagery that accompanied them and their placement as part of garden design.

Gemeinschaftsgärten were places where collectives worked *for* certain causes in their prefigurative politics, but also worked *against* other causes to do so. As they used imagery and language to articulate what values were being expelled to the cityscape beyond garden boundaries – consumer capitalism and the rationalities of urban land and development it implied – the collectives behind *Gemeinschaftsgärten* could be understood to simultaneously rearticulate urban life as it was being explored and reconstituted. They manifested a political ethos consistent with a democratic tradition of citizenship, advocating "active involvement in the political community [...] in accordance with a certain conception of the general interest" (Mouffe, 2018, p. 65). Whether statements of resistance to normative values or calls to 'build the city oneself', such messages called attention to the political character of social life and the role of individual and collective action in constituting 'a city worth living in'.

Tillsammansodlingar: Urban Ruralisation in Modern Cityscapes

Identifying gardens in Sweden was a different experience than it was in Germany. Firstly, there was no ready-made interactive map; the scavenger hunt to find gardens began while sitting in front of my computer, using a variety of terms in search engines, social media, and digital news to begin to develop a map of potential sites. Just as identifying *tillsammansodlingar* digitally was a different experience, so too was locating them on the ground; however, while identifying existing gardens was more of a challenge than it was in Germany, locating those I learnt about was much easier by comparison.

My fieldnotes from Gothenburg and Stockholm give a sense of the ease of finding gardens *in situ*, as well as being representative of the aesthetic features typical of *tillsammansodlingar* that were visited. Despite being at opposite ends of Gothenburg, Silverkällans kollektivodling (a collective garden in the Silverkällan neighbourhood) and Brunnsbo Trädgårdskollektiv (a garden collective in the Brunnsbo neighbourhood), shared several similarities:

> Silverkällan was in an open, green square surrounded by two- and three-storey apartments, just a block from the high street of Majorna [the city district in which it was located]. Comprised of a series of mounds and beds reinforced with thin wooden frames. Everything was grown direct in the earth, not in pallet boxes as observed at many of the businesses on the high street. It appeared to me more like a country garden, taking up the entirety of the square in which it was located. A red shed was situated to one side of the garden, used as a space for storing supplies. There were painted benches located around the perimeter of the garden as well. Clean and orderly, everything was arranged in rows. There were a couple of pallet boxes, I realised eventually; they were also painted red and had lids atop them. It turned out that these were used for storing compost, soil, and mulch, hiding them from view. (fieldnotes, 27 September 2019)

> Brunnsbo was located along a residential street with apartment towers on one side and single-family homes on the other, suggesting it was at the intersection of two neighbourhoods. The garden was quite expansive, enclosed by a high fence that lacked gates, appearing to have once been used for football or another sport. The space was filled with raised beds reinforced with wooden frames and a few planter boxes. There were also several wooden storage boxes located throughout, likely containing gardening tools and equipment. The entire garden was arranged on a grid and looked to be regularly weeded. The collective had set up a picnic area with benches under

> a large pergola. Small signs were posted throughout, welcoming visitors and encouraging them to become members to enjoy the garden's produce. (fieldnotes, 28 September 2019)

A similar experience was encountered at Bellevue Farm, a self-described 'citizen garden' and 'food park' located at the northern edge of the central Stockholm. It was located along a walking path at the edge of Brunnsviken, the lake at the Royal National City Park. As for its aesthetics:

> the first thing I noticed about the garden was an enclosure created out of woven branches. Following alongside the walking path for about 100 metres, I noticed that the garden was comprised of a series of small enclosures organised by different themes – perennials, annuals, meadow, field. With the exception of the meadow and field areas, most the others were formed into rounded keyhole-shaped garden beds, allowing one to walk into the centre and therefore access everything from one spot. The beds were at waist height, held together by pieces of wood with wire woven around them to form retaining walls. Woven branches were used to delineate a walking path that dissected the garden on a north-south axis. In the centre, but off to one side, they had constructed a pergola, seating and a table with plants growing up the support beams of the pergola. (fieldnotes, 18 October 2019)

As each example illustrates, *tillsammansodlingar* tended to be situated in high-visibility locations designated for public use – the common areas of apartment communities and in squares, parks, and other public green spaces. They were in well trafficked, well-cared for and protected spaces, on freely accessible, common-use land. Additionally, their plants were almost always rooted in the soil, not in planter boxes or other containers. Considering these details together, *tillsammansodlingar* appeared to be rather securely established where they were, growing plants *in terra*, and seemingly without need to secure or restrict access. More than that, they appeared to be in locations of prominence within their communities. This observable security was reinforced by realising that every garden was where I expected to find it, none having disappeared or been relocated. Also, digital ethnography conducted after my visits informed me that, although some were relatively new, most *tillsammansodlingar* were at least five years old by the time they were visited. Out of over three dozen visited, only two had relocated at some prior point, doing so only once – one due to the association deciding to relocate to a smaller, easier to maintain site (as stated in Svensson, 2018), the other due to a change of lessee combined with complaints about the maintenance of the site (as quoted in Lodding, 2018).

As with *Gemeinschaftsgärten*, a tendency towards urban commoning was also observed with *tillsammansodlingar*. Though not visible to the same extent at all gardens, there were structural features that emphasised a sense of place as being for common benefit, through features that suggested collective and non-commodified social interaction. As already described through reference to my fieldnotes, this included: (1) the absence or decorative nature of fencing, in contrast to fencing as security; (2) emphasis on social space and communal seating, which I interpreted to be encouraging of people remaining in the garden for purposes other than gardening; and (3) signs that welcomed people and provided information about the social goals of these locations. It also included features such as those noted at several more established sites around the country, which had greenhouses, plant nurseries and other structures used for community education, cultural exhibits, celebrations, and similar purposes.

Anti-Modernist Urbanism as a Political Ethos

Although at first glance *tillsammansodlingar* appeared to be extensions of their environments – gardens built within already existing green spaces and parkland – reflecting on fieldnotes and photos after completing site visits revealed different ways of using green spaces and contrasts with their surrounding neighbourhoods. This first became clear by analysing the aesthetics of *tillsammansodlingar* and those of their frequent neighbour – allotment gardens. About one-third of all *tillsammansodlingar* I visited were located on land along the periphery of allotment gardens, making such comparison particularly easy and readily apparent. Because of some commonalities in building aesthetics, and the recurrent proximity between *tillsammansodlingar* and allotments, it was at times uncertain which of the two types of gardens was about to be entered, doubting my aesthetic judgement until finding signs that indicated what type of garden it was. Even *tillsammansodlingar* that were not adjacent to allotment gardens often looked aesthetically similar, at least from the outside. It was the interiors of the two types of gardens where the differences became more obvious.

As Magnus Bergquist (1996) discusses in his ethnographic study of the Swedish allotment movement in Gothenburg, these gardens could be characterised by a rational, modernist design aesthetic reflective of ideas of land use and production coming into fashion in the late nineteenth and early twentieth century, when they were first being established across the country (p. 139). Allotment gardens were characterised not only by their parcelling into individual lots, but by grid layouts and arterial paths that maximised the space dedicated to individual parcels. They were designed with minimal common space, most of which was functional – such as playgrounds for children or thoroughfares only wide enough for people and wheelbarrows to move through the allotment area and access individual parcels (ibid., pp. 99–103).

Tillsammansodlingar, by contrast, were neither parcelled into individual plots like allotments, nor were they characterised by efficient grid layouts that limited common space in favour of maximising individual allotment areas and the overall number of allotments. Whereas allotments had perimeter fencing, as well as fenced borders enclosing individual parcels, few *tillsammansodlingar* had these; if they were present, they enclosed the outer perimeter or a limited area within the garden, and even then, appeared to simply demarcate the boundaries of the garden. Typically lacking gates – with a few exceptions, in which case they had no locks and therefore they could not be 'closed' – these could be described as decorative borders as they did not restrict access. *Tillsammansodlingar* tended to devote equal space to common areas and cultivation, almost always featuring seating that encouraged non-transitory use of common space for socialising and not just passing through.

As with allotment gardens, the landscape architecture of the parklands in which they and *tillsammansodlingar* were both situated to present rational, functional uses of space. Paths provided connectivity between these green spaces and adjoining neighbourhoods, and they were characterised by tree-lined walking paths, large green lawns, and a variety of purpose-built spaces designed for distinct uses – playgrounds, sports fields, picnic areas with benches, outdoor gyms and so forth. *Tillsammansodlingar*, by contrast, manifested according to an altogether different aesthetic. Seating was dispersed throughout, amongst vining vegetation or under the shade of fruit and nut trees, along pathways, and tucked behind tall grasses. Rather than purpose-built playgrounds, children and adults alike seemed to find entertainment in observing plants and wildlife. In contrast to the compartmentalised uses of surrounding areas, as places for outdoor dining, scenic thoroughfares, playgrounds, or sports centres, *tillsammansodlingar* appeared to serve all these functions simultaneously.

Just as the use and organisation of green space differed, these were also contrasts with the neighbourhoods beyond the parklands that gardens were located in. The majority of areas where I found *tillsammansodlingar* were characterised by dense apartment blocks, often as part of large complexes of housing units characteristic of the modernist functionalism of *Miljon-*

programmet[26] – with housing communities featuring concentrated commercial centres with a variety of public services surrounded by large areas of apartments set amongst landscaped paths and walkways and bordered by arterial roads that connect them to other parts of their respective municipalities. Most observable human activity in these neighbourhoods was concentrated on their peripheries or in their commercial centres. It was only upon finding gardens that this trend differed, with people spending time in them without the need for events or purchases from their cafés (if they had one). More people appeared to gather in *tillsammansodlingar* than the lawns around them, although both offered places to sit, sunbathe, or picnic. In contrast to the modernist ethos of both allotment gardens and the *Miljonprogrammet*, *tillsammansodlingar* could be argued to manifest an alternative ethos of urban design, what I would call an *anti-modernist urbanism*, given it reflected an ideal about ordering and inhabiting places in the city that was observably resistant to modernist ideals of spatial planning and use.

Rooted in History and Heritage

It was not only the contrast in layout and functionality through which *tillsammansodlingar* seemed to set themselves apart from their local areas, however. In addition to being rooted in the earth – quite literally – there were other aspects of their aesthetic vocabulary that characterised these gardens and differentiated them from their surroundings. A preference for natural building materials was one such example. While thin wooden frames or peat blocks were used to reinforce raised beds at some sites, at many more branches and vines woven together were observed to serve a similar purpose, as well as functioning as fences and enclosures. A technique that resembled basket weaving, it was an ancient construction method known as *flätverksgärdsgård* [wattle fencing]. Others utilised a method known as *hankgärdsgård* [roundpole fencing], where rather than woven together, horizontal poles were held in place between a pair of stakes by means of *vidjor* [withies], flexible branches that are shaped into *hankar* [coils] around the stakes (refer to figures 15 and 16, page 98).

Complementing this tendency towards traditional garden construction practices, the built environment of *tillsammansodlingar* also referenced the Swedish countryside through colour choices. Sheds, cottages, and other

---

[26] Miljonprogrammet (literally "the million programme") refers to a public housing programme undertaken by the Swedish government between 1965 and 1974 whereby over one million dwellings were constructed to address a nationwide housing shortage as well as replace substandard housing.

structures were typically painted in a particular shade of red, often with white trim (refer to figures 17 and 18, next page). If not using one of the more ancient fencing methods, fences employed a simple post-and-rail technique, also painted in a comparable shade; so too did planter boxes when encountered. This choice of colour could be associated with a stereotypically 'traditional Swedish' aesthetic, reminiscent of small town and rural settings as it was most common to see in connection with older buildings in Sweden. Such an aesthetic therefore articulated very differently in relation to the aesthetic of modern urban cities.

Upon reviewing images of structures in gardens, there were still other features that alluded to historical influences. For instance, at Vintervikens trädgård in Stockholm, there was both a stage with outdoor dancefloor (refer to figure 19, page 99) and a bee pavilion (refer to figure 20, page 100). Both types of structures became common in Sweden in the late nineteenth century – the former for social dances organised by social and workers' movement organisations (Frykman, 1988), the latter as a way of protecting both bees and beekeepers from inclement weather (Gerner, 1881, pp. 20–21) – but were less common to encounter in the current day.

As alluded to already, many features of *tillsammansodlingar* – particularly garden construction and enclosure techniques, their colour palette, and the presence of outdoor entertainment areas – were analogous elements of allotment gardens. As such, the aesthetics of *tillsammansodlingar* could be argued to reflect a continuation of an established heritage within urban agriculture in the country. However, like the various historical elements of their design, most allotment gardens were themselves heritage sites, their aesthetics being maintained from the time of their establishment over a century earlier. *Tillsammansodlingar*, by contrast, were the product of contemporary design choices.

Figures 15–18: *Tillsammansodlingar* often manifested traditional design and aesthetics, visible, for example, in enclosure techniques (**Fig. 15 & 16** top and second from top) and building design (**Fig. 17 & 18**, second from bottom and bottom). (*Credit*: Author)

Figure 19: Vintervikens trädgård, in Stockholm, featured a large outdoor dance floor and stage, a common feature of the Swedish social landscape in the late nineteenth and early twentieth centuries. (*Credit:* Author)

Figure 20: Vintervikens trädgård also featured a bee pavilion, uncommon in the current day, yet a typical feature of beekeeping in the late nineteenth century, as it protected bee colonies from exposure to harsh winter weather. (*Credit:* Author)

The closest aesthetic comparisons that could be made to *tillsammansodlingar* within their urban settings were thus with heritage preservation areas that reflected pre-twentieth century Swedish architecture and design aesthetics in their materials, colours, and techniques. Such an aesthetic remained a feature of the contemporary built environment to a larger degree in rural areas of the country, part of the normative design of small towns and country homes. In most urban areas however, it was largely restricted to allotment gardens and heritage districts that had been spared demolition during periods of redevelopment in the twentieth century. They could also be found in the country's open-air, living history museums, sites composed of 'collections' of buildings that had been physically relocated from other parts of the country and 'archived' in a single location within urban centres that were otherwise being redeveloped according to modernist planning rationales (see e.g., Arrhenius, 2010; Rentzhog, 2007).

Through their aesthetic vocabulary, *tillsammansodlingar* could therefore be observed to articulate a material and aesthetic equivalence with agrarian ways of life across time and geography, thereby constituting a degree of equivalence with small-town and historical Swedish idylls. Because of this, I argue that the aesthetic of these gardens rearticulated a rural or historical character into the urban cityscape, and that the subsequent redefinition of contemporary urban design and development ideals this involved was relevant to their significance. The relationship being expressed was not only an aesthetic or historical-temporal one, but also a spatial-geographical one, highlighting the importance of viewing a place through its relationships to other places – in this case, the countryside – with articulation being one means of entry to investigate those relationships insofar as the character of a specific place is a product of how it is articulated within the context of wider setting (cf. Massey, 2005, p. 130). The aesthetic of *tillsammansodlingar* represented a ruralisation of the urban environment as an aesthetic ideal, constituting a political ethos as it concerned a collective belief about the sense of place that should be provided in contemporary cities. Looking at their material construction alone, it wasn't clear what this significance might be. It was also necessary to investigate this in discourse with the local environment beyond the gardens themselves.

Considering *tillsammansodlingar* in discourse with their surroundings, their prototypical aesthetic appeared to materially resist the rationalities by which urban land was being used around them. Distinguishing themselves from modernist aesthetics in architecture, landscape, and urban planning, a spatial discourse concerned with modernist design and 'efficient' use of space was interpretable. By holding this rationality at a distance, *tillsammansodlingar* seemed to articulate an alternative idea about cityscapes and thus city life, one that was inclusive of inefficient places and inefficient uses. I would argue this anti-modernist urbanism reflected a *counter-conduct* of urban spatial practice (cf. Foucault, 2007, p. 201), as it manifested an alternate rationality of how to inhabit urban space that was contrary to the modernist design characteristic of the communities surrounding many of these gardens). Instead of rationalities of preservation or redevelopment and modernisation as normative 'truths' by which planning and design choices should be deemed right or reasonable, *tillsammansodlingar* reflected a valorisation of aspects of rural and traditional agricultural heritage as appropriate for integration into contemporary urban design.

In this manner, *tillsammansodlingar* can be observed to articulate alternative discourses about city life and of the relationship between individual and society, much like Bergquist (1996) observed in his study of the early decades of the Swedish allotment movement. The choices made in their design and layout are not independent of ethical judgements, whether those pertaining to the ideal organisation of urban space and food cultivation or the ideal social relationships to be encouraged and facilitated through gardens as public spaces (pp. 278–282). While sharing certain features that associated them with historical sites, rural heritage, and a stereotypical 'traditional Swedish' aesthetic, *tillsammansodlingar* were built in the present day and functioned as non-commodified spaces – open to all, without entry fee, waiting list, or mission to convey 'how life used to be'. And while the aesthetic genre of *tillsammansodlingar* may have had certain equivalences with some other sites in their respective cities, they contrasted with a normative urban design characterised by large apartment blocks built in the mid-twentieth century according to rationalities of density and compartmentalisation.

The application of traditional techniques of garden construction, and selective appropriation of traditional and rural aesthetic elements from their historical and geographical contexts, thus rearticulated Swedish vernacular architecture through its insertion as a feature of a contemporary urban design. In doing so, the aesthetics of these gardens blurred temporal and geographical distinctions between past and present, as well as rural and urban. Manifesting an alternate vision of urban life that articulated practices and aesthetics more familiar in rural and heritage preservation contexts into the contemporary cityscape, I argue that *tillsammansodlingar* reflected a projected social rationality of urban ruralisation. As an imagined alternative practice not yet materialised as normative, such a rationality could be understood to reflect an ideal for looking to the past, and to small-town and rural communities, to inform alternative norms of decision-making in relation to urban land use, planning, and design. Interpreted thusly, this projected rationality of urban ruralisation involved an aesthetic ethos that extended into a broader political one – that cultural heritage and rural life should be brought into the present as elements of contemporary urban living and spatial practice.

As this exploration suggests, in comparison to *Gemeinschaftsgärten*, I had a somewhat easier time making sense of the aesthetic vocabulary of *tillsammansodlingar*. It was already somewhat familiar to me, but not from prior visits to such gardens; rather, it was due to my prior experience of travels throughout Sweden, exposure to a similar aesthetic in small towns and open-air museums across the country, and through Swedish media. Having pre-existing context through which to relate the aesthetic vocabulary of *tillsammansodlingar* to other places and contexts (cf. Dufrenne, 1973), it was possible to interpret how they articulated within a broader social context, facilitating my ability to make sense of my observations.

As I noted in the material culture of *Gemeinschaftsgärten*, the commoning of urban space seemed to be equally significant in Sweden, manifesting in the form *tillsammansodlingar* took as an aesthetic counterpoint to their environments. Though a comparable rearticulation could be observed in the allotment gardens that were often located nearby, in many ways they had a more intermediate relationship in discourses of urban space. Although aesthetically similar to *tillsammansodlingar*, this was a continuation and preservation of an established allotment aesthetic. Also, they were compartmentalised like much of the cityscape around them, and only pseudo-public places; visitors were only meant to walk the paths between allotments, and only during designated times when the gates to these areas were unlocked.

Signs of Welcome and Working Together

Despite a contrast in rationalities of spatial design with their surroundings, analysing signs and banners at *tillsammansodlingar* nuanced how I understood the relationship between these gardens and their social contexts. Although their aesthetic appeared to deviate from the modernist tendencies of their surrounding cityscapes, the political character of signs at *tillsammansodlingar* did not suggest a similar relationship to their social context. Unlike the signs of resistance and solidarity at *Gemeinschaftsgärten* and their calls to action that accompanied these, the signs at *tillsammansodlingar* were characterised by logotypes highlighting sponsorships, partnerships, and membership. With few exceptions, these gardens appeared to be made possible and sustained through collaboration or sponsorship – most often with public sector organisations. In addition to municipal departments and local housing authorities, these at times included continuing education organisations or the Church of Sweden.

Often small, with a few sentences about the site and a couple of logotypes placed discretely along the bottom, the language of these signs distinguished sites from their social environment. Tending to be more descriptive than the statements, proclamations, and exclamatory manifestos encountered in Germany, they included paragraphs of text that provided information about becoming involved, historical context, or information about the mission of the *tillsammansodling* in question. Certain thematic commonalities were noted among these materials, including an emphasis on the fact that community residents had formed voluntary associations to care for their sites, language that expressed the significance of these gardens as natural meeting places, and words of welcome encouraging passers-by to contribute on their own terms.

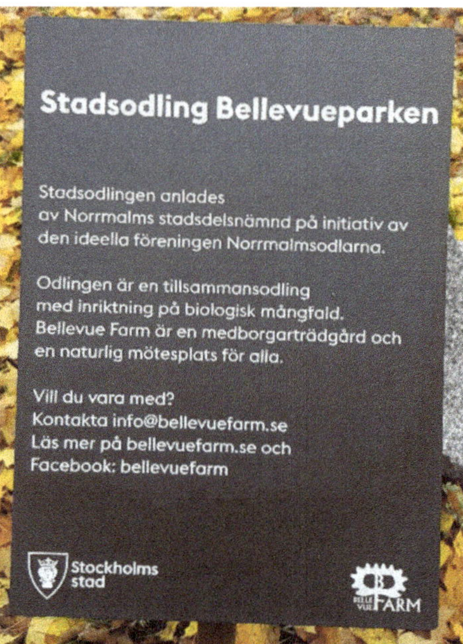

Figures 21–23: Typically found on public land, *tillsammansodlingar* would post signs that described their purpose to passers-by, encouraged involvement, and noted the municipal partnerships through which they became possible. (*Credit:* Author)

As I would argue, such messages situated *tillsammansodlingar* within discourses of civic engagement, both in their focus on taking collective responsibility for urban space and the anti-hierarchical social organising apparent in their relaxed approaches to participation. In both senses, this messaging reinforced my perception of *tillsammansodlingar* as places for urban commoning, providing a collective benefit via non-capitalist means through the community resources they provided and how they were operated and cared for (cf. Harvey, 2012). Language presenting a garden as *"en naturlig mötesplats för alla"* [a natural meeting place for all] (refer to figure 22, prior page, top right) conveyed what I considered as two complimentary senses of place – identifying *tillsammansodlingar* as places to meet *in* and interact *with* nature (in the sense of plant, fungal, and animal life), as well as the idea that urban commons such as these were natural (in the sense of being logical or innate) places for social life to occur.[27] Reflecting then on the logotypes on garden signage, they were interpreted to convey analogous agendas between the associations caring for these sites and their municipal or quasi-governmental sponsors and partners. To the extent that I could observe and intuit from the material cultures of *tillsammansodlingar*, associations and their sponsors seemed to work from a common discourse about the role of civil society in assuming responsibility for community life.

While their aesthetics did not convey explicit or contentious critiques of their surrounding cityscape, the emphasis of signage on providing natural meeting spaces and being open to all for involvement and contributions implied a constitutive outside – the garden characterised by its contrast with features of the city beyond it (cf. Laclau, 1990, p. 192) – that was lacking in such opportunities. It also reinforced an interpretation of these gardens as places for urban commoning, implicitly characterising a need in relation to the areas where these gardens were established. As one sign expressed, an identity for *tillsammansodlingar* could be reflected in their self-expressed mission: *"Här odlar vi grönsaker, blommor och gemenskap"* [Here we grow vegetables, flowers, and community] (refer to figure 23, prior page, bottom). Such a statement of purpose could be interpreted as advertising the collective ideals, or ethos, of those who were engaged in that garden, with the cultivation of food, flowers, and a sense of community articulated as values that characterised the sense of place by which *tillsammansodlingar* were able to be mean something as a particular type of place. Because this was being done collectively, in environments intended for other purposes according to different design principles, it could be understood to convey a political desire

---

[27] There were some exceptions to this trend of *tillsammansodlingar* initiated, sponsored, or otherwise supported by local organisations and municipal actors. A handful of gardens – primarily in rural communities and smaller towns – instead aligned themselves to the *Omställningsrörelsen,* the Swedish term for the global Transition Towns movement, as grassroot community projects to increase self-sufficiency to reduce the potential effects of peak oil, climate destruction, and economic instability.

sought through a particular way of knowing and relating to place as encouraged by these garden associations.

Based on the prototypical aesthetic of welcome and informational signs posted at *tillsammansodlingar*, I posit that they can be analysed as expressions of a political ethos to the extent that they explicitly communicate purposes for these places. Implicitly or explicitly, they express collective intentions about community and environmental benefit. They not only advertised themselves as initiatives that, in my estimation, had much in common with commoning; they also alluded to the embodiment of an ethos of collaboration between garden collectives and public institutions as fundamental to their commoning efforts.

Although the design and layout of these gardens tended to support an interpretation of modernist urban planning as a constitutive outside, institutions that were tied to the same political order that upheld these planning and development practices appeared nonetheless to be internally constitutive of *tillsammansodlingar*. In other words, despite observations that the aesthetic genre of these gardens tended to be constituted through the exclusion and subversion of the spatial compartmentalisation, densification, and efficiency characteristic of normative urban planning practice, this did not preclude the possibility that municipal planners were also amenable to a degree of non-normative urban spatial use. The fact of their partnership implied some degree of common interest between the associations and collectives that maintained *tillsammansodlingar* and the municipal bodies and decisionmakers permitting these gardens to be established on public land.

Accordingly, the discourses I observed as analogous with commoning, alongside the visual displays of collaboration between voluntary organisations and public institutions alluded to an interesting example of pericapitalist practice. Viewed from one perspective, *tillsammansodlingar* could be understood as pericapitalist because of the anti-capitalist commoning tendencies expressed through their material culture. From another perspective, this same material culture – not least the signs of partnership with municipal governments – offered an interpretation of pericapitalist tendencies within government institutions as well. They seemed willing to support commoning projects that, in some small part, gave residents direct involvement in determining the form and function of public space. Whether or not voluntary associations and municipal decisionmakers promoted *tillsammansodlingar* according to the same values or motivations, there was nonetheless an observable implication of analogous significance by which the partnerships advertised were possible.

Furthermore, the focus on partnerships apparent in their signs made it clear that these were places where people were actively engaged with political institutions, and thus the political life of their communities. As such, they could be argued to be consistent with a view of citizenship as an active political practice, to the extent that citizens were collectively partnering with local government to provide a place of community benefit. They took political positions in the values they advocated, and engagement with municipal institutions was implied by the partnerships they advertised.

Concluding Discussion

As I found, each country had a prototypical genre through which a common aesthetic vocabulary of materials, structures, and signs constituted most collective gardens. While I interpreted a pronounced tension between the aesthetic environment of *Gemeinschaftsgärten* and the cityscapes in which they were located, their DIY and recycling ethos nonetheless benefited from, and was made possible by, salvaging sites and materials discarded and abandoned in the course of capitalist production. And while *tillsammansodlingar* tended to look, at first glance, in harmony with their immediate environments, they manifested tensions of both spatial and temporal characters, rearticulating rural aesthetics and agrarian cultural heritage into contemporary post-industrial cityscapes. Both genres of collective gardening could thus be argued to be characterised by a similar political ethos. Although differing in their aesthetic vocabulary, both *Gemeinschaftsgärten* and *tillsammansodlingar* articulated relationships to place and material that stood in contrast to neoliberal capitalist rationalities by which objects and land were treated as disposable commodities, and by which land was subject to modernist principles of development. While *Gemeinschaftsgärten* manifested this through an aesthetic vocabulary that rearticulated and subverted materials that would normatively be considered waste, *tillsammansodlingar* did so, in large part, by avoiding such materials altogether, instead utilising traditional techniques and historicised aesthetics.

Whether turning to salvage or heritage to construct these gardens, the disarticulation and rearticulation taking place in their aesthetic vocabularies were illustrative of meaning-making as an interpretive process. Sarah Pink (2013) cautions that photographic surveys (such as I have included here) are not 'photographic truth' but 'represent a point of view' (p. 81). Consequently, the significance of the material repertoires of each genre of collective garden was contingent on the point of view from which I observed it and what could be interpreted from materials and land use practices in relation to other places and contexts. My observations led to me agree with Pink's claim that how the visual elements of our world make sense to us is inseparable "from other elements of sensory experience […] in relation to how we might use them to produce ways of knowing that acknowledge this interrelatedness of the senses" (p. 47). Sensory experience of salvaged materials and contemporary examples of vernacular architecture were each producing other ways of knowing the use value, potential applications, and appropriate locations for objects and design features.

As Laclau and Mouffe (1985) contend, "forms of resistance to new forms of subordination are polysemic" and thus capable of being articulated into a variety of discourses (p. 169). Correspondingly, I observed how there was no single meaning or discourse of resistance to capitalism or urban space being articulated in the aesthetic vocabulary of either genre of collective garden studied here; rather, the diversity of forms of aesthetic expression could only be analysed for what they signified relationally as products of negotiating a garden's character within a wider context (cf. Massey, 2005, p. 30). Through analysis of the material culture of gardens as built environments, and the signs and banners displayed within and around them, they were interpretable and therefore meaningful to the extent that they could be observed in relation to their surrounding environments, other use contexts (in the case of the materials used in *Gemeinschaftsgärten*), and traditional or historical practices (in the case of the built environment of *tillsammansodlingar*).

Rearticulated within the context of collective gardens, the normative association of their aesthetic vocabulary – of the bathtubs, grain sacks, and milk crates of *Gemeinschaftsgärten* with bathrooms and freight logistics, or the structures and design features of *tillsammansodlingar* with rural landscapes and heritage preservation – were still possible associations, but no longer the only ones. As Clifford (2005) phrases it, rearticulation has the result that a normative meaning "remains in the mix but no longer at the center" (pp. 43–44). In doing so, I understood my own perception of these materials to be reconfigured, and consequently observed their use in collective gardens in Germany and Sweden to desediment normative ideals of urban land use, urban design, and food cultivation practices.

Throughout this chapter, I've described my own process of aesthetic literacy, learning to "read the appropriate set of conventions" (Dufrenne, 1983, p. 209) to make sense of the material culture of collective gardens. Beyond merely describing my own experience, I argue that doing so is relevant to reflexive research, as my capacity for aesthetic interpretation, as with that of anyone else, is premised on the capability to interpret and articulate relationships between objects – in this case collective gardens and the environments in which they were located. The aesthetics of these gardens provides a practical example of discourse as a totality of linguistic and extra-linguistic elements whereby making sense of these sites relationally as objects (and amalgamations of objects) amongst other objects, required observing their surroundings to identify similarities, contrasts, and combinations of the two.

More obviously contrasting aesthetics – as seen with *Gemeinschaftsgärten* and their surrounding cityscapes, and the contentious language employed in their signs – became easier to interpret due to their juxtaposition. Those with seemingly more commonality – like *tillsammansodlingar* with parklands and allotment gardens, and their signs of partnership and collaboration – required an ability or willingness to look closer at specific details to make sense of the political ethos articulated. The ethos characteristic of each genre of collective garden consequently differed. Whereas *Gemeinschaftsgärten* manifested openly antagonistic political discourses with their urban environment, *tillsammansodlingar* – although differing from their environment – appeared to convey more amicable relationships with the political order. Following a line of enquiry that led me to investigate the precarity of *Gemeinschaftsgärten* and their explicit focus on solidarity and resistance, the complexity of their situation came into view. The conditions of existence for these gardens were not independent from the resources of land and post-consumer waste which were salvaged or otherwise acquired, each available due to capitalist production and land speculation that gardens simultaneously derived benefit from, resisted, and were made precarious by.

In contrast to the dense, winding, and untamed arrangement of plants typical of most sites in Germany I visited, most in Sweden articulated an altogether different aesthetic experience. Considering their locations, proclivity for planting in the ground, and signs that advertised partnerships with government institutions, *tillsammansodlingar* were interpreted to have more secure land tenure in comparison to most *Gemeinschaftsgärten*. I needn't necessarily have equated these elements with permanence but interpreted them thusly in contrast to *Gemeinschaftsgärten*, as well as through the aesthetic continuity observed between their built environment and the heritages rearticulated into contemporary urban space. This impression was strengthened by another clear difference between collective gardens in the two countries. The material culture of *tillsammansodlingar* was predominantly constituted by its plant layouts and built structures, whereas sites in

Germany featured signs and other forms of imagery as pronounced elements of their aesthetic genre. Additionally, while signs at *Gemeinschaftsgärten* tended towards messages of solidarity and resistance related to their preservation, signs at the entrances of *tillsammansodlingar* were generally informative about their purpose, institutional partners, and how to become involved.

Despite these differing messages, I argue that both genres of gardens, and their signs, located them within discourses of commoning and were therefore interpretable as critiques of – or reactions to – neoliberal capitalism. That said, the ethos they communicated had similarities and differences. While each genre of collective garden seemed to promote non-capitalist economies in the types of educational, material, and cultural resources present, *Gemeinschaftsgärten* had a clear re-use ethos in contrast to the preference for traditional techniques and natural materials that could be seen to characterise *tillsammansodlingar*. Though a nostalgic interpretation of *tillsammansodlingar* as an aesthetic genre could be argued, I focus here on how their design and use reflected pericapitalist values, albeit in a different manner than was observable in *Gemeinschaftsgärten*. The layouts of *tillsammansodlingar* turned away from the modernist planning and compartmentalisation of the urban settings in which they operated, just as the resources provided for common benefit suggested a break with the commodification of social life that characterised neoliberal capitalism and the consumer cityscape it conditioned (cf. Tsing, 2015).

Interpreting each type of garden as signifying a political ethos, however, required developing a foundation of contextual knowledge through which to make sense of discursive references conveyed through aesthetic forms of expression. It was in this manner that the aesthetic vocabulary of *Gemeinschaftsgärten* was interpretable in terms of discourses of salvage and waste reuse, and *tillsammansodlingar* with agrarian practice and late nineteenth century social movements and design features. Additionally, this contextual knowledge helped me to understand how the prefigurative politics of collective gardens could manifest through subtle or implicit forms of aesthetic expression through which collectives embodied a desired social reality (cf. Boggs, 1977; Yates, 2015). This included how they advertised the social value of partnership or cooperation through logotypes, how they rearticulated the value of salvaged bathtubs, or the use of contentious language to call for solidarity or resistance. Regardless of the specific values conveyed through their material cultures, both types of collective gardens demonstrated that the collectives caring for these sites considered themselves taking active involvement in the political community, not least through the messages of partnership, resistance, solidarity, and welcome that greeted visitors and passers-by.

Although quite different in their tone, messaging, design, and placement, I considered the signs displayed at both *Gemeinschaftsgärten* and *tillsammansodlingar* – like their built environments and spatial designs – to reflect a complex relationship with their urban surroundings. Illustrating the nature of discourse as a totality of linguistic and extra-linguistic elements, the words displayed on signs made sense by taking their aesthetic expression into account as well – as objects in space and thus in relation to other objects (cf. Dufrenne, 1973, pp. 135–155). Investigating the visual media displayed within collective gardens thus enriched my understanding of the discourses that gave meaning to their respective aesthetic vocabularies and their aesthetic genres as a totality. Similarly, the duality of material relationships such as those observed in *Gemeinschaftsgärten*, where salvaged materials could be interpreted as *both* a pragmatic solution to precarity *and* representative of a democratising DIY ethos, highlights the pericapitalist nature of such gardens as simultaneously premised on and subverting capitalist relationships to objects as commodities. Despite the different ways of relating to the practice of salvage as constitutive of *Gemeinschaftsgärten* (as pragmatic or political), they nonetheless share a common political ethos in terms of what they rejected – normative attitudes towards the use value and lifecycle of objects.

Having now explored aesthetics as an expression of (as I have illustrated, not exclusively) extra-linguistic elements, I continue my exploration of discourses concerning collective gardens by directing attention to narratives as examples of their linguistic expression. To do this, the empirical material narrows from a sampling of two genres of collective gardens to encompass two case studies, one selected from each genre. A case study approach benefits the exploration of collective gardens as sites of prefigurative pericapitalist practice because it enables productive dialogue between the context-specific analysis of individual gardens, nuancing and sobering the generalisations that may be possible (see, e.g., Eriksen, 2014; Nystrand von Unge, 2019; Passeron & Revel, 2005). In the three analytical chapters that follow, I therefore look at Prinzessinnengarten and Vintervikens trädgård as case studies of *Gemeinschaftsgärten* and *tillsammansodlingar*, respectively. Starting with analyses of founding narratives of the two gardens in the next chapter, the two subsequent chapters each take up the contemporary social context of one of the two case studies. These latter two chapters both explore the contemporary social antagonisms being articulated in narratives as an entry point to analyse how discourses of contemporary urban life and rationalities of late modern capitalism pertain to the future-oriented prefigurative politics being experimented with at each garden.

5. Reclaiming Land & Social Life
through Responsible Citizenship:
Narrating Gardens as Solutions

My focus in this chapter shifts from the aesthetics of *Gemeinschaftsgärten* and *tillsammansodlingar* as genres of collective gardens to narratives about the project's two case studies, Vintervikens trädgård in Stockholm and Prinzess-innengarten in Berlin. As discussed in the introductory chapters, Francesca Polletta's research on social movements brings to the fore a variety of roles for narratives, particularly in sustaining collective identity within movement organisations. Narratives, she asserts, help groups "to make sense of unfami-liar events, to engage as they explain, and to sustain identity during periods of rapid change" (1998a, p. 143). In the context of collective gardens, nar-ratives are also a way of conveying their sense of place, or character, as arti-culated within a wider context (see, e.g., Basso 1996b; Massey, 2005). Because a sense of place is partly constituted through how a place is remembered through its history (Feld & Basso, 1996, p. 11), the chapter begins with the histories of the sites where Vintervikens trädgård and Prinzessinnengarten were established, before proceeding to stories that narrate the actual estab-lishment of each garden.

As Polletta et al. (2021) argue, the discursive character of a narrative means that it "sets the terms for its own evaluation and how it constitutes speakers and audiences, doing both in ways that foreclose alternatives" (p. 71). Or, as Stuart Hall (1999) describes it, narratives are *encoded* with preferred, *associative* meanings, that are able to be *decoded* (i.e., they become intelligible) to the extent that they fulfil expected conventions of storytelling and narrative structure and provide necessary context (p. 510).[28] Narratives about collective gardens include details that convey how an audience should relate to these places, offering preferred interpretations or ways of decoding their relevance by associating them with values, themes, and events. "The story's end is consequential; it is not only outcome but moral of the events which precede it" (Polletta, 1998b, p. 423). As a researcher, it is possible to interpret the meanings associated with collective gardens to the extent that I

---

[28] Hall (1999) refers to these as 'frameworks of knowledge'.

can 'decode' the cues provided in narratives, and through the act of narration, as they work to convey a moral or resolution of events.

Analysing local histories as a form of pre-history for the gardens studied here, conceptualising narratives in this manner is useful to investigate collective gardens as solutions to social issues. Carol Bacchi's (2012) problem formulation approach to policy analysis is adapted and applied to narratives, as it provides a helpful framework for interpreting how people account for the social circumstances in which gardens were established, and the rhetoric by which they were portrayed as natural reactions and necessary solutions to problems that preceded them.[29] Like policy proposals, the histories recounted about places formed with an intent for social change are thus understood to "contain implicit representations of what is considered to be the 'problem'" (Bacchi, 2012, p. 21).

Applied here, the pre-histories of collective gardens can be considered to provide the terms of evaluation against which the significance of these gardens is to be interpretable.[30] Accordingly, narratives about these sites retroactively set up the problems they will come to resolve through their establishment, thereby articulating their social value in relation to a recounted past that preceded them. Like the findings of prior research on allotment gardens and community gardening, the analysis of narratives of collective gardens can provide insight into social critiques and the need for social change based on how the gardens are presented as solutions to the problems they have been constituted in discourse with. Just as the aesthetics of collective gardens were interpretable insofar as they were relatable to other places or use contexts for their materials, the narrative construction of collective gardens as results of the articulation of events and associations to other places also offers a means through which to understand their significance. As places involve the negotiation of intersecting trajectories, they therefore reflect the intersection of different stories in order to give meaning and convey a sense of place (Massey, 2005, p. 130). Taking each garden in turn, narratives concerning their prehistories and founding are investigated, applying Bacchi's analytical approach to explore how characterisations of the

---

[29] As discussed in Chapter 2, although Bacchi (2012) specifically developed this approach for the purposes of policy analysis, it is applied here as I consider it consistent with Polletta's (1998a; 1998b) discursive understanding of social movement narratives and the rhetorical strategies they employ to motivate or account for collective action and reinforce collective identity.

[30] While Polletta (2002) focuses on identity politics in social movements and Basso (1996a; 1996b) on place identities, both make similar arguments for viewing narratives as linguistic forms of discourse through which social knowledge is transmitted, conveying cultural beliefs, values, and ways of interpreting the past and thus the symbolic value of social and place relations in the present.

local community establish social problems for which the gardens come to represent solutions by contrast.

With Prinzessinnengarten, I had access to a detailed official history available on the garden's website, as well as a visual timeline, each of which provided insight into the official narrative of the garden's founding and social critiques deemed pertinent to understand the political significance associated with the garden. As for Vintervikens trädgård, I turned to a broader range of material available to me because of extended participant observation at the site – primarily oral histories recounted by participants, collected through interviews, participant observation, and documents available in Stockholm's municipal archive. Each of these sources of material enabled an examination of 'preferred readings', institutionalised or legitimate ways of understanding meaning (see, e.g., Hall, 1999, pp. 513–514) – in this case the meaning of two gardens as culminations of local histories preceding them. Although presenting certain limitations with regards to comparing like materials, this allowed for analysis of how participants and the municipal planning office each conveyed a particular sense of place relative to the medium of communication, use context, and audience.

In addition to fully formed or 'big stories' involving "a coherent temporal progression of events" with "a plotline that encompasses a beginning, a middle, and an end" (Ochs & Capps, 2001, p. 57), 'small stories' are also examined. The latter refer to non-elicited narratives including "tellings of ongoing events, future or hypothetical events, and shared (known) events, […] allusions to (previous) tellings, deferrals of tellings, and refusals to tell" (Bamberg & Georgakopoulou, 2008, p. 381). As the descriptor 'small' suggests, these tend to comprise fleeting narrative moments, brief asides when a narrative orientation arises in the course of everyday interactions. Rather than complete, self-contained stories, small stories tend to be disjointed, partial or fragmentary stories or allusions to stories (Georgakopoulou, 2015). They can reveal by not revealing, which is to say that small stories can be analysed through what the narrator takes for granted that their audience already knows, what they seem to avoid discussing, or how they are narrating and making sense of events as they happen.

Vintervikens trädgård: From Dumping Ground to Demonstration Garden

In telling the story of Vintervikens trädgård, both the association and municipal planners took credit for making the garden possible. Each considered it to solve problems affecting the city district in which it was located. While the collective narrative of the association was pieced together from interviews and casual conversations with informants, the founding as recounted by municipal planners had been summarised in reports to Stockholm's Executive Board. Each associated Vinterviken with the improvement of the city district surrounding it. While collective members and municipal planners alike shared certain assessments of the benefits brought by the garden however, they premised these on very different rationalities and relationships to the area. Analysing these differing stories of the garden's origins alongside one another, it provided a more complex picture of how the Vintervikens trädgård came to fruition, prompting considerations about the nature of responsibility and citizenship in the process.

A Solution to Destitution and Dumping

In researching the history of Vintervikens trädgård, a pair of reports from Stockholm's municipal archive discussed the garden as one of three sub-projects that were planned by the city as part of a revitalisation project called *Kulturpark Liljeholmen* [Liljeholmen Culture Park] (Gatu- och fastighets-kontoret Stockholms stad, 2001; Kommunstyrelsen Stockholms stad, 2004). While the founding narrative they provide will be addressed later, the second of these two reports briefly alludes to the prehistory of the garden by stating that "the City Executive Office considers that the city has carried out an urgent upgrade of the urban environment in the area and increased attractiveness in this part of the southern city" (Kommunstyrelsen Stockholms stad, 2004, p. 8; my translation). Through its assumption of a commonly known narrative or image of this area, this small story could be seen to imply that the location of Kulturpark Liljeholmen had previously been unattractive and in such a problematic state as to need the 'urgent upgrade' referred to in these reports. What was it about the city district that went unspoken in this historical allusion? What context helped to explain the need to improve the area, and how did this relate to Vinterviken?

This line of enquiry prompted an exploration into how long-time residents involved with the garden recalled the neighbourhood prior to the establishment of Vintervikens trädgård, and how they characterised changes to the area since then. Among those interviewed at the garden, two people reflected on the longer history of the area, recalling the adjoining neighbourhood of Aspudden as it was in the decades prior to Vinterviken's establishment. One of them, Stefan, had been born and raised in another nearby neighbourhood, moving to Aspudden as an adult. As he reflected:

It's changed quite a lot, Aspudden. It was just destitution and social deprivation, I mean that's what it was, just 30–40 years ago. [...] Back then, from a social perspective, they placed a lot of outcasts and *really* down-and-out people in Aspudden. And yeah, it was destitute. A lot of addiction, a truly tragic environment, in fact. There was talk about tearing the whole area down actually, because there was such a low standard of living and such [...]. my mom said this when I was 10–12 years old: "You *cannot* cycle to Aspudden". She said it was because of all the *ölkaféer* [beer cafés],[31] and they were all drunk and there were drugs and such. So of course, we'd cycle right over there to check out what it was like. It was totally fascinating. But yeah, it was like that.

[...]

But it's truly interesting because this area has changed completely. There used to be burned-out car wrecks here and it was more or less a dumping ground. I cycled past a lot back then, back and forth to the city, and it was pitch black at night down here. There wasn't any lighting at all. It's a *really* unpleasant feeling. When you think how today so many people are moving about in the area, this here has contributed so much to the sense of safety in the area, just developing the garden and its activities, that's for sure. (Stefan, interview, 10 March 2022; his emphasis; my translation)

Not unlike the narratives about the garden's role in relation to the improvement of the community, the prehistory provided by Stefan could be understood to set the terms of evaluation of Vinterviken's history within a context of community transformation and improvement. He did so by evoking the problem of a 'tragic environment' that was unsafe and unwelcoming, articulating several illustrative elements of Aspudden's once tragic nature to do so – housing quality, public safety, poverty, and drug and alcohol addiction. Set up as a story of transformation, the presence of Vinterviken and the increased pedestrian traffic connected with its activities solved a safety problem, providing a pleasant environment that offered more than places for alcoholics to convene.

Stefan also described the safety of the area in terms of the social dumping that occurred there and related problems that contributed to a *'tragic' sense of place*. As he expanded on later in our discussion, the dumping occurring was not limited to the concentration of social outcasts but also material waste:

---

[31] The term *ölkaféer* (lit. beer cafés) refers to businesses where beer sales constitute at least 50 % of overall sales (Hallberg, 1982, p. 30).

It was just like a nature area, or rather a trash heap, there were things like blast stone, parts of mattresses, old car batteries. There was just shit everywhere in the area, and undergrowth.

[...]

Well, they dumped so much crap and it was claimed that a lot of what was there came from building the subway system and the motorway. They'd come down here with freight trucks and just dump garbage. It's but I don't think one could dare do that today, at least not in the same way, I don't think. (Stefan, interview, 10 March 2022; my translation)

While Stefan's reflections could be interpreted to frame the problem as due to social dumping and waste dumping, this did not appear to be what he considered as the underlying problem. Rather, these issues were presented as results of bad social planning and waste management policies, suggesting the municipal government had failed in its responsibilities. Also, Stefan's articulation of a tragic sense of place was not only interpretable in relation to its historical association with waste and industry, but also its relation to other areas of town considering the disproportionate concentration of social exclusion by which he characterised the area's past, and the fact it was deemed acceptable to dump construction waste there. It was less safe or desirable than other areas not only because of its recent industrial past, but also because it had been acceptable to treat it as a dumping ground for waste and a neighbourhood for concentrating social marginalisation because it kept those problems from other areas of the city.

Additionally, through his reference to *ölkaféer*, done with the assumption that I knew what this term meant and symbolised, Stefan articulated elements such as the type of people, treatment of land, the darkness of the area, and lack of maintenance to portray a historical status quo. Expressing multiple social critiques, Stefan seemed to evoke a sense of place for the area that, in the decades preceding the garden's establishment, should be understood as unacceptable. The social conditions he described conveyed a criticism of the past and the norms of city management that characterised it, setting up a historical problem through which Vinterviken's significance could thus be evaluated (cf. Bacchi, 2012). In both the personal and local history that Stefan provided, implicit comparisons between past and present could be interpreted.

Speaking with Eva, who had lived in the area since the 1970s, she provided a similar account to Stefan's. In speaking about social life in the area when she first moved to Aspudden, one place came to mind as characteristic of where one might go to socialise in the area. As her description conveyed, it attracted a very specific demographic and wasn't appealing for a young family like hers to visit with their small child:

> Until not so long ago there was one restaurant in this area. […] I forget what it was called. It was like the world's biggest *fylleslag*[32] there, one could say. Because of that, it attracted so many people who had alcohol problems here. But it's changed *so* much. It's certainly gentrified, one might say. (Eva, interview, 30 October 2018; my translation)

What I interpreted from Eva's reflections on the area's past, like Stefan's recollections of local *ölkaféer*, was that the area lacked social life, or at least public social life, and the few people attracted to come to the area to socialise did not contribute to a welcoming or safe environment. Through the juxtaposition of before and after in the narratives of informants and municipal reports, the garden came to symbolise safety, social life, and respect for the environment. Attributing the transformation of the area in part to the garden's presence in the area, these narratives, like Bacchi's (2012) problem formulation, portrayed the time before as a problem or grievance, and the time after as a solution (or resolution) in the form of the garden's existence. The garden, as solution, was already in place at the time in which the story is told, with the problems associated with the neighbourhood presented as retroactive, historical facts.

In her analysis of social movement narratives, Polletta (1998b) suggests that a common feature of effective narratives is their ability to legitimate a course of action as a solution to moral grievances (p. 423; cf. Cashman, 2006, pp. 137-138; Koskinen-Koisvisto, 2016, p.174). By equating the area's past, as Stefan and Eva did, with a sense of place variously characterised as a natural dumping ground, scary, trashy, and unsafe, there was an implication that the city government was complicit in, if not actively responsible for, the social policies and waste management practices that contributed to these problems – even if the city government had later been active in 'upgrading' the area. Furthermore, neither Stefan nor Eva relied upon facts, figures, or reports (such as crime statistics, toxicity reports, or alcohol consumption per capita) to lend legitimacy to their interpretations of the changes seen in the neighbourhood and the social and political causes underlying them. Rather,

---

[32] This is a Swedish term describing a party where the only purpose is to drink as much alcohol as possible; a keg party or gathering of binge drinkers approximate the sense of the term.

they used descriptions of the past and how they personally experienced it, implicitly juxtaposing these recollections with the manifestly different character of the area in the present-day. Stefan's narrative of the area over time, and thereby Vinterviken's relevance in discourses of urban social and planning policy, relied upon setting up a critical past through which the garden was symbolic of the transformation of the overall character of the neighbourhood. Starting with how things used to be but no longer were, his and Eva's narratives portrayed a garden that had distanced the neighbourhood from this unpleasant past and in doing so changed the negative public perception of the area.

For her part, Eva was not involved in the establishment of the association but had followed events at the time before later becoming involved. As she reflected, it wasn't only the collective action of creating the garden but the collective labour of maintaining such a place for the neighbourhood and beyond that gave Vinterviken its significance:

> I think it is a *fantastic* organisation down in Vintervikens trädgård. I have such respect for what folks do there. *It's just fantastic* to see something like that going on twenty years now, basically through voluntary labour. The whole time its only grown, and it has such a *huge significance* for Aspudden as a whole, one might say. *And for the inner city even.* Plenty of folks come out here from the city centre too. (Eva, interview, 30 October 2018; her emphasis; my translation)

While her comments in this excerpt did not explicitly address the founding of the garden, Eva's reflection on the changes to the area were being juxtaposed with her earlier characterisation of Aspudden as an area where alcoholics congregated. By articulating volunteers and voluntary work as part of the significance of Vinterviken, it could be argued that her reflections presented the garden as a place that persisted in solving problems through its continued presence. Equally, she seemed to consider the garden as extending its reach, also solving problems related to social life for the inner city through its existence and proximity.

A Temporary Exhibit Becomes Part of a Long-Term Plan

While narratives and small stories about the history of the area characterise Vinterviken as part of a story of local transformation, founding narratives of the garden itself revealed how individuals and city planners alike made sense of the garden in contrast to this past. While both local community members and municipal leaders saw it as a valuable contribution to the area, what it represented to each differed. For participants whom I spoke with in interviews and informal conversations, Vinterviken's significance was rooted in the collective action through which a temporary exhibit became a permanent part of the local area. As recounted in municipal reports, however, the sense of place was articulated in terms of the successful reproduction of an existing garden model from another area of the city.

As I was informed on multiple occasions when speaking with garden members, Vintervikens trädgård was not simply the result of a comprehensive city-led initiative. On the garden's website, an official history was recounted, describing the location where it was built and offering a summary of the circumstances through which the garden itself was established:

> For a long time, the valley basin of Vinterviken, between Aspudden and Gröndal, was an industrial area where [Alfred] Nobel's various companies had an explosives factory and other activities all the way until the 1980s. Since then, the area slowly developed into a recreation area with walking paths, allotment gardens, bathing areas and our demonstration garden.
>
> The first parts of Vintervikens trädgård were established when the city was 1998 Cultural Capital of Europe. In Autumn 1999, a non-profit association was set up in order to operate and further develop the idea for a demonstration garden at the site. In the years since, the garden has changed and developed in an organic manner, always with through the work effort of volunteers at the core. (Vintervikens trädgård, 2017; my translation)

According to this description, Vintervikens trädgård was the outgrowth of a year-long city-wide cultural event, with an association stepping in after the event to develop the garden further. Despite its brevity, this founding narrative situated the garden and its volunteers as part of a transformation from industrial space to urban recreation area, echoing the problem-solution formula set up in recounting the prehistory of the garden. Its sense of place was evoked through being a place cared for by volunteers and which had developed organically over time.

This history piqued my curiosity, not least to learn how the organisational change at Vintervikens trädgård – from exhibition to association – was accounted for. What configuration of events were considered central to understanding the garden's significance? How could more context about the history of the site help to make sense of the garden as a particular location within its local community? The welcome signs typical of *tillsammansodlingar* had suggested unproblematic relationships based on partnership and municipal support. As I came to observe in the relationship between the association and Stockholm's municipal government though, there appeared to be a more complex relationship between the two parties.

"It was just *so stupid*": From Concern to Action

Explanations came through speaking with participants at the site, particularly those who were involved since the garden's early days or who had lived in the area long enough to recall the events surrounding Vinterviken's establishment. In the recollections and asides of informants, various rationalities were shared for why residents felt compelled to step in and take responsibility in the interest of community benefit. As I heard upon meeting with Karl during my very first visit to the garden:

> Karl explained to me how the original idea came from a woman working in city planning, explaining that it was done as a temporary exhibit for the year when Stockholm was 'cultural capital'. Sharing the story further, he stated that the theme for the garden had been "a garden accessible to all". He told me how at the end of the year, the city planned to demolish the garden. Many in the community wanted to preserve it, and a group of people in the community, including himself, initiated a demonstration to stop its demolition, petitioning the city to turn over care for the garden to the community. (fieldnotes, 27 February 2018).

Speaking with Karl about the garden and what went on there, he began our talk with this unsolicited founding narrative. I later overheard similar retellings on at least two other occasions, both during lunchtime conversation with people who had recently began to participate in working days at the garden. Though seemingly matter of fact, Karl's recollection hinted at a conflict or tension through his mention of a collective group taking a stance against the plans of municipal decisionmakers. It conveyed that demonstrators should be interpreted as a collective of 'concerned citizens' who saw the value in preserving the garden. Karl's summary of Vinterviken's beginnings suggested a tension between the intentions of municipal planners and the collective of demonstrators – the former only seeing the contribution or value of the garden as a temporary exhibit, the latter committed to its potential as a more permanent demonstration garden and community resource.

While Karl recounted events in what I found to be a 'matter of fact' manner, lacking explicit value judgements, Lars – another active member of the association since its establishment – explained the sentiment of the time quite bluntly when I spoke with him about the garden's early days. During a lunchtime conversation one working day, he reflected on how long he'd been involved, making a brief aside about the founding of the garden association. "The city built a garden as an 'exhibition' and then just wanted to tear it down. We thought it was just *so stupid* to tear down something that added to the area" (Lars, personal communication, 7 December 2018; his emphasis; my translation). As with Karl, he emphasised a shared value in speaking on behalf of a collective of demonstrators, which alluded to a presumed common narrative of how those involved experienced and made sense of the events which had transpired. In this case, there was an implied collective judgement of the need to come together and take responsibility. The collective of demonstrators were portrayed as having solved a problem – the threat of losing the garden – by becoming responsible for its preservation and maintenance.

When I interviewed Stefan, he recounted a similar narrative to Lars, with a similar expression of emotions, intonating his voice as he reflected on city planning policy relative to the original garden exhibit. The moral of the story he provided positioned the city as wasteful and careless, mismanaging public finances and public land:

> Well, it's interesting, you probably already know, of course, the background here… that the city set up a garden here in 98. And that was, you know, because Stockholm was the cultural capital that year, so they step up the whole area with lighting on the paths, renovating the Nobel factory and such, because it was completely dilapidated … and they also set up a garden here, as there wasn't anything. And it was intended to be temporary for the season. Then, they would tear it down. So, folks were livid, of course, and said "*What do you mean, you've spent 1.5 million crowns in taxpayer money just to take away this garden?! We're gonna set up an association and take it over!*". That was how it began, let me tell you. So, it was *truly short-sighted* on the city's part, just to do it to have something pretty for that year. "*Yes, then we can let the site go to ruin again*". (Stefan, interview, 10 March 2022; his emphasis; my translation)

Stefan nuanced his narrative by focusing on social values and critiques about normative practices of public financing. As such, I interpreted his comments to take issue with a governmental rationality, whereby the municipality was portrayed to be acting as if its actions should be reasonable and acceptable to the community. As Foucault (1988) discusses, dealing with governmentality involves analysing how people question and problematise self-evident, familiar, or accepted rules and habits (p. 265). By problematising the actions of the municipality, Stefan's criticism could be interpreted as a problematisation of the governmentality of urban planners. Through the implication that public officials were motivated by short-term city branding rather than a long-term investment in the local quality of life, he portrayed the planners responsible for the exhibition as taking for granted that wasting large sums of public funds on temporary projects was normal behaviour. In contrast to this characterisation of what the municipal government was seen to take as self-evident and acceptable governance, Stefan's narrative equated the association and demonstrators – and thus Vintervikens trädgård – as signifying a commitment to long-term community development. Consequently, Vinterviken was being portrayed as solving not only the problem of the area's past as a dumping ground, but also the problem of half-hearted municipal investment in the community.

As I interpreted from their recollections of events, Lars and Stefan were not only directing their incredulity towards the city of Stockholm and its urban planners and planning policies, but also towards me as their audience. Mindful that meaning is articulated as much via extra-linguistic as linguistic means (see Laclau & Mouffe, 1987, pp. 82-83), the emotional emphasis that each invested in their words contributed to understanding the significance of these narratives. This was apparent when Lars tensed with anger at the stupidity he associated with city officials, and when Stefan raised his voice with incredulity as he recalled how livid demonstrators (himself included) had been. The body language of both men was relevant for conveying the sense of grievance they equated with the threatened demolition of Vinterviken.

Regarding investment in causes, Laclau (2005) argues that emotional attachments cannot be dismissed "in the name of an uncontaminable rationality" as

> [t]here is no possibility of a language in which value relations would be established only between formally specifiable units. So affect is required if signification is going to be possible. But we arrive at the same conclusion if we consider the matter from the viewpoint of affect. Affect is not something that exists on its own, independently of language. (p. 111)

Applying this to the commentaries of Lars and Stefan, each can be seen to provide explicit examples of the affective dimension of meaning, and thus how emotions are indissociable from constituting the sense of place by which a garden such as Vinterviken comes to be known, imagined, and remembered (cf. Feld & Basso, 1996). Being moved emotionally and constituting something as significant could be understood as mutually interdependent. In their examples, it wasn't only the choice to characterise city planners as stupid or short-sighted that provided an affective impetus to take responsibility for the site, but how the recollections associated with these words and their stories overall encoded the narrative to be read in terms of frustration and a sense of grievance. Body language and the embodiment of an emotional state were part of the narrative moment in which I participated with informants, inseparable from the sense of place and significance of what these men recounted having demonstrated for. The emotional elements of both narratives came through in how they characterised people involved, doing so through value judgements which juxtaposed municipal representatives and local community members, thereby conveying a sense of antagonism.

Both men's commentaries, as totalities of word choices and bodily emphasis, thus provided discursive cues that encoded how I should interpret and feel about this event (cf. Hall, 1999). Recalling and reconstituting their narratives in the moments when we spoke elcited visceral, lingering expressions of anger and frustration while also suggesting this to be an expected reaction shared by me as their audience. Considering that interviews and storytelling are both reactive, intersubjective situations, where a speaker is emphasising how they interpret events and advocating this interpretation to their audience (see Howarth, 2005, p. 335–336; Linde, 1993, p. 98), such examples illustrate how narratives can be used to call forth feelings of suffering or aggrievement for narrator and audience alike (cf. Polletta, 1998a, p. 140). They represented themselves as members of a collective of concerned citizens who stepped up and took responsibility for what both Stefan and Lars attributed to a critique of the municipality's ability to effectively manage and provide for the best interest of the local community. Part of what constituted Vinterviken's sense of place to Lars and Stefan was its representation of sustainable community planning and community improvement, involving active engagement by the community to provide a place of common benefit. As such, it could be seen as meaningful for providing a place for practicing citizenship as an active involvement in political life (cf. Mouffe, 2018).

Both men recounted 'small stories', alluding to and omitting more detailed narratives because it was assumed that I already had this context (see Bamberg & Georgakopoulou, 2008, p. 381). The condensed nature of these provided compelling examples of how narratives operate as discursive totalities, self-legitimising constructions that contain within them their own terms of evaluation (cf. Polletta, DoCarmo, Ward, & Callahan, 2021, p. 71). In each telling, they took for granted, and I was expected to take as given, that anyone else who recounted the story would tell me the same, validating it as authoritative based on the details provided. In their recollections of events, the city wasn't just an antagonist, threatening demolition; rather, it was constituted as a stupid and short-sighted 'other', implying by consequence that demonstrators acted from shared values of common sense, thoughtfulness and 'actually caring' about the community. The judgements they furnished were not only critiques of the city's decision to demolish the exhibition, but also a claim for why the city was wrong to do so. Through the actions of demonstrators that led to the association forming to take over management of the garden, Vinterviken came to signify the potential of collective action as a solution to a moral grievance portrayed in the form of bureaucratic ineptitude.

As I began to note over time, similar versions of the founding narrative were told when new members joined the gardening working group. The lack of tension in the written public narrative, in contrast to the apparent tension in oral histories, was at first curious in its omission. However, as Polletta (1998a) discusses, collective histories such as these are one way in which groups reinforce an internal sense of identity, "to make sense of unfamiliar events, to engage as they explain, and to sustain identity during periods of rapid change" (p. 143), doing so by providing a chronology and interpretation of events considered formative to collective identity. In this light, the relationship between narrator and audience was not inconsequential in determining which story was told.

The constitution of antagonistic values between municipal decision-makers and garden members were absent from public-oriented, written narratives. This could be seen as a choice not to be perceived as too political when speaking for the garden in an official capacity – i.e., to not be critical of the government, even if the collective of participants may have expressed clearly political values when speaking with them on a person-to-person level. The written history thus appeared to be tactfully written to reach a broad audience of potential visitors. Consistent with Polletta's argument, the oral history could be interpreted to be an internal narrative, serving to foster and reinforce a sense of common purpose among those who had already taken interest in becoming part of the collective of volunteers; it functioned as a means of conveying and reinforcing common symbolic values related to what was at stake in preserving the garden. I would therefore speculate that my being privy to this narrative was related to my sustained presence as a participant observer, as it was recounted to me by people whom I already had established a rapport with.

Solving a Problem through Responsibilisation

While narratives from the garden association and its members told a story in which the garden was founded out of an exhibition, reports from the municipal planning department told another story. Written in the five years following the establishment of Vintervikens trädgård, they provided their own narrative of the garden's establishment, according to which the idea preceded the exhibition and the forming of the association by several years. I was particularly interested to see how the planning department accounted for the initial decision to demolish the garden and the ultimate transfer of responsibility to the association. The reports proved insightful for understanding the garden's founding from the perspective of city planners, not least how they interpreted the significance of Vinterviken in promoting the marketability or desirability of the area. Furthermore, these documents provided an external perspective on the garden's meaning, specifically how it was defined through the rationalities of city management and urban planning.

As discussed earlier in this chapter, according to a motion submitted to Stockholm's executive board in 2004, the city management office had considered the initiative to be "an urgent upgrade of the urban environment in the area and increased the attractiveness of this part of the southern town" (Kommunstyrelsen Stockholms stad, 2004, p. 1; my translation). In the final report submitted to Stockholm's *Gatu- och fastighetsnämnden* [Committee for Roads and Real Estate], it described how city planners had hoped to establish a garden in the area as early as 1996. According to these documents, a temporary exhibition was not the original intent, but rather:

> A market and demonstration garden along the model of *Rosendals trädgård* was proposed as a natural complement to the allotment area, with organic cultivation, a boutique, a café, as well as educational offerings and more. (Gatu- och fastighetskontoret Stockholms stad, 2001, p. 3; emphasis added; my translation)

Importantly, this report situated Vinterviken within the story of the city's work to transform the neighbourhood as a whole. It was one of a series of events in the long-term redevelopment of the property that had once been a Nobel dynamite factory. Not unlike the narratives of members of the garden collective, it constituted Vintervikens trädgård as a solution to a problem in order to retroactively motivate its establishment, presenting the area as previously unattractive and in need of an upgrade.

Additionally, there was reference to another garden to convey the intent that city planners had. The omission of any description of this garden suggested that the audience had a shared knowledge about what it meant to develop another site "like Rosendals trädgård". The name alone seemed to carry with it a symbolic value, expressing an identity for the site. Established in the 1980s within *Djurgården* [The Royal Game Park], located on an island east of the city centre, Rosendals trädgård was – like Vintervikens trädgård later became – a garden with a café and handicraft boutique, operating with a pedagogical purpose around food cultivation and sustainable living. The intent to model the use and activities taking place at Vinterviken by referencing Rosendal as a prototype meant they were considered analogous places.

This equivalence struck me as relevant to understand the values that might motivate the garden's development from a municipal perspective. The expressed intent of city planners was to 'upgrade' and 'increase the attractiveness' of the neighbourhoods surrounding what later became Vinterviken, suggesting that both were valued for their potential to contribute to neighbourhood improvement and beautification. In terms of solution then, Vinterviken wasn't itself the solution to the problems associated with social conditions in Aspudden; rather, it was the intended replication of an existing, already 'proven' concept that was being presented as the solution. Based on informant descriptions of the area prior to the parkland being formed, it was not a desirable area for living, rather one where those with financial constraints could find affordable housing due to the neighbourhood's association with multiple social problems. Therefore, the idea of upgrading the area could be understood in terms of an implicit desire to alter the social and economic character of the community. As such, it could be interpreted as part of a municipal strategy for gentrification, with the material transformation of the area intended to make it more attractive to people with higher socio-economic status (cf. Glass, 1964; Clark, 2005; Kohne, 2020).

However, as the narrative told in the report suggests, replicating this model as part of Kulturpark Liljeholmen did not appear to be a straightforward path from idea to realisation:

> Interest in the concept from the community and sponsors was insufficient. But in the spirit of the programme, and in collaboration with the allotment movement, the gardening exhibition *Odlarglädje* [Joy of Cultivation] was put on during the Capital of Culture year instead, with 15–20,000 visitors. Private stakeholders erected a café and organic allotment cottage [...]. Cultivation was carried out by gardening enthusiasts. [...] After [the Capital of Culture] the operation of the exhibition was taken over by a voluntary association of garden enthusiasts, Vintervikens trädgård. (Gatu- och fastighetskontoret Stockholms stad, 2001, p. 3; my translation)

Interesting in this summary of the exhibition was that the city – like the association – omitted any tension in the switch from exhibition to association, instead suggesting it was a natural progression of events. As I interpreted it, the report alluded to a problematic past that the garden had solved in retrospect, portraying the area as previously having been unattractive and run-down in comparison to other areas. This problem became solvable through the reproduction of Rosendals trädgård as a strategy for transforming the city district in alignment with municipal goals. Vinterviken was meaningful not in and of itself, but for what it represented for the increased attractiveness and desirability of the neighbourhoods around it. Reports seemed to mirror the significance of the site as described by informants as an amenity that represented neighbourhood improvement – an appreciated addition, as implied in the comments of Lars and Karl, a symbol of safety and social life according to Stefan, and a step towards a more desirable area from the perspective of city planners. Important from the perspective of city officials was that they appeared to understand their role as facilitatory, not responsible for planning, execution, or maintenance of the site. As stated in official reports, municipal decisionmakers had developed a plan that civil society was expected to realise.

These various narratives served to remind of the garden's polysemy, open to multiple interpretations of its meaning and thus able to be viewed as an element of multiple discourses – even those that may have appeared to conflict with one another such as top-down urban development policy or grassroots citizenship and civic engagement (cf. Laclau & Mouffe, 1985, p. 169). Although a distinct geographic location, it was constituted in rela–tionship to other places and times (cf. Basso, 1996b; Massey, 2005). The sense of place that could be articulated in relation to Vinterviken was variably associated with discourses of community improvement and transformation, as well as with critiques of social planning, urban land policies, and waste disposal. Rather than any single meaning, its varied meanings were dependent upon the context and concerns that informed one's narrative. At the same time, there were instances where the significance of Vinterviken was conveyed in relation to similar discourses – such as those of desirability shared between informants and city planning reports. While both interests considered the garden to improve the area, informants also viewed it as a site providing respite from social and environmental problems that they partly attributed to the municipality's historical and contemporary urban planning and land development policies.

Another aspect of this narrative is worth considering, not least considering the responsibility assumed by demonstrators who established the voluntary association that maintained Vintervikens trädgård. The reports from the city management office were explicit in the fact that the garden was a top-down idea, premised on the assumption that civil society take responsibility for realising it. As such, it was consistent with the rationality of *responsibilisation* characteristic of neoliberal governance. As Nikolas Rose argues, neoliberalism, as a political rationality, seeks to render the social domain economic, with a subject framed as "the author of their own misfortune [...] seen as potentially and ideally an active agent in the fabrication of their own existence" (Rose, 1996), and problems with the economy squarely placed on individuals who "need to stop thinking the State owes us a living" (1999, p. 145). Consequently, this rationality operates according to an ethos of responsibilisation whereby subjects "would carry out the ends of government by fulfilling them themselves rather than being merely obedient, and [...] obliged to be free in specific ways" (Rose, O'Malley, & Valverde, 2012, p. 124; my translation).

Accordingly, not unlike the narrative from city managers attributing blame to the local community for 'insufficient interest', it can be argued that the threatened demolition of the exhibition garden was made to be the fault of the local community for not taking an active role as responsible citizens to care for their community and contribute to its quality of life. Although demonstrators chose to take responsibility for the location that they had developed an affective investment in, the choice to do so could not therefore be isolated from the 'fear of loss' created by its threatened demolition as a force that motivated their choice to take control – and thus responsibility (cf. Pyysiäinen, Halpin, & Guilfoyle, 2017, pp. 221–223).

As defined from these perspectives, municipal and collective narratives communicated what I considered to be a similar ethos of citizenship in terms of taking an active involvement in the political community and its implications for quality of life in the city (cf. Mouffe, 2018). And yet, it was also very different in the rationality that this ethos was predicated upon. On one side, people from the local community autonomously took responsibility upon themselves in reaction to perceived municipal mismanagement; on the other side, city management had an expressed intent to make citizens responsible for carrying out their plans without government support. In both interpretations, a sense of place was constituted through an interpretation of citizenship as an active practice, though each was quite different. For the collective, this citizenship could be seen as freely assumed based on a desire to provide a place for common benefit. From the municipal narrative, it appeared to be a coercively realised citizenship elicited in service of strategic goals as to what the site could represent for branding and redeveloping the local area.

Prinzessinnengarten: From Urban Wasteland to Urban Oasis

Turning attention from Vinterviken's origins to those of Prinzessinnengarten, the recent history of the site was portrayed in somewhat similar terms, and the nature of the garden as a solution to social problems was also presented as a reproduction of an existing model of urban agriculture. However, they were by no means similar narratives in terms of how they were structured. In reviewing the founding narrative of Prinzessinnengarten presented on its website, telling the story of the garden's founding, and thereby conveying the garden's meaning, relied upon the convergence of several intersecting narratives. These included: (1) personal histories in which the founders' identities were important to interpreting Prinzessinnengarten's significance, (2) a century and a half history of the site itself, and (3) an approach to urban agriculture being 'imported', adapted, and reinscribed into a different political and economic context.

Timeline of a Contested Location

While the problems set up by informants in Stockholm concerned the neighbourhood where Vinterviken was located, the prehistory of Prinzessinnengarten seemed to focus more on the specific plot of land where the garden was located. As detailed in a graphic timeline on the garden's website, the 6000 square metre site had historically been at the centre of competing discourses of land use. This visual history recounted the history of Moritzplatz, from its naming until the garden was established and beyond. Recounting a history of land development and tenancy activism over a period of 160 years, it also calls attention to the inspiration one of the founders drew from his first visit to a garden in Cuba. From there, plant life grew forth in the image, implying the visit had planted a seed that eventually took root with the securing of a lease (refer to figure 24, next page).

This timeline is itself a representation of Prinzessinnengarten's history, employing linguistic and non-linguistic elements to configure selected events, imagery, and characters within a chronological progression. As a combination of aesthetic and linguistic choices used to constitute a discursive totality (cf. Laclau & Mouffe, 1987), the timeline can be seen as a visual form of storytelling, articulating a sense of place for Prinzessinnengarten through the causality implied by a historical progression of events. The choice of a visual timeline condenses the narrative, distilling it to key events and themes considered meaningful to know, establishing the constraints through which the history of the site can be interpreted and evaluated. Situating Prinzess-innengarten within a broader historical narrative, it was articulated within multiple discourses through equivalences drawn between the garden itself and the places, problems, and events selectively appropriated to tell the history that preceded and resulted in Prinzessinnengarten's establishment.

The timeline set the terms for evaluation for Prinzessinnengarten by providing a pre-history of the area that articulated multiple histories of Berlin, the district of Kreuzberg, and its specific plot of land into a common narrative, shifting to a narrative of Moritzplatz after the building of the Berlin Wall, and eventually becoming the history to-date of Prinzessinnengarten upon the garden's establishment. It thus exemplified how places reflect constellations of stories coming together, articulated to give specificity to a place as the site where these stories intersect (Massey, 2005, p. 130). From the time of the Berlin Wall onwards, the timeline represents a problem in the form of competing visions for the site – those proposed by the government, which owned the land, and of people in the community squatting and appropriating the site for a variety of purposes.

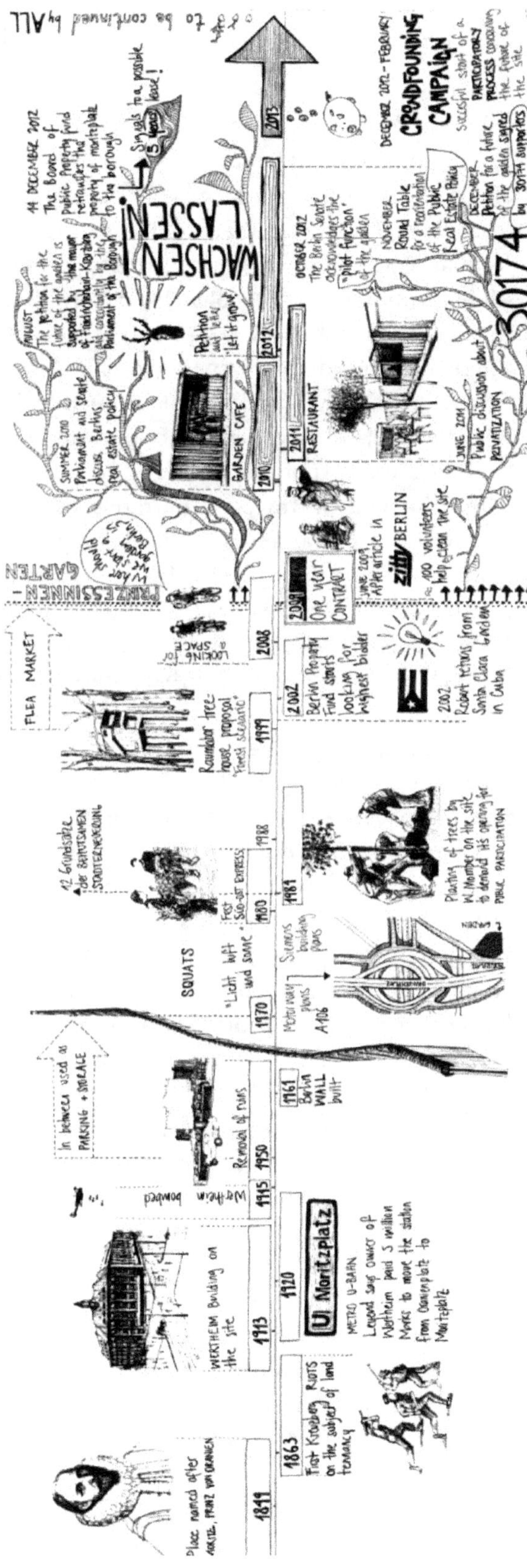

Figure 24: "History of Space, Prinzessinnengarten" by HosieWulff (2013). Licensed under CC BY-SA 3.0.

As portrayed in the timeline, government plans for the site involved building a large motorway or selling the land to Siemens (a German-based multi-national conglomerate) for them to build a factory at the site. For local activists, visions tended to involve various urban commoning projects – a public green space, a flea market, and a squat among them – through which the site could be accessible for individual and collective benefit rather than having its use dictated by market valuations (cf. Harvey, 2012, p. 79). On both sides of this discourse, there were thus different operative values and ways of interpreting the potential of the site, reflecting different rationalities by which the property could be most beneficially used – as a place of common benefit, or by making way for car traffic and corporations.

In such a manner, the timeline portrayed a narrative of ideological struggle, with the relative success of the garden as a solution to multiple long-term social and urban planning issues in Kreuzberg. Situated topographically at Moritzplatz, it was an intersection because it was a roundabout, but it was also metaphorically located at an intersection – one where discourses of urban planning, tenant rights, urban agriculture, urban commoning, commercial development, squatting, and automobile infrastructure converged and sought to prevail. The timeline articulated the site, and thus Prinzessinnengarten, within antagonistic values, with the history of the site representing a long-standing tension between property development and community benefit as competing rationalities of land use. Looking at the period after the garden was established reinforced this interpretation, as the same tension around privatisation were displayed as persisting. However, it also represented Prinzessinnengarten as impacting the re-evaluation of Berlin's real estate policy, in the process attaining more desirable lease terms and acknowledgement by the local borough as a project worth supporting.

The timeline thus provided an illustrative example for how a sense of place can be constituted through the combination of temporal equivalences and juxtapositions. Commonalities could be interpreted with past activism at the site, while it was set against the government and businesses when they supported incompatible proposals for developing the site. Visualising a relationship of equivalence in which Prinzessinnengarten was part of – and a culmination of – a common history of anti-capitalist and alter-urban activism concerned with to tenant rights and land development policy, urban capitalism was constituted as an historical problem, and Prinzessinnengarten could be seen as a solution to the ideological struggle that had long characterised the fortunes of its location. Prinzessinnengarten was thus inserted into land use discourses by retroactively constructing a story of competing projected social rationalities by which the value and use of the site should be determined (cf. Glynos, Speed & West, 2014). By gaining local acknowledgement of the garden's social significance, the *projected* social rationality of common benefit it was associated with thus became an *accepted* or *legitimate* social rationality, to some degree – at least for determining the use of that specific site.

In addition to the equivalence by which the timeline portrayed the history of Moritzplatz and the history of Prinzessinnengarten as analogous, an additional insertion stands out in the timeline in the form of the Santa Clara Garden in Cuba. In reading the official narrative of Prinzessinnengarten's establishment provided on its website, the first event recounted was the travels of one of the garden's founders in Cuba:

> How did this garden come about at Moritzplatz? Today, gardening is on everyone's lips in the city. When Robert Shaw and I developed the idea of a kitchen garden in Berlin in 2009, only a few insiders were familiar with terms such as urban agriculture and community gardening. On a trip through Cuba, Robert got to know the model of urban self-sufficiency through the communal cultivation of vegetables. In December 2008 he told me about his experiences there and the idea of building such a garden in Berlin. (Prinzessinnengarten, 2012; my translation)

Rather than suggesting Prinzessinnengarten was of indigenous or endemic inspiration or manifested *ex nihilo*, a choice was made in the founding narrative to articulate it as an extension of something bigger, as part of a global narrative and an international movement towards urban self-sufficiency. Equivalating it with Cuban urban agriculture as its source of inspiration, the gardens one of the founders had visited were *organopónicos*, self-governed cooperatives and government-sponsored, collectively operated, organic urban farms.[33] Inspired by the "idea of building such a garden in Berlin", Prinzessinnengarten and was presented as part of a common genre of collective agriculture with its Cuban inspirations. Furthermore, by describing *organopónicos* as representing values of 'urban self-sufficiency' and 'communal cultivation', and recounting these as inspiring attributes, Prinzess-

---

[33] *Organopónicos* became common across the island nation in the 1990s, as a nationwide response to severe food shortages that followed the dissolution of the Soviet Union, and with it the loss of preferential trade agreements and economic support (see Argaillot, 2014; McNamara, 2016). Until this time, Cuba was reliant on imports, the island's agriculture having largely shifted to sugarcane production under Spanish and later US occupation.

innengarten was inscribed alongside them in a chain of equivalence, implying that they promoted common values of urban living and food cultivation.

As Polletta (1998a) argues, social movement narratives have a normative function, constituting strategic actors and shaping legitimate strategies within a movement or cause (p. 154). As with the articulation of Prinzessinnengarten within the longer history of Moritzplatz, attributing its inspiration to *organopónicos* can also be interpreted to serve a legitimising function. It situates Prinzessinnengarten's history within another, larger narrative, claiming its validity by association with the Cuban model of urban agriculture as part of a common movement. Prinzessinnengarten's founders can be seen to portray themselves as what Polletta (2006) calls "legitimate heirs" to the extent that they acknowledged the formative work of *organopónicos* in making their own garden possible, thus positioning their own place as carrying forth that tradition in a new context (p. 152).

A Passion Project and a Place for Dilettantism

In addition to the attribution of the garden's inspiration from Cuban *organopónicos*, another aspect of the impetus for Prinzessinnengarten that is introduced is the personal trajectories of the garden's two founders. The founding story proceeds from the decision to adapt the *organopónico* model to Berlin by giving background on the founders and their approach to operating the garden. Providing this context suggests that knowing their personal experiences is relevant for understanding the significance of Prinzessinnengarten or evaluating its accomplishment:

> Although we were far from experts, we decided to work on it together. Until then, Robert himself had made films and realised video projects for theatre productions. I had a history degree and had experience in the hospitality industry. The fact that we were dilettantes shaped our project and favoured unconventional approaches as well as the willingness to cooperate and to continuously learn new things. A dilettante is not only a non-expert, but someone who does something for its own sake, for the joy of doing it. Robert and I brought different motives and interests to the joint project. Robert has a passion for the vegetable garden passed on from his grandmother and he dreamed of a place designed with his own hands, economically independent and with the opportunity to combine independent work, social and family life. I myself had previously dealt with questions of dealing with public spaces, had been involved in temporary use projects and had a passion for the unfinished and open of fallow and unused areas, which I documented photographically. (Prinzessinnengarten, 2012; my translation).

As expressed in this section of the history, the founders repeatedly position themselves as inexperienced and informal gardeners, describing themselves as 'amateurs', 'far from experts' and 'dilettantes' who are "doing something for the pleasure of it". Elsewhere in the narrative, they re-emphasise this point by referring to themselves as "budding urban gardeners without a professional background, with little capital, and an idea to make a social urban farm" (Prinzessinnengarten, 2012; my translation). In equating these descriptions of their approach with the garden, the story characterises Prinzessinnengarten as an egalitarian and easy-going space, shaped by desires to live, work, and socialise in another way. In other words, there was a sense of place conveyed through the articulation of family, work, and social life as elements of a single place, instead of compartmentalising them as distinct spheres of social life. Also, the significance of the garden was associated with an anti-elitist or anti-hierarchical ethos of learning through the collapsing of distinctions between experts and amateurs.

Based on this interpretation, the garden could be seen to foster the practice of a democratic conceptualisation of citizenship, with individuals coming together to shape a public place as well as impact social life within the broader community. However, in constituting this identity, expertise and commercial interests were articulated as elements of the constitutive outside of Prinzessinnengarten. Its non-hierarchical, DIY ethos was incommensurable with a neoliberal capitalist market rationality and the ethos of commodifying knowledge it entailed, even though the inspiration and creativity through which it came about was constructed through the presence of these as things to be resisted (cf. Duncombe, 1997, p. 194; Gunnarsson Payne, 2006, pp. 50–51).

Once again, these themes situated the garden within discourses of urban capitalism, associating it with (or characterising it according to) a negative sense of dependency and the splintering of different aspects of daily life that the founders desired to be better integrated. In addition to Cuban agriculture, the founders' prior experiences, and the history of Moritzplatz as a site of collective action, still other histories converged in constituting Prinzessinnengarten history. For instance, one founder's grandmother was also introduced as a source of inspiration, positioning her as a much earlier catalyst in the eventual realisation of the garden. As with *organopónicos* and land activism, the founders were portrayed as continuing and adapting multiple intergenerational heritages, seeking to carry those into the future in a new location, culminating in an orientation towards self-sufficiency and "the opportunity to combine of work, social and family life" (Prinzessinnengarten, 2012). Elements of family history and the founders' work histories also were selectively encoded within the garden's founding narrative, lending meaning to the latter by being associated with its history and intentions (cf. Hall, 1999).

The insertion of other stories into Prinzessinnengarten's history, and the articulation of other political demands as analogous and therefore pertinent, configured the garden as a logical result of the confluence – or meeting – of these various trajectories of people and places (cf. Massey, 2005). Doing so, the garden was polysemically situated, its significance capable of being interpreted within the context of a range of discourses, which according to its founders, included those pertaining to family life, communal labour, urban space, pleasure, dilettantism, and anti-hierarchical social organisation. Each of these could therefore offer a perspective through which to articulate and interpret the significance of the garden. By defining a need for these experiences and practices within the space of Prinzessinnengarten, an implicit critique of the normative experience of urban life could be intuited, by which discourses of expertise, obligation, hierarchy, and compartmentalisation of social life were implied to be the problems that could be resisted or resolved through engagement in the activities of the garden.

Cultivating Critical Consumers

From this background, and the inspirations it accounted for, the narrative then shifts to the intentions behind Prinzessinnengarten. By retroactively reflecting on the garden's goals and purposes, values and intentions were communicated:

> The most far-reaching decision we made was that the garden should support us and, ideally, other people. We didn't think of self-sufficiency with vegetables, but of a regular income. [...] But the garden that we had in mind, unlike a conventional farm, should not primarily serve production and be measured by yields. We saw the market garden in the city as a place that gives the people who live here the opportunity to learn more about cultivation and the variety of their food. Such a garden can create a sensory connection between the place where the food is consumed and the places where it is produced. And it was precisely through the contrast between the lively diversity of the garden and the standardization of the discounter offer that we hoped to get visitors to ask themselves questions. In the best-case scenario, they should start to be amazed. Amazed at the horseradish that grows in the middle of the city, but also amazed at the thousands of kilometres that our food travels and that we have learned to take for granted. Amazed at the low prices we pay for them, despite the resources that go into them and their

> often-destructive impact on the environment. [34] (Prinzessinnengarten, 2012;
> my translation)

In articulating the garden in discourses of food production, commercial agriculture, and environmental harm, it is envisioned to inspire and change people's behaviours by providing education and motivating them to think critically about their consumption practices. The repeated use of the word 'amazed' conveyed an emotional element to the re-evaluation and reorientation of relationship to food production and consumption.

Analysing the sense of place of collective gardens as a discursive or relational identity (see, e.g., Basso, 1996b; Feld & Basso, 1996), the intended emotional effects of the garden on visitors were thus put in focus, implying a role for sensory and practical experience in developing a critical mindset. Participation in the garden's activities was portrayed as a means of rearticulating relationships to food, with the implied critique being that the distancing of people from natural cycles of food cultivation contributed to uncritical and environmentally damaging consumption practices. Not surprisingly then, the narrative acknowledged the importance of sensory experience in achieving such a rearticulation. By providing a place to learn to be critical consumers, Prinzessinnengarten was represented to offer a solution to the problem of uncritical consumption norms whereby consumers passively enabled harmful industrial food production and distribution practices. It could thus be argued to reflect an ethos of responsibility-taking; its focus on critical consumption and collective food production implied that individual and collective responsibility were appropriate behaviours for addressing problems created by industrial food production and global logistics.

This responsibility-taking could be seen as an active, prefigurative political practice, reflecting a desire to explore the potential of urban agriculture as manifested in environmentally friendly and ethical relationships to food production and consumption as goals to enact collectively in pursuit of more general social change (cf. Boggs, 1977; Yates, 2015). Furthermore, I argue a political subjectivity was being enacted consistent with the conception of citizenship in the democratic tradition (cf. Mouffe, 2018; see even 1992a, 2000). Critical consumption and collective production of food could be seen as acts of citizenship because asserting agency in relation to food and transnational economic networks was represented as an individual practice in service of a common good. Personal behaviours were explicitly associated

---

[34] Originally published in *Prinzessinnengärten. Anders gärtnern in der Stadt* (Nomadisch Grün, 2012).

with political and economic impacts, suggestion that active involvement in the political community was a critical practice involving self-reflection, and that collective exploration and dialogue were means of facilitating this.

This reflects a certain continuity with the ethical orientation of allotment gardening, wherein part of the motivation (as I discuss in the introductory chapter) was a desire to effect behavioural change in people. While allotment gardens were often attributed a significance by their promoters to shape participants in line with values of industrial society or social democratic citizenship (see Baratay, 1997; Bellows, 2004; Bergquist, 1996), the narrative of Prinzessinnengarten articulated a pericapitalist subjectivity. Critical reflection and an ethos of responsibility-taking became central to a democratic enactment of citizenship. Participants in the garden should become inspired to take responsibility, individually and collectively, rearticulating relationships to food, nature, and social life according to a projected, non-capitalist, social rationality.

From 'Conquered Wasteland' to 'A New Place for Urban Life'

Shifting from inspirations and preparatory work, the founding narrative continues by mentioning how the founders spent half a year educating themselves in discussions with a range of professionals and creating a register of brownfields and other vacant sites, before being pointed to their eventual location at Moritzplatz by the borough mayor of Kreuzberg.[35] From there, they describe the clearing of the site that was necessary to construct the garden:

> With the contract in our pockets, we climbed through a hole in the fence onto the wasteland at Moritzplatz for the first time in May 2009 – after all these years without being used, we couldn't find a key. Vegetation typical of fallow areas had spread here, and the area was littered with rubbish. This almost forgotten place was used by dog owners as a space to exercise and by junkies as a retreat. There was no water, no electricity, and no toilets. At first glance

---

[35] While the visual timeline portrays Prinzessinnengarten the garden as a culmination of the history of its location, this written history states that it was the borough mayor who suggested the location to its founders. Rather than view this as a discrepancy, this rearticulation of the narrative illustrates that how the garden's story was being told and how its significance was thereby constituted were necessarily contextual and polysemic. One historical identity did not necessarily negate another (see e.g., Laclau & Mouffe, 1985, p. 121). Just as the inspiration for the garden could be attributed to Cuban *organopónicos*, it could also be portrayed as a culmination of a historical narrative of Moritzplatz. Similarly, the role of the borough mayor's advocacy did not negate the ability for the garden to be articulated within a history of resistance to top-down planning in favour of grassroots urban commons.

it was clear to us that we would only be able to do very little here on our own. We arranged to meet a journalist. A few days later, an article appeared under the headline: "The garden is growing above the pavement", which called for "collectively conquering the site, including rubbish clearing". For us it was impossible to assess if anyone would even come on a sunny weekend to clean up a wasteland. As a precaution, we had procured a couple of buckets and gloves. Nobody had expected what happened next: around 150 interested people, friends and neighbours came. They collected two tons of rubbish, old mattresses, tires, refrigerators, televisions, car batteries, and countless bottles and cans. But it wasn't just about the work. Cleaning up together was also an opportunity to exchange ideas and learn more about our ideas and visions. We began to suspect how many people are willing to get involved if you only dare to start. In the weeks that followed, we were to receive even more willingness to help – without them this garden would be unthinkable. Much of the help consisted of sweaty physical labour. (Prinzessinnengarten, 2012; my translation)

This section signalled a turning point in the narrative, transitioning from a focus on the founders' own histories in motivating the garden's relevance as a political project. While this was important as inspiration, the establishment itself focused on site conditions and the collective labour of volunteers, portraying the location as being in such a poor state that it needed to be 'conquered' rather than simply cleared or cleaned. By describing initial site conditions in detail, the narrative conveys an aesthetic judgement and through this, a moral one as well. Articulating the location with rubbish heaps, wastelands, and a 'retreat for junkies', the narrative characterised it as a place in need of significant labour to clear and transform it into something more acceptable and desirable.

As Polletta (1998b) reflects, "the story's end is consequential; it is not only outcome but moral of the events which precede it" (p. 423). Emphasising the turnout of volunteers as making a decisive difference in this transformation of the location as a material environment, the founding narrative demonstrates the possibility for change through collective action. Also, by appealing to readers' senses through an aesthetic description of the site prior to its reclamation, and the characterisation of the transformation in terms of a 'battle' that precipitated a 'conquest', I argue that the narrative legitimised the garden's presence on moral grounds. The encoding of the story with these details and word choices implied negative value judgements, retroactively explaining and justifying Prinzessinnengarten as a social institution because it could be decoded as a legitimate reaction to a moral grievance with the prior treatment of the location (cf. Blehr, 1999; Koskinen-Koivisto, 2016, p.

174; Polletta, 1998b, p. 423). Juxtaposing an abandoned wasteland with the results of collective action and care, the daunting and laborious task of salvaging an abandoned site was presented as a good and worthy cause.

Further down on the same page of the garden's website, a subheading entitled "What is Prinzessinnengarten" was followed by a description of the vision for the garden as it related to the local community. This context extended the image of the garden as a conquered wasteland to encompass Kreuzberg as a similarly bleak landscape:

> We started in the summer of 2009 when more than a hundred volunteers cleared this neglected area of rubbish. Since then, with the support of thousands of helpers, the forgotten wasteland has been transformed into a living market garden. In a district with high density, little greenery and many social problems, children, young people and adults, neighbours and interested laypeople – in a word, everyone who wants to – can learn together with us how to produce local, organic produce through social and ecological urban agriculture, and collectively create a new place for urban life. (Prinzessinnengarten, 2012; my translation)

The contrast between a thriving garden and a bleak characterisation of the city district of Kreuzberg underscored how the garden's sense of place was relationally constituted. Prinzessinnengarten was considered to matter, in part, because it was distinct from the rest of the city district, articulating housing density and lack of greenery as creating an inhospitable environment. Again, this posited the garden as a solution to a pre-existing problem being presented retroactively. The problem of an inhospitable community was 'solved' by establishing Prinzessinnengarten as a hospitable oasis, made so by providing opportunities for critical engagement as responsible (or responsibility-taking) citizens caring for an urban commons.

The results of capitalist urban development in the area were articulated as resulting in an unpleasant, unwelcoming, and even hostile urban environment, inconducive to well-being. With Kreuzberg characterised in these terms, the garden was presented as solving urban ills by providing an alternative sensory and social environment. Prinzessinnengarten was a space of hope and creation, 'a new place for urban life' juxtaposed against a dreary environment. It represented and prefigured its founders' vision of the future of urban living, seeking to reorient from a sense of place for Kreuzberg as a failed social and environmental experiment. In this manner, the sense of place of the garden could be characterised as a present-day, future-oriented oasis, its significance knowable in relation to activities meant to realise alternative social relations.

In situating the garden against critiques and judgements about the entire district, it also represented a shift within discourses of urban planning and social welfare. Viewed thusly, Prinzessinnengarten was posited as a corrective to its environment, using local food production and collaborative learning to counterbalance the bleak and problem-ridden status quo of the neighbourhood around it. Whereas the problem was attributed to rationalities of land use and social planning by which capitalist theories of value applied to urban space, the solutions being attributed to Prinzessinnengarten's activities were portrayed as bringing about a better future by cultivating alternative (i.e., non-capitalist and anti-capitalist) relationships to land, food, and other people.

Through this perspective, it could be argued that Prinzessinnengarten represented an attempt at rearticulating what constitutes an ideal urban space, itself conveyed as fostering alterative norms of urban design, social organisation, and economic relationships. Juxtaposed against a critical characterisation of Kreuzberg, Prinzessinnengarten was interpretable as a disarticulatory presence in its surrounding built and social environment, redefining the character of the city district and unsettling taken for granted ways of perceiving and valuing the area (cf. Clifford, 2001, pp. 477–478; 2005, p. 25). Because of this, the garden seemed to be presented as a place *apart* from its environment, rather than *amidst* it, but also able to change it.

Gentrification from Below?

Despite being portrayed as a place distinct from its immediate surroundings, Prinzessinnengarten was also described in terms that suggested it could serve a transformational role in relation to those same surroundings. The collective work of creating 'a new place for urban life', and the intention to nurture critical consumers, were not goals whose effects would be limited to the confines of the garden. Changing how people related to urban life and food production were matters with broader implications for social relationships, urban design, and economic behaviours, impacting the overall quality of life in the area. It can therefore be argued that the intention for Prinzessinnengarten to transform a socially undesirable area into a better place to live implied some amount of gentrification. Making a place more pleasurable and desirable would bring with it certain social and economic changes, whether or not those changes were intentional or 'desired' by Prinzessinnengarten's founders.

As I found in materials available on Prinzessinnengarten's website concerning a campaign organised in 2019 and read on flyers posted at the site when visited that same year, it appeared that such a tension with gentrification became apparent to the collective in retrospect. The campaign, *Prinzessinnengarten Kreuzberg für 99 Jahre als Gemeingut sichern* [Preserve Prinzessinnengarten Kreuzberg as a Public Domain for 99 Years] was focused on establishing a community land trust whereby the garden could secure a 99-year leasehold. As stated in the overview of the campaign on the garden's website:

> Together with users, initiatives, neighbours, and other interested parties, we want to formulate wishes, plans, and ideas for the next 99 years. Even against a background of displacement, privatisation and gentrification, our goal is to end the era of precarious interim uses.
>
> [...]
>
> We know now: temporary uses are precarious and contribute, intentionally or unintentionally, to gentrification. What can we do instead to permanently remove spaces from speculation and privatization? We no longer want to talk about the next 12 months, we want to talk about the next 99 years, and see the place as a generational project. (Nomadisch Grün, 2019; my translation)

Here there is an explicit position of being against gentrification, alongside an acknowledgement that places such as Prinzessinnengarten – with its temporary use of its plot of land – had a gentrifying impact. As such, the existence and success of the garden could be seen to contribute to a problem that it wished to solve, since improving the quality of life in Kreuzberg was associated with fuelling the increased privatisation and speculative development in the area. Urban sociologist Lance Freeman (2006) argues that there is an inherent duality in gentrification as it can bring benefits that existing residents appreciate while also negatively impacting an area's affordability (p. 207). Though residents may seek to improve their community for their own benefit, they cannot control the socio-economic repercussions this may have as they make a neglected area more desirable to developers and people with more social and economic resources (see also Clark, 2005; Kohne, 2020).

In the case of Prinzessinnengarten, the tension between improving quality of life and the potential for improvements to displace their intended beneficiaries illustrates what Tsing (2015) speak of in terms of 'unintentional coordination' between economies, whereby they may come to influence each other and even rely upon one another for mutual survival (pp. 22–23). In this case, the salvage economy of Prinzessinnengarten – which like other *Gemeinschaftsgärten* salvaged abandoned property and post-consumer waste – was being acknowledged as benefitting the capitalist economy of land development in Kreuzberg. By unintentionally contributing to gentrification when the founders and supporters instead sought alternatives to it, such a perspective underscores the porosity between anti-capitalist and capitalist economies, and consequently a porosity between improving an area for existing residents and leaseholders (such as Prinzessinnengarten) and contributing to their displacement.

Reflecting on Prinzessinnengarten's founding story and positioning within its physical and historical setting, the narrative was not only oriented towards recalling and making sense of the past to relate this to their audience; it could also be seen as a statement for the future, an interpretation of events seeking to convince its audience of the case for protecting and promoting spaces like Prinzessinnengarten – oases in urban wastelands, won through hard work and the commitment of hardworking volunteers. It was an appeal to respect the good done in the site, and an appeal to emotions by evoking the reasons one should be amazed and concerned, juxtaposing the labour of establishing the garden with a hostile environment to provide a refuge from its surroundings. It portrayed the garden as an oasis at the margins, constructing a discourse in which the status quo of neoliberal capitalism and its ethos of privatisation were responsible for creating the unwelcoming urban environment that constituted the garden's metaphorical and literal outside.

Concluding Discussion

The histories told of Vintervikens trädgård and Prinzessinnengarten conveyed what each garden signified by situating it as a historical product of its environment and the convergence of needs and values that had not yet come to expression. Not unlike the relationships of aesthetic objects I explored in the prior chapter, both gardens presented very different founding narratives, obtained and elaborated through different types of sources. Despite their differences, each could be observed and analysed for how they existed in discourse with other narratives, and in the relationships articulated with other places, people, and times through which these stories constituted the significance of each garden. Furthermore, there were similarities in how each garden was recounted as solving local social problems. These similarities reflect interesting tensions, I believe, in the relationship between prefigurative politics and gentrification, and the role of responsibilisation in simultaneously creating alternatives to and contributing to neoliberal capitalist processes of urban development.

In both cases, local histories provided stories of neighbourhoods with problematic pasts, setting up terms of evaluation for each garden's founding narrative (cf. Polletta, DoCarmo, Ward, & Callahan, 2021, p. 71). Notable in the narratives of both gardens was how the historical sense of place for each location was central to interpreting the sense of place that the gardens were attributed. The areas surrounding Vinterviken and Prinzessinnengarten had both been characterised as inhospitable wastelands, abandoned due to lack of capitalist economic value. By salvaging among this capitalist detritus, they were each recounted, in their own ways, as cultivating a different sense of community. Among other things, these juxtapositions between characterisations of past and present, and between the gardens and their surrounding cityscapes, reinforced my conviction that the setting of a narrative is important to making sense of the values that emerge in relation to that environment (cf. Basso, 1996b). Whether obtained from informants, garden websites, or government documents, each founding narrative relied on juxtapositions with the past of the area to evaluate these gardens in contrast, thereby legitimating them as solutions to moral grievances with urban development and social planning.

Vinterviken and Prinzessinnengarten were both associated with critiques of normative social values, allowing for and providing conditions that called attention to governmentality, offering places to "disturb people's mental habits [...] to dissipate what is familiar and accepted" (Foucault, 1988, p. 265) – in this case as pertinent to relationships to land, place, social organisation, and economic activity. But just as salvaged property (and in Prinzessinnengarten's case, post-consumer materials) existed because of consumer society and capitalist land development rationales (see Tsing, 2015), so too did the founding narratives of each garden underscore that anti-capitalist and non-capitalist politics necessarily occurred in discourse with capitalist-oriented political and economic systems. The constitution of these gardens simultaneously inside and outside of extractive capitalist market economics, what Tsing (2015) describes in terms of pericapitalism, helped me to examine how collective gardens both reproduced and resisted normative social practice.

Considering how both gardens had come about through the efforts of their collectives *and* the active involvement of municipal government representatives in their local districts, they illustrated how, much like different forms of economic activity are often interdependent (Tsing, 2015), so too were partnership with and resistance to hegemonic political institutions. Vintervikens trädgård and Prinzessinnengarten work within the frameworks of local government while simultaneously engaging in prefigurative politics that challenged the normative practices of urban development which those same institutions enabled and enforced. Consensual participation in institutional politics and consumer capitalist economics coexisted with resistance to the authority of these and critiques of their legitimacy. Furthermore, the former made the latter possible, exemplifying how anti-capitalist or non-capitalist practices relied on pericapitalist relationships.

In the narratives of informants at Vinterviken and the founders at Prinzessinnengarten, implicit and explicit critiques of normative urban planning practices were portrayed as having contributed to social and environmental problems. The histories they told could thus be read as part of a reclamatory process, with founding narratives recounting land reclamation as part of a process of reclaiming the narrative of their local communities from the stigma attributed them. Gardeners and public officials alike provided interpretations of how they saw themselves reclaiming urban space. In doing so, each promoted an ethos of responsibility as central to what is arguably an active, democratic conceptualisation of citizenship being fostered in these places (cf. Mouffe, 2018). By narrating histories of community transformation through the establishment of both gardens, critical political engagement and 'taking responsibility' were implicit in transforming their respective 'wastelands' or 'dumping grounds' into desirable locations.

In the case of Vinterviken, municipal decisionmakers had an expressed intent for the local community do bring about this transformation, thus demonstrating that responsibilisation can operate as something done *to* people as well as an active choice *by* people. Whether based on individual and collective motivations, beliefs that community development shouldn't be left to institutions, perceived failures of urban development and social planning, or a combination of these, responsibilisation was implied to have solved the problem of urban wastelands through asserting democratic agency. Collectives took responsibility for public property to actively render their neighbourhoods more desirable places to be.

Observable in the reclamatory and transformational nature of their narratives, the collective action of those involved was attributed to have brought about positive changes to the quality of life in their respective neighbourhoods. Because of this, I argue that Prinzessinnengarten and Vinterviken alike could be interpreted as examples of gentrification 'from below', illustrating that gentrification was not purely a negative occurrence impacting the affordability of a neighbourhood, nor a strategy imposed upon it (see Clark, 2005). It could also be understood to result from collective efforts to sustain an urban commons for the benefit of the local community – regardless of whether increased desirability of the area may also have contributed to demographic shifts (see Freeman, 2006, p. 207).

A sense of place for Prinzessinnengarten and Vintervikens trädgård was informed in relation to Berlin and Stockholm, respectively. Despite conveying a sense of tension with their local environments and normative social practices in each city, narratives of both gardens acknowledged working within prevailing political, legal, and economic frameworks for the gardens to come into being. Even if collectives caring for these places acted in accordance with hegemonic economic practices in certain respects, narratives of their establishment conveyed how these places could also provide space for resistance, constituting 'new places for urban life' premised on pericapitalist relationships to urban space. Capitalist and non-capitalist economies were co-occurring at both gardens, giving way to blended economies through which financial obligations to the cities of Berlin and Stockholm as leaseholders coexisted with and enabled the exploration of non-capitalist practices and relationships. Each played a part in processes of gentrification based on their respective motives and audiences vis-à-vis community improvement.[36] In the next two chapters, I examine the relationships between each garden and their social context in more detail.

---

[36] With Prinzessinnengarten, an additional example of pericapitalism is noteworthy in the founding narrative. The founders earned their livelihoods from the garden, doing so alongside voluntary labour by like-minded people who shared an interest in creating a free space for learning and experimentation. Volunteers exercised agency in making a choice to be involved, hence the voluntary nature of their engagement. Their salvaged labour was not extracted under duress or compulsion as was the case with *colonies agricoles*, for example (cf. Foucault, 2007, p. 234; Tocqueville & Beaumont, 1833).

6. Co-opting the Commons: Land Rights and Global Citizenship at Prinzessinnengarten

The political and economic circumstances in which Prinzessinnengarten operated are the focus of this chapter, starting at the neighbourhood level before analysis of citywide and global contexts. Drawing on resources including the collective's website, local government webpages and planning documents, news reports, photography, and observational notes, the garden is studied in terms of its articulation within city branding strategies, contemporary urban planning discourses, and themes of global social justice. Through these themes, the garden's sense of place is explored as constituted through the confluence of local discourses of co-optation, government financing, and urban development, alongside global discourses of land rights each interpretable in materials. Investigating these discourses, the chapter provides an in-depth case study of political antagonisms and solidarities pertaining to *Gemeinschaftsgärten*, enriching an analysis begun in Chapter 4.

With Prinzessinnengarten as a prototypical example of *Gemeinschaftsgärten*, this exploration provided insight into how a sense of place among this genre of collective gardens was fostered in relation to neoliberal capitalism as a set of political and economic practices with transnational impacts (see, e.g., Harvey, 2012; Mouffe, 2015). To the extent that local government policies were interpretable as serving to "bring the interests of a challenging group into alignment with its own goals" (Trumpy, 2008, p. 480), an apparent co-optative relationship on the part of local businesses and political institutions is investigated. From there, I examine how the popularity and desirability of these places paradoxically contributed to their precarity through gentrification processes and emergent urban planning strategies that rearticulated the value of *Gemeinschaftsgärten* within Berlin's political economy. Finally, the political messaging, demonstrations, and solidarity events hosted at Prinzessinnengarten are analysed. Reflecting on how the garden was simultaneously articulated in local and global discourses through these, a chain of equivalence with a range of causes around the globe became interpretable despite the fundamentally different circumstances of activists elsewhere.

Co-opting Dissent for Consumer Lifestyle and City Branding

A trend that quickly became apparent during site visits throughout Germany, and especially in Berlin, was the seeming popularity of the aesthetic vocabulary of *Gemeinschaftsgärten*. An aesthetic vocabulary like that found in these gardens was observable elsewhere in the city, being used however in commercial design and marketing materials. Through later digital ethnography, Prinzessinnengarten and other *Gemeinschaftsgärten* were explicitly promoted for city branding purposes, used by Berlin's government and its subsidiary entities as a selling point to promote a particular image of the city. Whether through their aesthetic vocabulary, specific gardens, or the phenomenon itself, such uses came to be interpreted in co-optative terms to the extent they defused the political force of an aesthetic associated with urban commoning, rearticulating it as part of the consumer cityscape (cf. LaForge, Anderson, & McLachlan, 2017, p. 675; McRobbie, 2009, pp. 50–52).

"Watch Out! New Perspectives Emerging"

Leaving Prinzessinnengarten after my first visit to the site, I walked along the exterior of its perimeter wall, taking in the garden's surroundings anew. Having not attended to such details prior to entering the garden, the wall along the garden's western side was then observed to be covered by two billboards advertising a well-known local beer company (refer to figure 25, next page). Minus the beer bottles, the staging of these advertisements was akin to scenes observable in one of the city's many *Gemeinschaftgärten*. One showed two men, appearing to be in their early thirties, working on their bikes while using plastic crates as makeshift furniture; just on the other side of this wall, the garden featured a DIY bicycle repair workshop, and employed plastic crates and similar materials as makeshift planters and garden furniture. The other billboard showed a couple of a similar age taking a break from tending to vegetables. Additionally, both billboards were accompanied by the slogan *"Berlin, Du bist so wunderbar"* [Berlin, you are so wonderful].

Figure 25: Billboards on the exterior of Prinzessinnengarten's wall made use of an aesthetic and practices that would not be out of place within the garden itself. (*Credit*: Author)

While other interpretations were certainly possible, these billboards could be argued to encode an aesthetic vocabulary associable with *Gemeinschafts-gärten* (as the city's most noticeable form of urban agriculture) as an element of a particular discourse of a 'wonderful' Berlin lifestyle, thereby depoliticising urban farming and DIY cycle repair through their rearticulation within commercial contexts (cf. Gunnarsson Payne, 2006).[37] That marketers opted to locate these billboards directly outside such a garden was not irrelevant, instead suggesting a particular idea of the target demographic they sought to reach. This interpretation was further reinforced by the fact that participants and visitors to the garden appeared demographically similar to the people portrayed in the billboards, as well as having similar clothing styles.

Despite being sites that reflected anti-capitalist values, the presence of billboards was also illustrative of the garden's precarious, pericapitalist position. Even if the space within its walls was non-commercial in character, its physical exterior was not immune from operating as a commercial space – much like its aesthetic vocabulary was not off limits from being adapted for commercial purposes. This offered a rather unambiguous example of the porosity of boundaries between capitalist and non-capitalist (or pericapitalist) economies and thus their fundamental enmeshment (see Tsing, 2015).

---

[37] See also Duncombe (1999).

Similarly, I observed that restaurants, cafés, and other businesses in Kreuzberg – as well as other boroughs – had made use of wooden-crate and pallet-like planter boxes as part of their landscaping aesthetic or to construct outdoor seating. Unlike those observed in *Gemeinschaftsgärten* however, these appeared to be made of new materials rather than reclaimed wood or salvaged post-consumer materials. Also, rather than herbs, vegetables, strawberries, and bee-friendly wildflowers, these planters were more often filled with ornamental flowers. I therefore would argue that these billboards and the landscape design aesthetic observed in local businesses reflected a co-optation of the aesthetic vocabulary common to *Gemeinschaftsgärten*, appropriating elements associated with urban commoning and re-presenting them as part of a consumer lifestyle and commercial design discourses (cf. Trumpy, 2008, p. 480).

In both advertisements and commercial landscape design, the DIY ethos and salvage aesthetic that characterised *Gemeinschaftsgärten* such as Prinzessinnengarten could be understood as disarticulated from their typical association with the anti-capitalist, non-commercial context of urban commoning. Marketable elements of their aesthetic were appropriated, and thus rearticulated, within a commercial profit-oriented advertising strategy, while elements signalling their political critique were excluded (cf. Clifford, 2005, p. 25; 2011, p. 477). These aesthetic choices encoded aesthetic vocabularies normatively associated with Berlin's DIY subculture within advertising and commercial landscaping, observably different than their encoding within non-commercial sites like Prinzessinnengarten. Rather than support anti-elitist and non-commercial practice, this aesthetic had become appropriated in service of corporate profit, rearticulating it therefore within consumer discourse. Such a shift in context of use demonstrates that disarticulation occurring through corporate co-optation not only can appropriate anti-capitalist practice to serve ideologically contrary corporate goals (cf. Trumpy, 2008), but in doing so "devalues, or negates and makes unthinkable" the political significance of this aesthetic by promoting normative values at its expense (McRobbie, 2009, p. 26). In both advertising and commercial design, the political ethos this aesthetic vocabulary symbolised was displaced, substituted with a consumer lifestyle that undermined efforts to nurture alternative economic forms (cf. LaForge, Anderson, & McLachlan, 2017, p. 675).

As observed at Prinzessinnengarten and other sites, there was a clear sense of concern about these practices. Inside the garden – as well as many others visited throughout the country – a manifesto titled *Die Stadt ist unser Garten* [The City is Our Garden] was posted. Through later digital ethnography, it was learned that the collective at Prinzessinnengarten were one of several initiators of this political statement, which had been signed by over 150 *Gemeinschaftsgärten* and support organisations in Germany and Austria. Making a case for politicians and urban planners to recognize and strengthen the legal position of *Gemeinschaftsgärten*, the manifesto lamented how "large corporations and brand representatives, who want to utilise this 'cool' scenery for photo shoots", as well as "guerrilla gardening and knitting events [...] staged for commercials, linking 'applied practices' to the sale of their products" (Urban Gardening Manifest, 2014; my translation). As this text suggested, corporate co-optation was portrayed as part of a common grievance among *Gemeinschaftsgärten*, their precarity being linked with their popularity and appropriation of activist repertoires in a manner that undermined their associations with urban commoning.

Concerns of precarity seemed well-founded just by observing the immediate neighbourhood. The relationship of Prinzessinnengarten to the surrounding city was, like *Gemeinschaftsgärten* in general, characterised by its contrast with how commodified land took form. The garden of reclaimed wood, plastic buckets, and shipping containers was almost entirely surrounded by an architectural aesthetic characterised by steel, glass, and concrete – all of which appeared to be no more than a decade old. The age of these buildings was confirmed when I later pulled up street-level Google Map images of the area. Predating the garden's establishment, these images showed that, like the garden's site, most adjoining plots of land were then vacant lots, or older buildings that had since been demolished and redeveloped.

Across the road and just down the street however, one large gravel-covered plot of land did remain undeveloped. There, a large banner placed on it alluded of Prinzessinnengarten's impending future, as I interpreted it considering the general precarity of such gardens. In addition to the notice *"Achtung. Hier entstehen neue Perspektiven"* [Watch out. New perspectives are emerging here], the building company's slogan informed passers-by that they were creating space for the future (*"Wir schaffen Platz für die Zukunft"*) (refer to figure 26, page 155). Observing the signs and directories of buildings in the direct vicinity of Prinzessinnengarten, they were largely filled with software companies, design and consulting firms, coworking spaces, or corporate offices, and it appeared that these things had found their way into the garden itself. It was not uncommon to find people dressed in office attire sitting and working on their computers in the grove where Prinzessinnengarten's café was located. On one occasion, I was even approached in that grove by a group of university students, training to become app developers, who were doing user experience research with a prototype of an app they were developing.

There were thus aesthetic dualities and contrasts between Prinzess-innengarten and the immediate area, signifying contrasting social values. It could be said that the aesthetics of the garden and its surroundings articulated very different ideas about what a 'new perspective' was in the context of urban planning and land development, and thus two very different articulations of urban space and how it should be designed, inhabited, and experienced. A stark contrast could be observed between an aesthetic of DIY and salvaged post-consumer materials, and one that of the creative economy rising within a built environment of glass, concrete, and steel. Despite their overall contrasts, however, the latter did appropriate elements of the former's aesthetic vocabulary into its structures. As such, I consider pallets and related elements of the DIY aesthetic of *Gemeinschaftsgärten* to function as *floating signifiers*, capable of being articulated into different discourses that were otherwise in tension with one another (cf. Laclau, 2005, p. 133). They were able to become part of a DIY aesthetic or a corporate one, regardless of the divergent political and economic values each espoused.

This observation complexified the relationship commercial enterprises could be interpreted to have with *Gemeinschaftsgärten*. Their design embraced these sites as seeming aesthetic inspirations, yet they did so from different ideological positions, insofar as the ethos constituted in *Gemein-schaftsgärten* represented a critique of the capitalist rationalities such companies represented. Even more symbolic, I found, was how the aforementioned billboards literally constituted the outside of Prinzessinnengarten by their placement on its exterior wall. This was a rather clear illustration of how competing visions formed this boundary, as well as how the garden made the advertisements possible by being a use of land that permitted the billboards to be erected there (and arguably provided an appealing aesthetic to co-opt).

Figure 26: A sign of things to come. The last remaining plot of land in the immediate vicinity of Prinzessinnengarten, other than the garden itself, that had not been redeveloped. (*Credit*: Author)

Gemeinschaftsgärten in the Tourist Marketplace

The popularity and reputation of Prinzessinnengarten further complicated the relationship between *Gemeinschaftsgärten* and the city of Berlin. On visitBerlin [sic], the city's official travel portal, the garden had its own dedicated page under the website's sightseeing category, as well as being described on a separate page highlighting the city's urban gardening initiatives (Berlin Tourismus & Kongress GmbH., n.d.). Listed under a subcategory for parks and gardens, which primarily focused on municipal green spaces, the Tourism Board used these pages to tout the social and environmental work of *Gemeinschaftsgärten* generally. On the page highlighting urban gardening initiatives in Berlin, the international interest Prinzessinnengarten had garnered in its dozen years of operation was immediately acknowledged. Then, the text provided a general characterisation of it and other sites that were each profiled further down on the same page:

> Berlin's urban gardening projects are organised by a range of associations, initiatives, and groups of volunteers, and all have one thing in common: they aim to make city life brighter and more beautiful, adding a little bit of nature to the urban jungle while bringing people together and encouraging a sense of community spirit. Along with sharing the pleasures of gardening, many projects also offer a range of workshops and cultural events. We're happy to share a number of these urban gardening projects with you. (Berlin Tourismus & Kongress GmbH, n.d.)

Although describing the gardens as the work of "associations, initiatives and groups of volunteers", the Tourism Board was speaking for *Gemeinschafts-gärten* as a collective unit and marketing a particular representation of them. They conveyed their own interpretation of what these gardens represented for the city. While some of this may have intersected with values internal to the collectives maintaining Prinzessinnengarten and other *Gemeinschafts-gärten*, the Tourism Board produced its own meanings of these places. "[Inscribing] an interest in a complex reality different from that in which the interest was originally formulated", as Laclau (1996b, p. 98) describes the process of rearticulation by co-optation, the Tourism Board's mandate to market Berlin as a desirable destination for tourists and conference organisers meant that they constructed a different sense of place for these gardens, encoding them in a context meant to appeal to a tourist demographic in service of economic development goals.

In doing so, their actions could be understood as an instance of *appropriative representation*, as it "strips situated, cultural practices of symbolic meanings and historical specificities" (Finlay, 2022, p. 8). The Tourism Board produced its own symbolism for these gardens as part of an overall image of Berlin's social and environmental profile, marketing a sense of place by which the city and its gardens should be known or understood – in this case as an appealing place to visit and spend money. Aspects of Prinzessinnengarten and other *Gemeinschaftsgärten* that made them desirable to visit were reappropriated, while the non-commercial and anti-capitalist ethos that impinged upon their compatibility with a consumer capitalist tourism economy were excluded from descriptions of these sites. Prinzessinnengarten became rearticulated, grouped alongside other similar gardens as analogous with museums, city parks, and the city's nightlife. Together, these became selling points of city branding whereby Berlin was portrayed as a place with a good quality of life, and therefore worth visiting, investing in, and selecting for hosting conferences or other events.

Prinzessinnengarten and similar gardens were explicitly advertised and highlighted alongside city-managed green spaces and cultural facilities, integrated into Berlin's capitalist economy through its promotion of tourism as a source of economic development. Berlin's marketability as a place worth visiting could be understood to extrapolate values of beauty, pleasure, and community associated with these gardens as qualities synonymous with the city. This rearticulation involved a certain governmental rationality, I would argue, as the consumerist premises of tourism promote a particular way of thinking and behaving. Tourist marketing conditions people to relate to

Gemeinschaftsgärten as selling points in selecting Berlin as a place to spend time and money, and thus influences people to behave in a manner conducive to the city's economic development agenda. This was particularly striking considering the commercialising ethos of neoliberal capitalism, criticised as it was in the material cultures of *Gemeinschaftsgärten* and the founding narrative of Prinzessinnengarten. Commercial and private property development were portrayed as threatening to the non-capitalist economies and anti-capitalist values promoted in these gardens. Prinzessinnengarten and other *Gemeinschaftsgärten* signified alternative ways of living in and inhabiting urban space and had made these desirable enough for businesses and the Tourism Board to co-opt. Doing so, their sense of place was rearticulated as something compatible with neoliberal capitalist economic imperatives that collectives were observably at odds with.

Rearticulating *Gemeinschaftsgärten* in City Planning

And yet, while the Tourism Board benefitted from advertising existing gardens, including Prinzessinnengarten, materials from other agencies and government bodies promoted planning policies that could contribute to the erasure of the very sense of place that made them appealing for marketing purposes. Specifically, a ten-year strategy plan adopted by the Berlin Senate suggested that the significance of *Gemeinschaftsgärten* could become increasingly conditioned and determined by the commodification of land for development. Berlin's urban development strategy involved plans that would subsume this predominantly grassroots approach to urban agriculture and urban commoning as part of top-down development policies, fundamentally rearticulating their significance according to a political ethos that was incompatible with the anti-capitalist premises of commoning they fostered. Their popularity and the desirability of what they represented thus further contributed to the precarity of existing *Gemeinschaftsgärten* in Berlin and the sense of place constituted within them. Government plans and reports, and news interviews with local politicians, could be understood to suggest another manifestation of co-optation that would diminish their political potential.

Co-opting the Future of *Gemeinschaftsgärten*

The Tourism Board actively included and celebrated Prinzessinnengarten and several other *Gemeinschaftsgärten* by name on its website and promotional materials. So too did the city's Environment Office and the Berlin

Senate – the executive political body governing the city-state – seem to have a positive attitude towards them in terms of urban planning discourse. A key difference, however, was that the latter two had orientations towards the future rather than a focus on existing gardens. In 2019, the Senate approved a ten-year charter and action plan drafted by the Environment Office of the Senatsverwaltung für Umwelt, Mobilität und Klimaschutz (SenUMK) [Senate Administration for Environment, Mobility and Climate Protection]. This document, *Charta für das Berliner Stadtgrün* [Charter for Berlin's Urban Greenery], set out guidelines and goals "to promote the security, strength and development of Berlin's urban greenery as a self-commitment by the state of Berlin" (Senatsverwaltung für Umwelt, Verkehr und Klimatschutz, 2020, p. 5; my translation). In doing so, the Senate recognised that:

> the services and functions of urban greenery contribute significantly to the quality and attractiveness of Berlin as a place for living, working, leisure and business, as well as a travel destination.
>
> [...]
>
> Citizens need access to urban green spaces close to where they live, which gives them relaxation and encounters and allows movement. This is also a contribution to environmental justice. (ibid., p. 4; my translation)

As with the Tourism Board, the charter positioned Berlin's green spaces as part of what constituted Berlin as a desirable place, articulating the city's greenery with discourses of physical and psychological health, social inter-action, and environmental justice. In the supportive statements from the Environment Office, and their ratification by the Berlin Senate, a chain of equivalence could be interpreted whereby 'green spaces' or 'greenery' were articulated as analogous with values of attractiveness, relaxation, public health and environmental justice. This confluence of discourses contrasted with the focus on community and sustainability present in the discourses produced by the social enterprise responsible for Prinzessinnengarten, underscoring the polysemy of urban green space as a concept open to multiple meanings and thus possible to articulate as consistent with different – and even conflicting – discourses (cf. Laclau & Mouffe, 1985, p. 169).

Another theme of note in the charter was that of security, which can be interpreted as a projected social rationality sought by the government in relation to urban greenery. The Senate was using the idea of providing a more secure future for such gardens and green spaces as an intended, imagined norm for planning policies and decisions that had not yet occurred (cf. Glynos, Speed, & West, 2014). According to this rationality of security, the services and function of *Gemeinschaftsgärten*, as part of Berlin's urban greenery, were mostly being presented as significant in relation to economic concerns – "the quality and attractiveness of Berlin as a place for living, working, leisure and business, as well as a travel destination" (Senatsverwaltung für Umwelt, Verkehr und Klimaschutz, 2020, p. 4; my translation). Though there was an implied relevance to public health and environmental concerns, the attractiveness, appeal, and potential for urban greenery to encourage new residents, businesses and tourists seemed to constitute the primary goals. As this example demonstrates, sense of place, having to do with how places come to be expressed and experienced, and thus knowable through the meanings, stories, and trajectories associated with them (cf. Feld & Basso, 1996, p. 11; Massey, 2005), can also be articulated by 'outside' interests – in this case, city branding and consumer marketing. Government institutions, politicians, and corporations made sense of gardens like Prinzessinnengarten through their own interpretative schema. How *Gemeinschaftsgärten* were knowable and imaginable was contextual, subject to rearticulation and conflicting interpretations based on the nature of the interests and rationalities applied to them.

Examining the charter more closely, it referred to *Gemeinschaftgärten* repeatedly, citing them as one of the core elements of the city's green infrastructure, "part of Berlin's quality of life" and, alongside allotment gardens, "an essential contribution to the furtherance of the 'edible city' being realised" (Senatsverwaltung für Umwelt, Verkehr und Klimaschutz, 2020, pp. 7–8; my translation).[38] The plan stated an intent to create more "collective parcels for the use of multiple parties" and to see that "community gardening is promoted and conceptually integrated into the development of open spaces citywide" (p. 8; my translation). Through such statements, *Gemeinschaftsgärten* were articulated within a discourse of the sustainable city promoted by Berlin's government. Being a political document ratified by the Berlin Senate, the government could thus be seen to constitute its own sense of place for *Gemeinschaftsgärten* in relation to institutional strategies for urban development. Integrating these gardens into normative urban planning discourses from a position of legal authority, they could rearticulate and

---

[38] In referring to the 'edible city', the document references Berlin's role within an international network of cities committed to increasing the cultivation of edible plants in public areas for self-harvest, as a matter of promoting food security, sustainable development, and social cohesion (Edible Cities Network, 2018).

regulate these discourses through zoning laws, building regulations, development policies, and other means. Complementary elements of gardens could be retained while excluding the anti-capitalist political ethos they represented in their current state.

Through a chain of equivalence whereby government documents portrayed the government, *Gemeinschaftsgärten,* and other stakeholders in urban agriculture as representing common, shared values, the concepts of urban greenery and *Gemeinschaftsgärten* could both be understood to operate as floating signifiers. The two terms were ambiguous enough to be able to associate with any number of political projects, use contexts, and articulatory schema (cf. Moraes, 2014, p. 30), as they were observable in discourses of public health, ecosystem services, and tourism development as well as through the meanings and significance conveyed in the material culture and narratives of Prinzessinnengarten and other *Gemeinschaftsgärten* collectives. The rationality according to which Prinzessinnengarten and other such gardens were articulated within discourses of urban greenery and the edible city constituted their significance in terms of public health and the economic desirability, becoming a normative interpretation to the extent that its ratification by the Berlin Senate lent it the authority of political institutions.

However, despite being articulated as "an essential contribution" in the charter and action plan, existing *Gemeinschaftsgärten* appeared to be omitted from this discourse. Instead, it envisioned future gardens – i.e., ones that did not yet exist – as part of a forthcoming urban cityscape. As a future-oriented document, the charter emphasised the integration of *Gemeinschaftsgärten* and other edible and social gardening forms into developments and projects that did not yet exist but were intended to be realised by 2030. Furthermore, neither the charter nor action plan addressed the precarity of existing gardens, silent on how or if support for them would figure into the city's plan – this being the specific demand of the manifesto observed at Prinzessinnengarten (see Urban Gardening Manifest, 2014). Therefore, while the documents stated that the city was supportive of *developing* new collective gardens, "integrated into the development of open spaces" (Senatsverwaltung für Umwelt, Verkehr und Klimaschutz, 2020, p. 8; my translation), plans did not seem to be inclusive of a commitment to preserve existing ones.

This impression was reinforced in my search for initiatives which appeared to be, at least in part, oriented towards existing *Gemeinschaftsgärten*. One was the online *Plattform Productive Stadtgrün* [Productive Urban Greenery Platform], which in addition to an interactive map and links to research, was intended to serve as a forum for "the direct exchange between gardeners, community garden initiatives and projects as well as the Senate Administration for Environment, Mobility, Consumer and Climate Protection (SenUMVK)" (Senatsverwaltung für Umwelt, Mobilität, Verbraucher- und Klimaschutz, n.d.; my translation).[39] In 2022, already two years after its implementation, it did not appear that the forum was actively used; there were but a dozen forum postings, few of which invited discussion or received responses. The second initiative, *Berliner Gemeinschaftsgarten-Programm* [Berlin Community Garden Programme], was a participatory planning process operated by a pair of landscape architecture firms on behalf of SenUMVK (Senatsverwaltung für Umwelt, Mobilität, Verbraucher- und Klimaschutz, 2021). Involving a series of workshops and events, it appeared focused on gathering information from garden stakeholders on how to best support them, particularly through legal and funding mechanisms. At the time of publication, it is unclear how the information gathered, and discussion had, may translate into policy changes and practical supports for existing or future *Gemeinschaftsgärten*. This would require a longitudinal evaluation of the implementation and impact of as-yet undeveloped policies.

Because of this distinction between present and future *Gemeinschaftsgärten* in the charter, achieved through the omission of references to the former, I argue that existing collective gardens became *collectively* marginalised and excluded from the projected social rationality of security. While the existence of *Gemeinschaftsgärten* apparently provided a source of inspiration for the strategic plan, those which already existed had often emerged in the interstices of urban planning, premised on interim, and thus insecure, land tenure. As such, they were inconsistent with the rationality presented in the charter, according to which secure urban agriculture was to be an intentional, planned element of property development projects to ensure its continued presence in Berlin. A discrepancy could therefore be noted between (1) the rhetoric of the Environment Office and Berlin Senate, according to whom these gardens worth securing as a core element of the city's environmental profile, and (2) the situation in which *Gemeinschaftsgärten* actually found themselves due to the circumstances they were compelled to operate within.

The charter thus implied a disarticulation of *Gemeinschaftsgärten* through their co-optation, as they were to be "disempowered through the very dis-

---

[39] SenUMVK, cited here, succeeded the SenUMK with the addition of consumer protection to the department's portfolio.

courses of empowerment they are being offered as substitutes" (McRobbie, p. 49). Existing gardens could be understood to become even more precarious in the name of a secure future for as-yet undeveloped ones. Integrating *Gemeinschaftsgärten* into the city's normative practices of private property development would occur at the exclusion of the urban commoning and collective benefit they fostered in their current forms. While stating that *Gemeinschaftsgärten* were a valuable contribution to Berlin's quality of life, the Charter for Berlin's Urban Greenery established a relationship between the Berlin Senate and *Gemeinschaftsgärten* in an abstract, future-oriented sense, not as a relationship between the Senate and extant gardens. *Gemeinschaftsgärten* and supports for urban agriculture would be inscribed in Berlin's future, their place in the present left ambiguous.

Furthermore, this co-optation of *Gemeinschaftsgärten* could be interpreted to governmentalise the phenomenon, making these gardens more conducive to the ends of government by inducing their existence to be conditioned by inclusion in development projects (cf. Foucault, 1982, 2007, 2008; Rose, O'Malley, & Valverde, 2012, p. 124). Such an outcome, I argue, could change the conditions by which people had access to *Gemeinschaftsgärten* in the future, and the nature of their organisation, as the implication of the Senate's charter was that they would come to manifest in accordance with normative rationalities of urban development. As features or amenities of *private* development, they would no longer be urban *commons* premised on critiques or rejections of private property.

City for Sale: Cultivating Gardens in the Interim

Considering the circumstances in Berlin, and the fact that many *Gemeinschaftsgärten* there or elsewhere in Germany were already relocating, scaling down or mobilising to preserve their sites, it was unusual that Prinzessinnengarten had remained in its original location for an entire decade by the time of my first visit. Despite the seemingly high profile they had in city branding, as part of the cultural, ecological and creative identity of the city, at the time of writing several of the oldest and largest *Gemeinschaftsgärten* that I visited in Berlin were in the process of either downsizing or fully relocating Social media accounts and news stories explained this as being due to short-term land leases with the city – most often annual or biannual – that were not being renewed. Others had experienced periods of uncertainty, threatened with ceasing operations, but managed to remain through last minute extensions from the city. Whether finding reprieve or not, it appeared to be a common feature of Berlin's *Gemeinschaftsgärten* to regularly be in search of new garden locations, meeting and negotiating with local officials and potential property owners, and mobilising supporters.

In exploring Prinzessinnengarten's comparable resilience, it turned out the social enterprise was not so different in this regard; however, it had been more successful in securing continued and longer lease extensions for its location. As referenced in the founding story on the garden's website, the property was then "managed by the Liegenschaftsfonds Berlin, a city-owned real estate firm, whose mission is to privatise municipally owned land and buildings with the highest bidder" (Prinzessinnengarten, 2012; my translation). As I learned by investigating further, this was known as a *Zwischennutzung* [in-between use], an interim or temporary use lease, which meant that the city expected to sell or develop the property, allowing it to be used for gardening in the meantime. This type of lease was typical for sites in Berlin and elsewhere, and even encouraged by the federal government in guidance materials (see Bundesministerium für Umwelt, Naturschutz, Bau und Reaktorsicherheit (BMUB), 2015). As mentioned earlier, Prinzessinnengarten was surrounded by buildings that were newer than the garden itself, with the little remaining land already slated for development. It therefore appeared to retain the last plot of land that was neither city park nor built (or under construction) structure, and in doing so seemed at first glance to be something of an outlier. Despite being designed with mobility in mind, due to the intended sale and development of the location, the garden had held its ground, outlasting many similar gardens.

Looking closer at how the leasing situation of Prinzessinnengarten changed over that decade, it complicated this initial impression, proving insightful for understanding the challenges involved in protecting gardens like it. Between 2009 and 2012 the social enterprise which managed the garden had a lease which was renewed annually. The property owner at the time, Liegenschaftsfonds Berlin (LFB), was a wholly owned subsidiary of the State of Berlin. Central to the mission of LFB was facilitating the sale of surplus government-owned property, primarily through public auction, in order to help pay down the tens of billions of euros in debt that the Berlin government had accrued as a result of reunification and the assumption of East German government-owned property (Silomon-Pflug & Heeg, 2013).[40]

---

[40] To give a sense of the scale of its holdings, LFB had sold over 14 million square meters of land and property – over 5000 properties – within ten years of being established (2001–2011) (Lautenschläger, 2011; Der Tagesspiegel, 2011); there were still 4 million square meters remaining in the states surplus property portfolio as of 2020, a decade later (BIM Berliner Immobilienmanagement GmbH, 2021).

[41] While a majority of the LFB property portfolio was transferred from the East German government upon reunification, Prinzessinnengarten was situated in the former West Berlin, where LFB holdings included many sites that had been destroyed and left abandoned since the Second World War. The majority of *Gemeinschaftsgärten* visited in Berlin were also located on government-owned property of this type. While some were in parks, and therefore comparably protected from the possibility of property development, many more were on surplus property or co-located with schools and cultural institutions that could eventually decide they needed the land for other purposes.

Analysed with this context in mind, the interim leases that Prinzessinnengarten and other *Gemeinschaftsgärten* had were interludes in official discourses of land development. The legitimate value of the properties where they operated were, from the perspective of the government (via LFB), associated with their development potential. Prinzessinnengarten and other gardens like it were precaritised as a legal precondition of their existence while the government awaited a time when these sites could be sold at a sufficient profit. This was not irrelevant context through which to understand the significance of the mobile, DIY, and salvage character of garden construction and design observable at sites like Prinzessinnengarten. The in-built precarity of their legal circumstances necessarily conditioned how they were designed and planned; further, it also made it difficult for these collectives to operate without being in tension with the capitalist rationalities that enabled their interim use at the same time as threatening their continued existence.

To give context to the extent of this precarity, the government was selling large areas of land and a significant portfolio of properties at a steady pace – approximately 5,500 properties in the period 2001–2011 alone (Lautenschläger, 2011). It was therefore not surprising that *Gemeinschaftsgärten* located on government-held land left in ruins for decades – which were a considerable number in Berlin and elsewhere – were at risk. Prinzessinnengarten itself was threatened by the planned auction of the property in 2012, three years after it was established. However, several fronts of political action coalesced to save the garden. Firstly, a campaign was started to spare the site from auction and commit to a longer-term lease agreement, gathering over

---

[41] In 2015, Liegenschaftsfonds Berlin was absorbed into BIM (Berliner Immobilienmanagement GmbH), a subsidiary company of the State of Berlin which manages the state's real estate, including government buildings, rental facilities, multiple cultural institutions, as well as property held in trust for the LFB.

30,000 signatures to their petition. Alongside this, the borough mayor stated his support, having meetings with multiple Senate departments, citing Prinzessinnengarten as "an urban laboratory [...] a nucleus of urban sustainability" (Martens, 2012; my translation). Also, as mentioned in a news interview regarding the success of the garden's lease extension, the Senator for Urban Development positioned Prinzessinnengarten as "a good example for how urban agriculture can be realised through site-based engagement", describing the outcome – by which the borough took over the lease from LFB – as "extremely desirable because green spaces have a very positive effect on the urban climate, especially in the densely populated inner-city areas" (Die Welt, 2012; my translation).

Despite the precarity of their legal right to remain in their location, the garden was simultaneously celebrated as the type of place that the city was motivated to develop in the future. But it wasn't just that *Gemeinschaftsgärten* were seen as compatible with the government's priorities vis-à-vis sustainability and urban gardening. Gardens like Prinzessinnengarten benefitted in some ways from their positive association with these concepts as floating signifiers, applicable to seemingly contradictory discourses of urban commoning and urban development. The Tourism Board and Environmental Office each expressed a positive inclination towards *Gemeinschaftsgärten* – and Prinzessinnengarten specifically in the case of the Tourism Board – in line with their interests. However, at the same time, gardens were also valued according to their provision of short-term rental income, as marketable goods in the tourism economy, or as ecosystem services fulfilling the city's environmental aims.

There was thus a seeming duality in how *Gemeinschaftsgärten* were simultaneously valued and being pushed out to accommodate property development. As a floating signifier, different institutions, and even competing mandates within the same institutions, worked from divergent discourses of urban development. They weren't being seen as places, nor their sense of place significant because of its DIY and salvage ethos; they were rearticulated as commodities, with their 'floating' nature making it possible to co-opt them by rearticulating the significance of Prinzessinnengarten and other *Gemeinschaftsgärten* in a manner aligned with institutional mandates and goals (cf. Trumpy, 2008, p. 480). In this case, the significance of a garden like Prinzessinnengarten to the city was relative to its potential for serving capitalist land development or its desirability as an amenity or 'selling point' for tourists and businesses. *Gemeinschaftsgärten* and public land were commodities that could generate income and were also valued according to a rationality that constituted them as *securities*, tradable assets to be sold off.

The borough mayor addressed this tension between different government discourses in an interview where Prinzessinnengarten was discussed in relation to Berlin's real estate policy. Calling attention to what was implied to be common knowledge at the time, he alluded to a tension between the positions of the Senator for Finance and the Senator for Urban Development:

> I am cautious about the assessment that Berlin wants a new real estate policy. You know the dispute between [Finance Senator] Nußbaum and [Urban Development Senator] Müller. The Senator for Finance won 95 percent of the proposals for the new property policy. The proposal has a clear focus on selling even more plots of land. I think it's worse than the current model. (Heier, 2012; my translation)

As the borough mayor's allusion to a political antagonism suggested, the preservation of Prinzessinnengarten was not a singular issue, inserted rather in a struggle over the values of the city. In his comments, Berlin's sense of place was at stake, headed either towards a future that prioritised land sales or one that focused on urban development.

The consumer rationality of neoliberal capitalism, by which income and profit were equated with quality of life and welfare (see Harvey, 2012; Mouffe, 2015), was thus seemingly also an internal struggle within the government, with greenery and *Gemeinschaftsgärten* portrayed as competing interests. Even government departments and some local politicians could be seen to express counter-normative values and rationalities regarding reasonable and appropriate land policy. They worked within the authority they had to promote and support existing *Gemeinschaftsgärten* but lacked the legitimacy to supersede the ethos of speculative development that the borough mayor implied was characteristic of the Berlin Senate's normative land policy. Although expressed through different discourses, there was nonetheless some sense of ideological alignment through which politicians and collectives like Prinzessinnengarten lobbied the Berlin Senate to realise policy changes.

Global Grievances

Developing this contextual understanding about the multiple forms of precarity experienced by collective gardens in Berlin helped to make sense of the global character of Prinzessinnengarten's material culture and events hosted at the site. Analysing discourses of global solidarity being articulated through flyers and other materials posted in relation to demonstrations and discussions held there, it was possible to interpret certain concerns whereby global justice movements and local activism on urban development policies could be equated as part of a common discourse. Although locally specific, Prinzessinnengarten's precarity became interpretable within the scope of broader demands and grievances concerning land rights and global capitalism.

Solidarity Against the Violence of Global Capitalism

Where local themes were concerned, materials suggested that demonstrations and other political events taking place at the garden had a commonality in their focus on the impacts of luxury housing and the expanding IT sector on the availability and affordability of housing development in the area. One example was a flyer for a *Straßenfest* [street party] stating "*Solidarisch im Alltag – solidarische Nachbarschaft*" [Solidarity in the everyday – a neighbourhood of solidarity]. The flyer was for an event organised by Basta Berlin, an organisation which advised, assisted, and advocated for people who were unemployed or low-income earners, as well as students, largely focused on preventing evictions, advocating for a living wage and rent control, and assisting in legal claims against job centres regarding the withholding of social insurance (Basta Erwerbsloseninitiative, 2022). Another image, a brightly coloured, text-dense flyer with the title "*Wurzeln schlagen!*" [Take root!] turned out to be a manifesto calling to "[p]reserve Prinzessinnengarten as a common good for ninety-nine years", with the text specifically criticising the city for privatising land, selling off municipal housing, and displacing residents. Signs and stickers posted at the garden and throughout the neighbourhood also alerted to a movement called "Fuck off Google", which had mobilised in Kreuzberg in 2017 and 2018 in response to Google's attempt to develop a 'start-up campus' in the borough, fearing the project would exacerbate rising rent costs in the area and overall gentrification – as well as criticism of the company's surveillance and data management practices (which remain particularly controversial in Germany) (see Kaiser, 2017; Knight, 2018).

Messages such as these emphasised a sense of precarity, not only for the garden, but for residents of Berlin and their quality of life. They alluded to the sense of tension – and outright antagonism – towards employers, landowners, the IT sector. and the city government, who were articulated as threats to people living on the margins of society, equated in their focus on profit through which they were depriving people of basic needs such as living wages, housing, jobs, and urban commons. Taken together, the promotion of this range of issues within the garden could be understood in terms of cultivating and realising a projected social rationality of security for urban commons. Threatened by property speculation and achievable through defending land and housing rights, acting on privatisation was reasoned to secure the future of the garden and a more liveable future for residents of Berlin.

In addition to these local issues, many of the most prominently placed messages in the garden were those expressing solidarity with land activists or demanding accountability for the victims of political assassinations in other parts of the world. With adjoining text that provided more context for some, and through follow-up research in other cases, these materials detailed grievances with corporations, police, and (para)military forces, along with claims of either government complicity or outright corruption, who were characterised as inflicting violence in the name of land dispossession. The size, location, and visibility of these signs gave the impression that they were purpose-made for advertising and using during demonstrations hosted at Prinzessinnengarten. Expressing solidarity with such causes implied a relevance to being informed and acting in solidarity with contemporary political struggles elsewhere in the world. Despite their focus on geographically distant issues, their association with the garden made them salient to understanding the garden's significance to its collective and visitors.

Among the most prominent of these signs was a large banner hung from atop the garden's multi-storey tower calling for "*Solidarité mit der ZAD*" – employing a blend of French and German in reference to the French *zones à défendre*, a movement of militant open-air squats that have defended various sites across France from development projects consider to be environmentally damaging (as reported in Kerinec, 2018; Willsher, 2018). Another, along the side of the same structure, was written in Portuguese with an image of the person in question, stating "*Executada - Quem matou Marielle Franco*" [Executed – who killed Marielle Franco], referring to a Brazilian politician, feminist, and human rights activist whose assassination was largely believed to be tied to her criticism of police brutality against favela residents and extrajudicial killings by individuals with close ties to the country's then president Jair Bolsonaro (as reported in Cowie, 2019). A poster with a large Spanish-language heading that read "*El silencio nos hace cómplices*" [Silence makes us complicit], and provided information and a call to action, in Spanish and German, supporting victims of political assassinations in Columbia, which have disproportionately targeted indigenous and Afro-Colombian community organisers in rural communities (as reported in UN News, 2020).

Associated with demonstrations and discussions hosted in the garden, these materials alluded to events that those involved at Prinzessinnengarten would have participated in or likely been aware of and were thus considered relevant to understanding the character of the garden's significance internal to its community. All of the events were recent or ongoing at the time of my first visit to Prinzessinnengarten in summer 2018; Marielle Franco's assassination and the clearing of a ZAD by French authorities both had occurred earlier that same year, and political assassinations in Colombia were stated to be ongoing at that time. As with the circumstances of Prinzessinnengarten and other *Gemeinschaftsgärten* – in Berlin as elsewhere in Germany – these causes shared an element of conflict over the viability of commoning, some in urban locations, others in rural settings. The extent of precarity may have differed in relation to the conditions in Berlin, with activists in some cases exposed to violence or the threat of violence. Nonetheless, all were related to concerns about corporations taking control over and developing land – either for property speculation or industrial agriculture.

This dynamic presents another way of imagining the global city, a concept typically understood to refer to a city that operates within a network of other cities across the globe that, through their influence over the flow of information and capital have direct effects on global socioeconomic affairs (Sassen, 1991, 2000). At Prinzessinnengarten, it seemed important to develop responsibility-taking and critical reflection on a local *and* global level, as evidenced by the types of political demonstrations and discussions being hosted. Relating to the global political community in such a way could therefore be seen to reflect a conceptualisation of democratic citizenship characterised by being globally informed and actively engaged in practices that support global justice as inextricable from local justice. Through the example of Prinzessinnengarten, a global city then might also be conceptualised in terms of global networks of solidarity through which cities like Berlin become articulated with other places that together influence the global flow of anti-capitalist values and political education consistent with the democratic expression of citizenship. In other words, by assuming the role of globally responsible citizen, individuals could be understood to contribute to solving the problems of global capitalism through personal responsibility for consumption practices and reducing dependence on transnational industrial agriculture and global logistic networks. Rather than separate from the normative capitalist concept of the global city, this way of conceptualising it reflects an interconnected but contrary trajectory of globalised resistance.

A Precarious Alliance

Analysing the local and global mobilisations hosted at Prinzessinnengarten in relation to one another, the common theme through which the circumstances of *Gemeinschaftsgärten* and movements elsewhere could be considered analogous was in their precarious land rights. As Laclau and Mouffe (1985) argue, a political discursive approach helps to explain how people who may be perceived as aligned to different interests or causes can in fact come together and identify (or be understood to identify) behind a common cause (p. 105). According to them, it is through experiences of suffering, the perception of threat, or the opportunity for action that people articulate chains of equivalence to create a narrative of common suffering or common interest with other causes considered to be comparable. Taking this argument further, Laclau (2005) describes this common interest in terms of an *empty signifier* – a concept or demand that is sufficiently empty of meaning to allow multiple meanings to be attributed, thereby enabling people to see themselves as united behind a common cause (p. 71 & 105).

The disparate situations of gardeners in Berlin, favela dwellers in Rio de Janeiro, rural homesteaders in Colombia, and *zadistes* in France could be articulated in a chain of equivalence, implying some sort of commonality between them, because land rights provided just such an empty signifier. Though meaning different things in practice for these different social movements and collective mobilisations – whether in terms of the right to land for anti-capitalist commoning, homes for the urban poor, or non-industrial cultivation by peasant farmers – each situation was analogous through a common desire to not be exploited or controlled by corporations or the greed and corruption of those placing money before human or environmental welfare. Whether asserting or protecting land rights, each concerned the ability for people to exercise greater control or freedom over their lives through non-exploitative relationships to place.

In this manner, Prinzessinnengarten was articulated within a common global struggle against dispossession and precarity. Though the extent of the threat differed – for gardeners in Berlin limited to eviction, while elsewhere risking physical violence and even death – in each case, global capital posed a threat as an antagonistic other. While the lives and livelihoods of rural farmers were threatened by global capital in the form of violence in support of industrial agriculture, Prinzessinnengarten's existence, like the housing of favela dwellers in Brazil or *zadiste* settlements in France, was embedded in struggles with political institutions that involved global networks of property development that sought to transform the city according to a rationality of economic liberalism privileging private property, free markets, and free trade (cf. Harvey, 2005, 2012; Mouffe, 2018). In a similar vein, the concern over the assassinations of Marielle Franco and Columbian community organisers, as well as the expulsion of the *zadistes* who squatted proposed development sites in France, can be seen to have a common link in their focus on land rights and human rights, and the abuses and neglect of these at the hands of corporate and government interests that did not consider their demands as legitimate ones. Furthermore, each also conveyed a grievance with government complicity in economic interests taking precedence over collective uses.

The political and economic critiques expressed in relation to each of these international issues had a commonality with the precarity of *Gemeinschaftsgärten* that made sense through analysis in terms of governmentality. In Berlin, the Charter for Berlin's Urban Greenery could be interpreted to signal a shift in the direction of governmental rationality, by which the conditions under which urban agriculture could be practiced would be altered in furtherance of the government's economic interests (cf. Foucault, 2007, 2008). The violence in other parts of the world (that demonstrations at Prinzessinnengarten were being organised to demand action on) was itself described as the result of people who resisted complying with what I would argue are the governmental rationalities of nation-states and transnational corporations seeking to condition specific ways of using and relating to land. The social movements in Brazil, Colombia, and France that were being addressed were, like Prinzessinnengarten and similar gardens elsewhere in Berlin, resisting the influence of neoliberal capitalism and what it meant for their collective and non-capitalist ways of life. Each could be understood to reject the imposition of land privatisation because it threatened the possibility of alternative economies and practices of commoning.

Although Prinzessinnengarten's social values were site-specific, constituted in relation to Berlin's political economy of land development and the commodification of green space as tourist sites, marketing backdrops, or ecosystem services, the sense of place the garden represented in relation to Berlin was simultaneously constituted through the context of global social justice through which shared demands for land rights could be interpreted. The social values promoted at the site were articulated within a chain of equivalence that connected international and local issues as analogous and relevant to the social issues the garden was understood to address. Differences were circumscribed to construct a common identity and sense of solidarity, exemplifying Laclau and Mouffe's (1985) semantic understanding of how this occurs, by "subverting the differential character" of each groups' struggle (p. 128). Simplifying geo-political space, Prinzessinnengarten's potential eviction and violence against land rights activists elsewhere functioned paradigmatically as "elements that can be substituted for one another" to articulate common anti-capitalist and anti-corporate grievances (p. 130).

Concluding Discussion

Prinzessinnengarten's existence was premised on its integration into the normative legal and political frameworks through which it functioned as a business and leased land from the government through a publicly owned corporation (and later the borough itself). These same circumstances also put it in the position of being used by multiple government institutions and policymakers as a selling point to advance the capitalist economy that also threatened the garden's persistence. Viewed in light of the pericapitalist interpretation of *Gemeinschaftsgärten* arrived at through analysis of the aesthetic vocabulary typical of this genre of collective gardening, this added another layer of complexity to the relationship places like Prinzessinnengarten had with capitalism. While the garden could be read in pericapitalist terms because of its existence pursuant to a lease agreement with the city, and through its dependence upon salvage accumulation, it was also pericapitalist to the extent that the city – whether in the form of developers, businesses, or government institutions – incorporated places of urban commoning into its own rationalities, benefiting economically from salvage capitalism occurring on the periphery of neoliberal capitalist economic activity and urban redevelopment.

While Prinzessinnengarten signified a resistance to capitalist values and practices through the activities and sense of place constituted within its walls, it also had a precarious dependence on the city of Berlin due to interim leases with the city. The garden operated in a state of duality, threatened by the commercialisation of its aesthetic and the site as a tourist amenity, but also benefitting from the marketing that brought more attention to the garden as a valued element of city branding. The pericapitalist character of Prinzessinnengarten thus emphasised that the boundaries between capitalist and non-capitalist economies and economic practices were not clearly defined but porous and subject to *contaminated diversity*, "collaborative adaptation to human-disturbed ecosystems" that can be cultural and biological in nature (Tsing, 2012, p. 95; see also Tsing, 2015, pp. 30–34). The presence of economic diversity in Kreuzberg was interpretable in the contamination of the 'purity' of a non-capitalist urban commons by adapting to its circumstances, engaging in some capitalist economic relationships that enable the garden's lease and minimal staff to be paid. Equally, it could be seen in the economic benefit that neoliberal city branding derived from urban commons such as Prinzessinnengarten. Seen in such a light, co-optation begins to look much less clearcut, as both the garden and Berlin's political institutions could be understood to reflect at times porous or 'contaminated' economic ideologies.

As such, while the collective within the garden appeared to promote discourses of urban commoning, as a floating signifier *Gemeinschaftsgärten* were also articulated within marketing, economic, environmental, and land use discourses by corporations and various government offices and politicians as relevant to their respective mandates and agendas. In being rearticulated thusly, Prinzessinnengarten and other *Gemeinschaftsgärten* in the city were co-opted, their political significance disarticulated to bring them into alignment with the neoliberal capitalist interests of Berlin's government (cf. McRobbie, 2009, p. 26; Trumpy, 2008, p. 480). I maintain that this was present not only in the rearticulation of elements of their aesthetic vocabulary into normative city planning and city branding discourse, but also in the sense that these gardens were portrayed in official government discourses as civic resources, tourist amenities, and ecosystem services, suggesting the government was taking credit for enabling or supporting the grassroots actions of these collectives.

Whether by local politicians or the tourist board, Prinzessinnengarten was positioned as a popular destination; so too was the neighbourhood of Kreuzberg itself, as evidenced by the building surge observed during fieldwork and property sales carried out by LFB indicative of rising property values in the area. Even as it contributed to and was acknowledged in narratives of state priorities, it also conflicted with others, as the borough mayor for Kreuzberg alluded to in discussing a tension between the city's financial and urban development policies. The polysemy of Berlin's *Gemeinschaftsgärten* meant that there was no unified or universal way of making sense of their significance, neither within the community of gardeners nor, as government discourses demonstrated, within the institutional policies and official positions of various departments, subsidiary corporations, and political offices. Each articulated these gardens with a sense of place that served its own internal environmentally and economically informed discourses of ideal urban development practice. In doing so, the latter also disarticulated these gardens from discourses of grassroots urban commoning through their use to market an urban consumer lifestyle and subsume them within strategic plans, thereby undermining and dispersing their prefigurative political significance as critiques of, and alternatives to, the normative conditions of social life.

While several government bodies and politicians actively promoted *Gemeinschaftsgärten*, thereby bringing more public attention to them, they nonetheless threatened those which already existed to the extent they were permitted as interim land uses and therefore not conducive to the development discourses influencing the long-term strategic intentions for their salvaged sites. As the concept of these gardens was co-opted through their rearticulation into city planning, existing ones were not consistent with the normative rationalities of urban development that had adapted to be inclusive of *Gemeinschaftsgärten* as part of top-down planning. Furthermore, in the arguments for promoting the security of *Gemeinschaftsgärten* through the Berlin Senate's approval of the Charter for Berlin's Urban Greenery, their situation had commonalities with what Angela McRobbie (2009) describes in efforts to disarticulate feminism as being "disempowered through the very discourse of empowerment they are being offered as substitutes" (p. 49) which "has implications for the foreclosing on other radical political imaginaries" (p. 50). Prinzessinnengarten, like many other gardens, thus existed in an antagonistic state where multiple discourses and values intersected and competed, many of them between different government agencies, subsidiaries, or political representatives. A tension internal to government institutions could therefore be seen to become externalised, each working within their own mandates, with Prinzessinnengarten and other *Gemeinschaftsgärten* left to navigate their way between competing discourses and demands.

In relation to the socio-political context of Berlin, the example of Prinzessinnengarten exemplified how ideological tensions within local government can play out in the example of a single garden as well as Berlin's *Gemeinschaftsgärten* more broadly. As a floating signifier, *Gemeinschaftsgärten* were articulated within multiple discourses among Berlin's government institutions and policymakers. These institutions were not monolithic entities, rather assemblage of departments, agencies, politicians, and bureaucrats with varying mandates, interests, and priorities that were conditioned by different normative ideas about economic, environmental, and land development. Correspondingly, the significance of these gardens varied according to how they related to departmental or other political agenda – as a temporary source of income for the LFB, as an ecosystem service for the Environmental Office, or as a civic amenity according to the Tourism Board.

While these competing discourses contributed to the precarity of places like Prinzessinnengarten, as its future would be shaped by prevailing discourses, the garden was nonetheless constituted through this same tension. It was able to be established at the interstices of each discourse, seen as beneficial to different institutions and offices for context-dependent reasons – lifting the profile of the borough and city, providing additional publicly-accessible green space without cost to the environmental office, contributing to tourism and therefore economic development, and generating profit for LFB until the site became desirable for purchase and development.

Turning once again within the garden, the globalised elements of its material culture provided terms of evaluation through which to interpret the chain of equivalence articulated between global solidarity and local land development politics. It was through an empty signifier of land rights that global space was collapsed and articulated as analogous to local politics despite materially different circumstances. Although, the physical safety of gardeners in Berlin did not seem to be a concern, as it was elsewhere, the threat of eviction in the face of global capitalism could be interpreted as a shared concern through which grievances and solidarity against a common threat could be articulated. As such, investigating the discursive intersections of local and global discourses, through the example of Prinzessinnengarten, highlighted how sense of place involves a fundamentally relational character, constituted through associations made between places. The garden was articulated as part of a transnational anti-capitalist – or anti-global capitalism – movement because local experiences were possible to be made sense of through their relatability to broader global occurrences.

The concept of an empty signifier was thus informative for understanding how comparable circumstances are not prerequisite for bonds of solidarity to be articulated. Rather, comparable grievances, as observed in the discourses on display at Prinzessinnengarten, were sufficient to articulate common threats and common antagonists, with the differing levels of violence or threat serving as examples of the capitalist land grabbing that favela dwellers, rural farmers, *zadistes* and Berlin's community of *Gemeinschaftsgärten* could all relate to. What Prinzessinnengarten meant and the type of place it pro-vided, at least as promoted within its own cultural production, pushed the normative values of urban capitalism and commodified social life in Berlin outside of its walls, while bringing within it a global discourse of land rights and social justice as an alternative norm. To make sense of Prinzessinnen-garten, local context could not be analysed in isolation from global discourses through which the claim to legitimacy of their grievances was articulated. The garden was self-precaritised to a certain degree, I argue, by knowingly entering into an interim land tenure agreement, and by rejecting the norms that they criticised in their local environment in favour of aligning with the anti-capitalist, social justice, and land rights movements they expressed solidarity with.

Sense of place is not limited to being constituted by a collective however, as it can be appropriated and co-opted by other interests - even those whose premises for doing so may differ greatly. This process, it seems, occurs at the level of articulation, being able to benefit from certain associations by rearticulating them with others in line with their own interests. Through the examples of Prinzessinnengarten and other *Gemeinschaftsgärten* in Berlin, this the security of these gardens, as a phenomenon, could therefore occur at the expense of the sense of place or significance they represented for their current collectives. As gardens 'float' from significance defined in terms of commoning to significance defined in terms of city branding and economic development, collectives cannot control the direction in which these meanings shift. However, the openness of meaning that allowed *Gemeinschaftsgärten* to be co-opted by government and corporate interests could also enable them to make sense of their significance at a global scale. With land rights as an empty signifier, collectives like Prinzessinnengarten could articulate their local cause as part of a global movement, constituting solidarity through shared grievances with other causes, even if the conditions under which each struggled were far from similar.

7. A Reprieve from Neoliberal Rationalities?
Responsibility, Resistance, and Recovery
in Vintervikens trädgård

Vintervikens trädgård is returned to in this chapter, shifting focus from how and why the garden came about to what it represents in relation to contemporary social and political life in Stockholm. Working primarily from interviews and participant observation of working days and board meetings, historical narratives and small stories are analysed to explore how the approach to work within the garden was contrasted with organisational models and work norms attributed to the city beyond it. Throughout, I interrogate how concerns and criticisms made towards urban life and working life focused on external conditioning of individual and group behaviour, as well as tensions with concepts of responsibility, compulsion, and obligation.

This exploration begins by situating the voluntary association's legal circumstances in relation to other *tillsammansodlingar* and with the municipality of Stockholm. From there, a conflict with a local park planner is examined, looking at how informants characterised their ethical position in relation to said planner to convey a moral grievance. Enquiry then turns to characterisations of the garden itself in contrast to the city's overall urban development policy, and how this juxtaposition operated to articulate Vinterviken as a place representing an alternative rationality of urban planning. Narrowing in from municipal discourses, the association itself then becomes the site of analysis, investigating how board members rationalised the association's ethos of voluntary work based on specific conceptualisations of obligation and compulsion. Additionally, an event that led to the departure of multiple board members is analysed. Looking at how remaining, new, and one departing board member (who remained an active volunteer) made sense of what had transpired, I consider the divergent ways of thinking about organisational sustainability and responsibility that seemed to underlie the disagreement within the board.

Finally, the focus narrows even further to that of individual informants, investigating how they attributed significance to Vinterviken's approach to voluntary work through juxtapositions with reported experiences of work and social life. Among other things, this involved exploring how informants made sense of their relationship to Vinterviken as a place of recovery from social conditioning attributed to neoliberal capitalist working environments and commercial development. To this end, governmentality is employed as an interpretive framework to understand how the garden's significance was related to distinctions that informants made between social conditioning and independent motivation in their experiences of life in the city. Reflecting on municipal, associational, and individual perspectives through which the significance of Vintervikens trädgård was articulated, a sense of place is discussed as interpretable through the intersecting trajectories of legal requirements and discourses of work, volunteerism, and enjoyment through which alternative ways of organising social life were being experimented with in the periphery of the neoliberal cityscape.

Responsibilisation and Responsible Citizenship

Founding narratives of Vintervikens trädgård recounted the establishment of the garden as taking place through the transfer of responsibility for the site from the municipality to the voluntary association formed by community members (see Chapter 4). A similar theme of responsibility was present in the legal relationship between the association, as lessee, and the municipality as lessor. Such a reading was interpretable in the contractual relationship between the two parties as well as through recollections of events as told by informants at the garden.

Tillsammansodlingar: Conditions and Constraints

Stockholm was the only of Sweden's three largest cities that did not have an official network for *tillsammansodlingar* and similar forms of urban agriculture. Stockholm's municipal government did provide support for such projects through its parks department, but this was decentralised, with policies and the extent of support varying by local district office. Contacting a designated staff person in one's district office, it was possible to receive suggested locations or request a location to be considered, and agreements allowed for the possibility of growing individually or as part of an *odlarförening* [growers' association].[42] Some district offices even offered start-up

---

[42] By comparison, in both Gothenburg and Malmö the municipality provided start-up kits as a matter of course, and both cities had support staff who coordinated relevant workshops and served as municipal representatives to local associations (see Stadsodling Malmö, n.d.; Göteborgs stad, n.d.).

kits that included pallet boxes and organic soil (Parker och natur, Stockholms stad, 2021).

Despite the lack of centralised organising, the city had no shortage of *tillsammansodlingar* or other gardening initiatives. However, they were typically smaller than those visited elsewhere in the country. Most often operating pursuant to a *brukaravtal* [user agreement] with their local borough office, signatories were given permission to carry out work on municipal property – usually parkland – but were held to certain standards of access and aesthetics as terms of their use of public land. Upon review of several such agreements, the standard expectations appeared to involve conditions for public accessibility, site care and maintenance, and use of the provided pallet boxes or otherwise approved planter boxes. They also included an expectation that any damage by third parties was the responsibility of the growers' association to remedy (see, e.g., Hägersten-Liljeholmens stadsdelsförvaltning, 2020; Skärholmens stadsdelsförvaltning, 2014, 2019; Södermalms stadsdelsförvaltning, 2016).

As these legal terms suggests, the constraints typically enforced by the city meant that there was a certain degree of visual uniformity and orderliness to most *tillsammansodlingar* in the city. It also appeared that the long-term viability of these gardens could be somewhat precarious, as they were commonly annual agreements that could be terminated with one month's notice; they could even be terminated with immediate effect if those responsible didn't maintain the terms of their agreements, or if the city determined it had other uses for their locations. At the same time, few of these collectives of growers paid to lease their location, with the primary exception being those who were utilising sidewalk space or public squares (see Parker och natur, Stockholms stad, 2021). Only a few gardens across the city appeared to be exceptions to the pallet box rules or short-notice termination of use agreements. In each case, they appeared to have additional requirements in their agreements – for example, being required to provide cultural and educational activities, or fulfil biodiversity and ecosystem service requirements (see, e.g., Norrmalmsodlarna, n.d.; Vintervikens trädgård, n.d.).

Based on my observations, it appeared that providing public-oriented programs and activities – even without being outlined in user agreements – correlated with being able to secure larger areas of land and greater flexibility and legal rights in terms of how it could be used compared to other *tillsammansodlingar*. The normative rationality, it seemed, was to treat such initiatives as a privilege and responsibility, with those who had more permanence and advantageous land use rights also having more responsibilities, even though what they were doing was situated in discourses of public benefit and transference of maintenance responsibilities for public land (see e.g., Södermalms stadsdelsförvaltning, 2016). Interesting in both typical use agreements and more flexible ones was an apparent duality, with the willingness of the city to permit food cultivation on public land coexisting with what could be viewed as a strong element of oversight in terms of how these gardens were permitted to take form and be organised and maintained. Despite the absence of a direct role in these gardens (beyond that of oversight and enforcement), they could nonetheless be interpreted, from the duality of the government's legal relationship to them, as articulated within an official image of the city. Though not managed by the municipality, they nonetheless needed to be compatible with the municipal government's vision for the aesthetics and practice of urban agriculture.

The municipality's urban agriculture strategy can therefore be interpreted as a manifestation of a neoliberal ethos of responsibilisation, as the existence of these gardens was often made possible through government strategies that appealed to Stockholm's residents to fulfil the ends of government themselves. As Pyysiäinen et al. (2017) argue, responsibilisation works by "ascribing freedom and autonomy to individuals [...] while simultaneously appealing to individual responsibility-taking, independent self-steering and 'self-care'" (p. 216; see also Rose, O'Malley, & Valverde, 2012, p. 124). According such an interpretation, district offices were replacing municipal *responsibility* for public space management with municipal *oversight*. By giving residents the freedom to grow food in public space, the city expected those same people to take responsibility for maintaining their locations as if they were public spaces managed by the municipality, despite lacking the municipalities resources and infrastructure. Their freedom to do so would be taken away if they didn't maintain aesthetic and access requirements. In providing the opportunities for collectives and associations to use public space for agriculture, gardens were thus not independent of a governmental strategy or rationality that conditioned residents to take greater responsibility over public space in exchange for rights to use it.

An Exception to the Rule, with Strings Attached

With this context in mind, my interest turned towards examining Vintervikens trädgård, as a specific example, to understand how the voluntary association that maintained the garden made sense of their political context. This was a particularly interesting case considering that the association had formed to preserve a garden that the city had established, unlike other associations which formed with the express purpose of creating gardens themselves. The conditions placed on Vintervikens trädgård, it seemed, were of an entirely different nature than most *tillsammansodlingar* in the city. The association's core areas of work were conditioned by stipulations set out in its lease agreement with the municipality, with Vinterviken's articles of association enumerating lease terms that required:

- The association will operate a *visningsträdgård* [demonstration garden] according to organic principles
- Activities are to include cultivation, a café, courses, and exhibits
- The café shall support the association's other activities financially
- The activities of the association will be externally oriented
- The organization will work to actively engage different groups of citizens in the area
- The organisation will be operated without subsidy from the city (Vintervikens trädgård, 2017; my translation)

These stipulations could be understood as legally binding elements of the garden's sense of place, according to which it was obligated to function as a garden, a café, a cultural centre, and even an educational institution. And while they did not constitute the limits of the garden's significance, they resulted in a conditional freedom. The association was free to shape the site within these constraints, dependent upon having the time, energy and resources remaining to do so once these basic obligations were met. Although the terms of their lease may have constrained or partially determined the garden's constitution through the requirement to provide these specific services, it was not however determinative or absolute. Rather, it provided a normative understanding of the type of place Vinterviken should be and the social benefit to be provided.

This is not to suggest that there was not an interest among those who formed the voluntary association to provide such things to the community. As explored in Chapter 5, informants, city planners, and the city council alike had all considered the garden to solve a problem with the desirability, safety, or pleasantness of the local area. Instead, it underscores the complexity of the relationship between the association and the municipality, through which it is difficult to extract one institution from the other. Both parties could be understood to have interests at stake, and although these may have been different, they nonetheless relied on one another for the provision or fulfilment of a more desirable and attractive area – whether from the perspective of city planners for redevelopment purposes, or of community residents for a better quality of life. Much like the city branding of *Gemeinschaftsgärten*, there appeared to be a duality in this relationship. The association was legally required to offer certain amenities to the public as a condition of its operation and lease, as per the will of municipal planners and decisionmakers, but the agreement also explicitly outlined that the association must do so without financial support from the municipality.

That said, the obligation that public programming be provided by the association without public (i.e., municipal) financial support, reflected a strategy of responsibilisation by which cultural programming and public space management were reframed as the responsibility of citizens and voluntary associations rather than government institutions (cf. Lemke, 2001, p. 201). In this sense, the 'freedom' the association enjoyed – not unlike that of other gardens where collectives took responsibility for public space management – had been commodified by the city of Stockholm. In the case of Vinterviken though, the municipality could be seen to have monetised this transfer of responsibility, with the association paying for the privilege and responsibility to provide an urban commons for the local community. The association thus paid, in more than one way, for its conditional freedom.

Although subject to comparably more demanding stipulations, the association also enjoyed noteworthy legal 'freedoms' in contrast to comparable gardens, not least in terms of the collective responsibility and autonomy possible within these constraints. Rather than the more common use agreements of other gardens, the organisation *leased* the property, doing so according to a *tomträttsavtal*, or right of superficies, giving the association legal right to use the land and erect structures on it, the association owning structures they built with the municipality retaining ownership rights over the land. As of 2009, it was also included in the *stadsplan* [city plan] for Stockholm, an official document outlining land use and zoning permissions. This meant the garden had the benefit of being able to plan and invest in longer-term projects.

Unlike the contractual precarity of *Gemeinschaftsgärten* or other *tillsammansodlingar*, with their temporary, interim, or easily terminated use agreements, the right of superficies and insertion into Stockholm's city zoning plan protected Vintervikens trädgård from a similar precarity of land rights. It also meant, however, that the garden was a strategic element of the government's vision for the local area, and thus not entirely outside of institutional oversight. The role of Vintervikens trädgård as a demonstration garden, and what this role entailed, was thus co-constituted between the association and the city in multiple legal documents and the discourses of urban development articulated within them – the association's statutes and lease agreement, the city zoning plan, and the strategic plan for Kulturpark Liljeholmen (discussed in Chapter 5) that the city had already planned as early as 1996.[43]

As such, analysing this legal relationship through the lens of power dynamics provides insight into how governmentality and responsibilisation can operate in situations that are mutually beneficial, as seen here in the transactional cooperation between the association and municipality. The municipality had an expressed interest in developing a garden on the site with the intent of making the area more attractive. In bringing this about by seeking out local stakeholders who would create and operate such a site, there was an explicit rejection by the municipality of direct responsibility for bringing its own plans to fruition. This could be seen as an illustrative example of Foucault's (2007) conceptualisation of governmentality, as well as Rose's (1996, 1999) extension of this in terms of responsibilisation, as city planners intended for community residents to take on a city strategy of their own accord. Vinterviken's significance as a place was in part constituted by the activities and amenities it provided, but these were inseparable from the conditions set out in the association's lease agreement with the city. Looking at Stockholm as a whole, one commonality between Vinterviken and other *tillsammansodlingar* – whether leasing or allowed use of the site for free – was that in exchange for permission to cultivate, individual growers and collectives were expected to take care of public property that the municipal government would otherwise be responsible to provide landscaping, litter removal, and maintenance services for.

"Making Trouble": Bureaucracy, Bees and Biodiversity

While the garden was relatively secure in its land tenure, due to its inclusion in Stockholm's official plans for land use and zoning, the association's relationship with the city was not without the potential for moments of tension. The municipality was willing to give over responsibility for the site, with the stipulation that the association assume responsibility for providing public access, programming, and amenities; however, it could be problematic when

---

[43] Considering the authority of the municipality in each of these documents, the city had the institutional legitimacy to set the terms of leasing the site, meaning that whatever ideas the association may have had for the site were necessarily conditioned by a willingness to compromise. This is not a criticism of such a choice, rather an acknowledgement of transactional cooperation. As Polanska and Piotrowski (2015) contend, it can represent an ideological openness and plasticity that may benefit the adaptability and longevity of a movement (p. 278). In Vintervikens case, it wasn't just a matter of longevity or adaptability, but a precondition of its existence. The facts of the garden's existence and the association's willingness thus make the question of ideological consistency a moot point.

visions of how those were provided did not align. It was in one such instance that I encountered a critique of the municipality's regulatory role. This came to the fore when a tension arose with the local district's planning office over the garden's recently completed bee pavilion (refer to figure 20, page 100). Observing a board meeting one evening, a board member provided an update about a demolition order that had come from the city planning office, instigating a larger conversation and expression of criticism:

> The board were frustrated that the city seemed to be contradicting itself, saying that bees and biodiversity were important, and at the same time were making trouble about the bee pavilion. Apparently, the board was told that they hadn't been permitted to set it up as a permanent structure on that portion of land – which was beyond the area covered by their right of superficies. Their permission to use that area of land was terminated by the city, stating that the bee cultivation area was considered illegal according to their usage agreement, with the stated reason for this being that a fence was built to enclose the space, and was therefore understood to limit public access. Listening further, someone made mention of it being reported by a local resident who often made spurious reports that went nowhere. They then joked about "how unpopular does one have to be to evict *bees*?". (fieldnotes, 18 August 2020)

In partnership with the local beekeepers' association, who cared for the site and its bees, the garden's association had already had usage rights over that space for the purpose of beekeeping. Until then, this had only comprised a collection of hive boxes. The bee pavilion it turned out, had been built for a rather unfortunate reason:

> Karl presented a sketch of the planned bee pavilion and surrounding enclosure to the board, having worked with the beekeepers' association to design it. As the sketches were passed around, he reminded the group how the entire colony of bees had frozen to death because their hive boxes had not been properly sealed to keep out the sub-zero temperatures. When recalling this event, the sorrow was evident in the faces of attendees – both among those who already knew about the mass death and those, like myself, who had learned of it in that moment. In addition to housing the bees during the winter, the pavilion and its surrounding meadow were planned for use as a bee education centre where the public would "be informed about the things that are important for bees" in terms of their well-being and survival. (fieldnotes, 12 March 2019)

Several motivations and intents could thus be interpreted to have influenced the project. In addition to an emotional investment – as many of those I spoke with displayed sorrow in recalling or learning of the mass death which had occurred – there was also a motivation to return to traditional, sustainable solutions and to educate the public about the plight and needs of bees. Respect, care, and appreciation were thus equally present. While this may have been, in part, motivated by an awareness of the role of pollinating insects in ecosystem viability, as well as an appreciation for their honey, it was also a more general concern for their welfare. Demonstrating and educating people on traditional ways of beekeeping was also a way to educate about respectful practice – respectful of other species, the ecosystem, and the survival of future generations (see Sherfey, 2020).

The topic came up again a couple of years later when I interviewed Stefan, after the matter had been resolved. According to his explanation, the concern was less with the city *per se*, as it was with an individual person and how they were characterised to understand their own role as park planner:

> It's interesting because the municipality, or the local district council here, suddenly changed *parkingenjör* [park planner]. The park planner was involved a bit in the project here and the new person came in and just said *"this here is svartbygge* [illegal construction]*! You've got to tear it all down. Take it down!"*. It was all just a fucking mess! [Someone] wrote a big piece in the local news. They didn't reply to it, and we even invited them here, but they didn't come either. Then we just received a letter where he said: *"You've got 30 days to tear it down, otherwise you'll be reported to the police"*. That was the culmination of it, and then we went another way via the police somehow. And it seemed that those involved sorted it out that the police outflanked the municipality, so now we had permission to be there, but they still wanted us to tear down everything. And it's so remarkable, really, when you think about what bees mean from a symbolic and societal point of view…or just in terms of sustainability. That's what we're doing here, working towards sustainability. […] There are many municipalities in Sweden that are investing millions in building up a sustainable environment for pollinators. And here he just said: "Tear it all down or get reported to the police", you know. It was like we were criminals. They want sustainability in their plans, but not in practice. It's just awful, really. (Stefan, interview, 10 March 2022; his emphasis; my translation)

Describing further, Stefan pointed to the fact that if they wanted bees, there needed to be a fence for public safety purposes. Echoing the discussion of the board on the matter, what could be gleaned from his expressed frustration with the situation was a seeming conflict between two different interpretations of citizenship. On the side of Stefan and the board it appeared to involve active, critical engagement in the political community and thus taking responsibility for the plight of bees as they saw consistent with a common good (cf. Mouffe, 2018); in the portrayal of the park planner, it suggested a reading in which this person was perceived to interpret citizenship as a passive legal or bureaucratic status, involving a set of rights and the obligation to adhere to rules and regulations (cf. Mouffe, 1992a, pp. 3–9).

Portrayed as unconcerned with sustainability and bee survival, this narrative articulated an antagonism in which one person, through their institutional authority, sought to assert control over the association through what could be interpreted as an expectation of compliance. Accordingly, the role of the association was to adhere to the law as interpreted by a particular park planner. The two positions on the issue could therefore be understood to reflect a conflict between compliance and freedom, with the situation overall illustrating multiple discourses that Vintervikens trädgård was being inscribed in by different actors. Reports, lease agreements, and zoning plans each articulated the garden in discourses of responsibilisation, intending to bring about an 'attractive' community and promote biodiversity by having citizens take responsibility – or be 'made responsible' – for providing a public amenity as the fulfilment of an institutional political strategy (cf. Rose, 1996, 1999; Rose, O'Malley, & Valverde, 2012). For others, like the park planner referred to in Stefan's account, the garden appeared to be reduced to its obligations and expected behaviours of compliance. Finally, within the association, the issue was a matter of sustainability and interspecies relations, understanding themselves to be taking responsibility for the survival of bees as a global environmental issue, and more locally to avert the unnecessary mass death of another colony due to freezing temperatures.

The fact that the association was able to find support from the police in this apparent standoff between the association and park planner – as recounted by Stefan – also calls attention to the interpretive nature of laws and regulations. What was interpretable as a failure to comply by one park planner was interpreted as perfectly acceptable by the police, who resolved the standoff over the bee pavilion's future in the association's favour. The association, as well as bees and sustainability by extension, could thus be seen in Stefan's recollection of events to have benefitted from competing regulatory rationalities and the authority of the police interpretation over that of the park planner. In this light, the regulations were not themselves the focus of informants' grievances, but rather an individual person's rationality, according to which the 'right' application of regulations could be 'wrongly' determined.

In this example, board members did not act as passive recipients of rights and protections, obedient to rules and authority, or consumers of lease privileges. They portrayed themselves as challenging a regulatory decision based on their own ethos and interpretation of their obligations to bees and biodiversity. Doing so involved contesting and rearticulating the limits on the freedom that the association had to make decisions in the interest of the garden, consistent with its broader legal and environmental responsibilities. As such, I argue that the situation, as portrayed by informants, was illustrative of a democratic conceptualisation of citizenship premised on a *critical* engagement in the political community, acting for the common good and thereby taking responsibility for its realisation. In this case, it meant extending responsibility beyond the wellbeing of human society to include bees and an entire ecosystem of species by implication. The association and park planner could be seen in informant narratives as representing conflicting responsibilisations, association members portraying themselves in terms consistent with 'taking responsibility' as a critical, autonomous political practice, the planner portrayed as a governmentalised bureaucrat, conditioned to behave in a manner consistent with regulatory enforcement at the cost of biodiversity.

"A Natural Meeting Place" Amidst Commercial Monoculture

Like the frustration expressed about city officials regarding rigid compliance to rules at the expense of sustainability, in conversations with most informants there were criticisms – explicit and implicit – of the normative practices that characterised Stockholm's urban development. Their criticisms could be understood to convey the values that were being rejected in order to constitute their own sense of Vinterviken as a place. For instance, although for many the site had an implied political significance through what it represented for the overall transformation of the local area, its political significance could be stated more explicitly. Ida, a member of the garden who lived nearby, and was involved in another local *tillsammansodling* as well, expressed it thusly:

> I think it's important, maybe this is a little political, but I think it's important that there are public spaces where one doesn't have to pay, like with libraries, that one can…that it's not just large shopping centres where one must shop in order to be there. Rather, that people who don't have so much money can just be there. I think it's important to have this and important that these types of places exist. (Ida, interview, 10 March 2022; my translation)

For Ida, Vinterviken and similar places were associated with a problematisation of the pervasiveness of consumer culture in city planning and how it was interpreted to condition and constrain social life. For her, the significance of places such as Vinterviken could thus be understood in contrast to how other places in the city were characterised by her. Unlike elsewhere, the garden represented a place for non-commodified forms of cultural and social life in an urban environment otherwise treating social life as a commodity. Requiring one to spend money to be in public was deemed inequitable from the perspective of personal and household economy.

Based on Ida's juxtaposition of the garden and Stockholm more broadly within discourses of urban space and the type of social life they result in, Vinterviken could be interpreted as an urban commons, portrayed as it was in terms of a non-commodified community resource (cf. Harvey, 2012). Criticising what I understood to be governmentalising tendencies of the 'city-as-shopping- centre', a cityscape that conditioned people to behave as consumers in order to experience social life in commodified public space, Vinterviken and similar gardens could be interpreted as places to counteract such governmentality. Such an interpretation is interesting in that while the garden may have functioned as an urban commons, and thus as a non-commodified space for the local community, its ability to operate as such had been commodified through the privileges and obligations outlined pursuant to leasing the site, fulfilling the intentions of city planners for the site to elicit responsibilised neoliberal subjects.

This duality elucidates a lack of clear distinction between values like autonomy and resistance and those such as obligation and compulsion. Recalling that both municipal documents and informants recounted the transformation of the area in a manner consistent with gentrification through the 'upgrading' and increased desirability attributed in part to the presence of Vinterviken, it also demonstrates the complexity and diffuse nature of processes of gentrification. Although the initial motivation to make Aspudden and the surrounding areas more desirable through the redevelopment of a brownfield into parkland may have come from local government, so too did the collective action of community members to preserve and sustain Vintervikens trädgård contribute to making the neighbourhood a more appealing place to live.

When I spoke with Kerstin and Eva, their focus was less explicit on Vinterviken's role as an urban commons, and more so on what it represented in resistance to normative discourses and practices of land development. In their reasoning, land development policies in Stockholm, and Sweden more generally, seemed to be reflective of a particular rationality, or normative way of thinking, according to which the 'reasonable course of action' that informed development policy was premised on short-term economic values that disregarded the need and value of urban agriculture and agricultural land more broadly:

> But think about this now, how much good agricultural land near the city has been built on? It's truly quite interesting to think about. This whole thing that one wants to have agriculture near to the city, but… (Kerstin, interview, 30 October 2018; my translation)

> It's becoming denser everywhere, with more concrete and houses and such. There's really not any land for allotments anymore, I find. And it's just such terrible city planning, as I see it… One should be able to go much further out and blend…have parks and allotment areas, housing…see to it that there are opportunities for farming…nearby, for everyone… not least in the suburbs where there is still some land and green areas, but one doesn't plan like that in Stockholm, not now in any case. (Eva, interview, 30 October 2018; my translation)

Kerstin and Eva, like Ida, each conveyed a sense of frustration and disappointment regarding urban development practices in Stockholm, characterising the normative approach as an irresponsible one. While Ida explicitly critiqued the commodification of social life, the statements of the other two women articulated concerns with the densification of the city and its impact on the availability of arable land.

Despite different preoccupations, all three informants could be seen to critique a rationality of urban development characteristic of neoliberal capitalism, according to which land was equated with ground to be developed upon. Their critiques of such a rationality in contemporary urban planning situated it as part of a constitutive outside through which Vinterviken and similar types of places were presented as a necessary alternatives and correctives – potential solutions to the problems of commercial development and densification. All three informants articulated elements of a counter-normative rationality of urban development, in which a better city was imagined by blurring the boundaries between built environment and agriculture. Such a projected social rationality of urban development was implied to decentre the privilege afforded to commercial development and urban infill, better accounting for a variety of social and environmental demands alongside economic and housing pressures.

Importantly, these critiques emerged in speaking about what Vinterviken represented to each of them, each doing so through contrasts. Speaking explicitly of the garden in relation to the city, rather than implicitly through reference to urban planning in general, Eva impressed upon me her view that:

> Nature is lacking. It's a constructed nature…but [at Vinterviken] there's birds, butterflies, and plants. One has the possibility to sit there and relax in a calm, car-free environment. Plus, it's also been a cultural centre. So many good activities take place there…and people can go without it costing anything more than the price of a *fika*. (Eva, interview, 30 October 2018; my translation)

Reflecting further, she considered Vintervikens trädgård to be:

> a rather natural meeting place for the area. It's so easy to just go down there and sit yourself down. You don't even need to buy a coffee, just sit in a little grove there. Or watch the salamanders [*chuckles*] in the pond. (Eva, interview, 30 October 2018; my translation)

With these reflections, Eva articulated a complementary sense of place to Ida's interpretation of the garden as an urban commons – serving a variety of social needs in a collective, non-commodified manner. Yet she extended this reflection with a sensory contrast to the city in general, providing plants, wildlife, and a sense of calm in contrast to the portrayal of car-filled streets beyond. Vinterviken was understood to offer a refuge or sanctuary from the neoliberal city while simultaneously fulfilling a neoliberal policy of responsibilisation by providing this place of reprieve.

While Eva's discussion of contrasts focused more on the experience of visiting the garden, Stefan reflected on contrasts related to how he experienced volunteering at Vinterviken. Specifically, he expressed deriving a sense of personal fulfilment from spending time working in the garden, attributing this feeling to the informal nature of social interaction the garden afforded:

> When I'm down here for a few hours working with the plants or checking on things, I always end up chatting with folks who comment, ask questions, and it becomes a sort of community or fellowship here. In a totally informal way, and we're doing a social service by maintaining this here for people. We create a common…a common ground for community, simply. It's incredibly valuable and it gives me so much more on a personal level than if I had my own little garden. Not only that, but I don't have total responsibility, I can just come on by and work when I feel like it. But it's the social aspect, I think…It's so obvious down here that one realises "this here *really does* means something for people". (Stefan, interview, 10 March 2022; his emphasis; my translation)

Interesting in Stefan's reflections is the duality interpretable in relation to responsibility. Part of what was meaningful about the garden was the fact that, for him, one could contribute without having 'total responsibility', relating this to a sense of pleasure and enjoyment. At the same time, he also seemed to value how volunteers as a totality were "doing a social service by maintaining […] a common…a common ground for community" and thus took responsibility for public space. In this sense, the responsibilisation through which the city expected the association to provide public services was articulated as something positive, for people who, like Stefan, found fulfilment in contributing to a place that "*really does* mean something to people". Considering this to be the case, a sense of place for Vintervikens trädgård could be interpreted in terms of enjoyment. The garden's social significance was conveyed as a matter of experiencing pleasure and fulfilment gained through collective responsibility for providing a place of common benefit. In other words, its meaning was inextricable from what volunteers did there, how they did it, and who they understood it to be for.

Rather than being fundamentally negative and coercive, the basis of responsibilisation in "discourses that tap into and resonate with [people's] desires of personal freedom, quality of life and fulfilment of self-realization potential" (Pyysiäinen, Halpin, & Guilfoyle, 2017, p. 219), can also operate from rationalities that are conducive to counter-conduct, understood here in terms of "struggle against the processes implemented for conducting others" (Foucault, 2007, p. 201). In other words, counter-conduct can be seen to encompass any counter-normative ethos that is fostered or promoted in resistance to normative, governmentalising ideals and ways of thinking. I would therefore argue that there is no fundamental incompatibility between the two; instead, to borrow the phrasing that Tsing (2015) uses to discuss the enmeshment of different economies, there is an 'unintentional coordination' whereby different rationalities of responsibilisation come to influence each other and even rely upon one another for mutual survival (see, e.g., pp. 22–23).

This interpretation was reinforced through reflections that Eva made about the social aspect of volunteering at Vinterviken and how she considered it to impact quality of life in the area:

> It's about doing something, feeling some sense of belonging in one's area without one just residing and working. [...] And then it's, one can say, a group that's existed for years. It's a way to live and not just reside. (Eva, interview, 30 October 2018; my translation)

In what could be seen as an implicit critique of the normative characterisation of everyday urban life, Vinterviken represented, for Eva, a place of belonging and autonomy in a place not constrained or conditioned by consumer capitalist rationalities of urban space. How she articulated the significance of the garden could be interpreted in terms of its contrast to governmentality, as a place nurturing counter-conduct by enabling people to be more than home-dwellers or workers conditioned by the constraints of those places where they would otherwise spend their time. A sense of place for the garden was thus attributed not just through the positive associations Eva had with the garden itself, but discursively through the contrast it represented with her characterisation of the broader urban environment of Stockholm.

Like Stefan's appreciation for Vinterviken as providing a "common ground for community" that "*really does* mean something for people", Eva too articulated a social problem by juxtaposing the garden against an implied lack of similar places elsewhere in the community. A collectively managed urban commons was the solution to the problem of an incomplete or bifurcated life, in which one otherwise moved between a public sphere of work and the private one of personal residences. Vintervikens trädgård was thereby associated with offering a reprieve from the demands of working life. As a public space not defined by obligations or consumption, it implicitly solved these problems by its existence as an urban commons shaped in contrast to these features of the neoliberal city. Although managing the garden in a manner that resonated with responsibilisation – because taking collective responsibility for public space was compatible with neoliberal governance strategies for the retrenchment of institutional service provision (cf. Pyysiäinen, Halpin, & Guilfoyle, 2017; Rose, 1996) – it could nonetheless be seen to reject the behavioural conditioning implicit in this same neoliberal rationality of governance.

Resisting Obligation in Voluntary Work

In Stefan's comments about Vinterviken as a common ground for the local area, he also brought up the informality of the association's approach to voluntary work and how he interpreted this to promote personal fulfilment without the burden of 'total responsibility'. The themes of enjoyability and responsibility in relation to voluntary work were similarly used to articulate a sense of place among board members, not least during board meetings, where interpretations of both were reinforced through discussions. While the informal approach to work was apparently appreciated among those who gardened and aided in maintenance, it was not without its tensions or struggle within the board. Different ideas about responsibility and sustainability – concerning both the garden as a physical place and the continued viability of the association's way of operating – created conflict over the appropriate organisational model for managing Vintervikens trädgård into the future. Though all seemed to share a desire to protect what the garden represented and provided for the community, ideas differed about what the most important attributes of its sense of place were. Because of this, opinions differed about where the collective energy of the association should be focused to ensure that its social value would persist.

Recounting events considered significant in the association's history, informants tended to motivate and reinforce a particular vision for, and set of values about, voluntary work. I found it pertinent to examine grievances and threats expressed in relation to these events through the concept of 'obligation', as this term was often invoked in discussions about the significance of Vinterviken's approach to voluntary work and the legitimacy of the association's board. Obligation was, as I learned, a floating signifier, capable of being articulated into different discourses about the roles, responsibilities, and appropriate limits of the voluntary association.

While there was hesitance or resistance towards making people feel a sense of obligation, the maintenance of the garden nonetheless required – or relied upon – that people assume some sense of obligation to care for it and contribute to the continued operation of the site. Attending to expressions of antagonism in these discourses, the concept of governmentality is again informative, in this case for analysing the perception held by many informants that business rationalities were an existential threat to the garden's voluntary work model. In exploring these themes, the tension between taking responsibility and being made responsible is revisited as relevant to understand the relationship between responsibilisation and democratic citizenship.

Desire Over Obligation: Anti-Professional Voluntary Work

As was discussed at a meeting where new board members attended with continuing members for the first time, the association was considered to have a relationship of mutual care with Vintervikens trädgård, taking care of the garden so that it could also take care of them:

> One of several returning board members reflected how *"trädgården sköter människor, inte tvärtom"* [the garden takes care of people, not the other way around]. Another member added that the statutes provided them with something to come together and gather around – a reference point for their actions and decisions – keeping them accountable to the garden rather than passing whims. There seemed to be an understanding among the group that those who didn't agree with what was written in the statutes had left the board. (fieldnotes, 12 March 2019)

Of note in this excerpt from my fieldnotes is the opinion that the statutes were interpreted to be something that should not be tampered with. By making a passing reference to prior events that returning board members were assumed to know about, it was interpretable that the possibility of changes to the statutes had resulted in a significant event in the association's history. This discussion at the board meeting gave a sense that the issue in question – here being the board's normative relationship to its statutes – was a resolved question, as those who disagreed with this perspective had left the board. However, the repetition of this story suggested a need to reinforce this relationship among the current group to ensure that they operated from a shared sense of purpose (cf. Polletta, 1998a). The intended sense of place that needed to be protected, it seemed, was interconnected with a sense of responsibility towards a particular relationship to the association's statutes. The revisiting of an apparently resolved matter thus begged two questions: Why were the statutes so contentious? And why did the board believe they needed to be preserved as they were?

Interview transcripts and fieldnotes from conversations the year prior helped to provide context for this, particularly recollections wherein Karl and Eva touched upon the board departures alluded to at this board meeting. Speaking with Karl early in my research, he had told me that there had been a particularly contentious period in the board's history:

Karl recounted how a few years prior some board members had sought to 'professionalise' the board, in part by adding more specific commitments into the statutes, contrary to norms which had already been in place for several years by that point. An ideological split emerged as more established board members were concerned. As he expressed it, statutorily committing to do specific things would force the association into obligations without any guarantee that they would always have volunteers who wanted to do those things. The changes would have been, as I understood him, premised on the interests of those same board members, and therefore dependent upon their continued involvement to ensure that there were volunteers willing to be told what to do. Also, there seemed to be a concern that in order to make good on those commitments, the association would become obligation bound, rather than having the flexibility to shift focus in line with changing circumstances. He then told me that those board members resigned in protest. While seemingly threatening its future by lacking enough people to constitute a quorum, enough people stepped in to fill the sudden vacancies, enabling the board – and thus the association – to continue to operate. (fieldnotes, 21 March 2018)

In my conversation with Karl, the tension appeared to come down to organisational visions – an antagonism between a 'professional' organisation or a flexible, adaptive one. The situation he recounted could be interpreted in terms of an antagonism towards an ethos of professionalisation and the threat it was considered to represent to the identity of the garden, and thus its approach to voluntary work.

On the question of whether the association itself should nurture what they considered to be a counter-normative organisational model or operate according to normative rationalities of 'professional' organisational management, it seemed to constitute an identity crisis: would the ethos of the garden move in a direction aligned with neoliberal values or would it operate in a manner considered contrary to them? Within this 'identity crisis', the concern of those who prevailed appeared to be framed in terms of protecting the values they associated with Vinterviken against normative values from beyond the garden. Rather than assume the association operated in a vacuum apart from the neoliberal city beyond, this could be better understood as a concern over the balance between obligation and freedom as the predominant ethos by which their working model operated.

Eva had been a member of the association on and off since its establishment and was one of several people who joined the board after the mass departure of prior board members. As she recalled that period:

> … the question was whether to shut down, such a crisis it was for a time. […] There came to be a proper schism within the old board, I understand, about which way we should take and how tightly controlled it should be. That which unites those who remained is that one should not force or obligate anyone, but rather everything should happen on a voluntary basis. In principle, one should go there out of a desire to do so, to not be forced to do so, in a manner of speaking. (Eva, interview, 30 October 2018; my translation)

Considering both her and Karl's comments, there seemed to be a tension between an ideal of voluntary work and the need for some degree of structure or workload to make sure things operated smoothly. The failure of the advocates for a more 'professional' model of leadership to get their way, leading to their resignations and replacement by new board members who shared the remaining members' commitment to the existing organisational model, was thus the resolution of this story of crisis. Reflecting on the board since then, Eva agreed with those who had not left the board, believing

> [t]hey have a very relaxed and good attitude, [the board] works much better now, I think. A few kind people [laughs] who try to help put things in order…tidy up things and not, you know, control and stall things so much. Help out to solve problems, quite simply. (Eva, interview, 30 October 2018; my translation)

Speaking thusly, Eva, who had joined the board at what she considered to be a crisis point in the association's (and thereby the garden's) history, reinforced an interpretation of the statutes as incontrovertible and inalterable in the minds of those who protected the status quo. But in protecting this status quo internally, what they perceived themselves to advocate for can be interpreted in terms of an anti-corporate ethos of organisational management. Informants made sense of their own positions and rationalised the direction the board maintained by characterising it according to a rejection of professionalism, obligation, and control that they associated with for-profit businesses. Implicitly, these values were also being ascribed to the board members said to have left the board in protest. Both Karl and Eva's comments suggested this event was representative of the values that prevailing and incoming board members prioritised and would defend.

Even if it caused tension within the board or with other members, it was considered important to ensure that the association's operating model be defined by an approach that respected peoples' willingness, interests, and abilities to inform what took place. This contrasted with what those who prevailed characterised as a 'controlling' approach that, according to them, would interfere with the intended sense of place they associated with Vinterviken. In an interesting duality, despite comments articulating a criticism of neoliberal governance, the board could nonetheless be considered to operate in a manner consistent with a neoliberal imperative, as volunteers should want to give their time and energy as something meaningful and fulfilling for them, rather than feeling compelled or coerced to do so.

Disagreement over how to manage the association, and its implications for the relationship between association and volunteers, was positioned as a significant threat that the garden ultimately survived. In articulating two antagonistic factions, the perception given by those who remained suggested that this had to do with a resistance to a particular governmentalising interpretation of obligation, insofar as an obligation to meet deliverables was associated with a rigid organisational model that would condition volunteer gardeners and board members in a manner that served the organisation as legal entity rather than the garden as a type of place. The fear was that voluntary work would cease to feel voluntary, risking that the garden would be stuck with responsibilities that nobody wanted to carry out, or that if they did, it would be done out of a sense of duty rather than personal fulfilment.

It was accordingly reasoned that Vinterviken's board should avoid committing themselves in their statutes to more than the baseline requirements of their lease agreement. As Karl discussed, he considered it a practical consideration related to a concern about obligations:

> If we add something to the statutes that obligates us to take on certain activities, it reduces our ability to reflect where volunteer interest lies. It requires us to deliver something whether or not those who originally wanted it are still here to help sustain it. If the interest is there, people can do those things without them needing to be written into the statutes. (Personal communication, Karl, 21 March 2018; my translation)

In line with this concern, Eva provided a cautionary tale as an example of what could happen when an initiative relied too much on someone who no longer remained active in the association:

> Well, I believe that there's a rather humble attitude towards what one can offer…I believe anyway. Because so much of it is voluntary. Before, there was much better order in the garden, and it depended *a lot* on one person who stopped a few years back, who was busy with everything to do with plant choices. She really worked hard to keep the garden pretty and had sort of a good group around her that were really knowledgeable as well. So, she got a lot of folks interested who came and worked in the garden. Then it was a little bit of a crisis when she disappeared. A very important force in the association disappeared too. It was a *proper* demonstration garden at that time, now it's not been in quite the right shape to call it that, not really, at least not from a professional gardener's perspective. (Eva, interview, 30 October 2018; her emphasis; my translation).

Eva's comments highlighted another fundamental tension in the association's relationship to freedom and flexibility as promoted by board members who remained. On the one hand, her comments expressed a concern with being over-reliant on a single individual, echoing Karl's worry about becoming obligated to sustain projects driven by individual interest without continuity of willing volunteers; in this sense, her characterisation of the association as humble in outlook reflected a value in protecting its relaxed approach to voluntary work, even if it resulted in the garden being perceivable as less 'professional' from a horticultural perspective. On the other hand, she did also lament the deterioration of it as a 'proper' demonstration garden, emphasising that the choice to not have a more robust routine or structure for maintenance, relying instead on volunteer interest, had its drawbacks. Despite this sacrifice of quality, however, I interpreted her comments to only problematise the direction taken by the garden, not question or criticise it.

The board's 'crisis' was inscribed within a number of discourses related to collective identity and the threats that those who remained concerned themselves with. For the 'post-crisis' board, the ideal organisational model for the association articulated a flexible organisational model and a 'hands-off' board as elements conducive to the sustainability of their approach to voluntary work. Connected with these were certain conceptualisations of enjoyment and desire, where the status quo was articulated as providing an 'enjoyable' volunteer environment, enabling volunteers to do so on their terms, according to what they felt like doing.

Conversely, those who resigned from the board were attributed antagonistic social values by those remaining; a 'strong' board and deterministic statutory obligations were inscribed as threatening this enjoyment, associated with a directorial model of volunteerism that was feared to make the survival of the association uncertain. Rather than speak to this discourse in terms of verity or accuracy, as those who left the board would themselves likely offer other interpretations and arguments for their positions and ultimate decisions to leave the board, what *is* possible to take away from their comments is how Eva and Karl characterised their own positions. Both did so in terms of respecting volunteers and ensuring a certain conceptualisation of voluntary work as critical to the sustainability of the garden as the type of place they understood it to represent.

Differing Visions of Organisational Sustainability

Suffice it to say that, just as Eva and Karl's comments suggest, the resolution to the crisis did not appear to be the end of the discussion. As was heard and observed, concerns about the potential for values considered antithetical to Vinterviken's sense of place were persistent themes at meetings and in working day conversations. They constituted an 'outside' for the association's board, implicated in the ongoing rearticulation and reaffirmation of the association's values against values being actively excluded.

Concerns with potential changes to the organisational model were thus not fully contained within the association itself but instead situated within broader discourses and interpretations of social relationships playing out in places beyond Vinterviken. For instance, during a meeting I attended where the board discussed the association's business plan for the coming year, board members began to talk about Vinterviken in comparison to another garden in the city that was also a demonstration garden with a café. Interestingly, this was the same garden that city planners had taken as inspiration for what they hoped Vinterviken would become (as discussed in Chapter 4). Here, a more detailed discourse emerged of the prevailing interpretation of voluntary work within the garden, enriching the picture of the constitutive outside that was inscribed in their discourse as an example of what not to become:

> Karl noted that Vinterviken was *not* like Rosendals trädgård, a well-known garden elsewhere in the city. Whereas Vinterviken was a voluntary association, Rosendal had at some point become a foundation with a professional, paid board, and was no longer collectively managed but fully staffed. He categorised it, in comparison to Vinterviken as a business-driven organisation. He continued by referring to a tendency he saw for non-profit and voluntary organisations to adopt the mindset or rationality of for-profit businesses, and in doing so forget the initial motivations for their causes. Others nodded in agreement. (fieldnotes, 10 December 2019)

In this excerpt, the negation of this 'other' garden, Rosendals trädgård, was premised on its organisational model as a foundation, and how such a model was articulated with for-profit businesses in characterising the rationality they operated from. In Karl's estimation, the elements that made such an articulation possible were having a paid board of directors and a management style according to which the direction of the garden was decided by its board rather than volunteer interest and willingness. It was this, as Karl described it, which had caused Rosendals trädgård to lose sight of its original values when it became a foundation.

Rosendals trädgård could be understood to function as a floating signifier in this example, capable of being articulated into different discourses that were in tension with one another (cf. Laclau, 2005, p. 133). It could be interpreted as a model for Vinterviken, as well as its antithesis. For the municipality, Rosendal was portrayed in a chain of equivalence with Vinterviken, the former as a successful model of responsibilisation and attractiveness that the latter should be interpreted as analogous with. For Vinterviken's board members, Rosendal could be argued to represent the garden's constitutive outside, incomparable because it was a foundation, and therefore representative of a professional managerial approach deemed more appropriate to the business sector than the voluntary sector.

By cultivating a voluntary model that resisted a sense of obligation, compulsion, or professionalisation, informants seemed to attribute a sense of place to Vinterviken constituted through values it rejected. An implicit belief could be surmised in comments and conversations with informants that anti-professional operations and promoting desire to volunteer over obligations to contribute enabled Vinterviken to act as a counterpoint to for-profit rationalities of organisational management. Portraying a business mindset as naturalised in public and non-profit organisations elsewhere in the city, it could be said that the association saw themselves as promoting counter-conduct. As Foucault (2007) argues in discussing governmentality, dominant cultural values can affect people by conditioning them towards certain ways of thinking and reasoning. Rather that exert control, those in positions of power are able "to arouse, facilitate, and *laisser faire,* [...] to manage and no longer control through rules and regulations" (p. 451). By framing Vinterviken's approach to voluntary work in terms of its rejection of sedimented organisational norms, the garden's sense of place was constituted not just through its rejection or exclusion of these, but through its association with an active struggle to question and desediment these norms.

The tension expressed in the critiques of board members could thus be understood as related to concern with the pervasiveness of governmentality. Rationalities of profit-based business management were understood to threaten the sense of place of the garden and what it meant as an urban commons that should be seen as a place apart from the focus on rationalisation, efficacy, and results that were argued to condition ways of working. Implicit in this critique was an understanding of Vinterviken's significance as represented in the appeal to freedom its voluntary approach was premised upon. Interestingly, this could be interpreted as promoting responsibilisation within the association, as the board sought to appeal to volunteers' desires for personal fulfilment and autonomy (cf. Pyysiäinen, Halpin, & Guilfoyle, 2017, p. 219; Rose, 1999), fostering an environment in which volunteers would contribute according to interest and ability rather than being compelled or coerced to contribute in a particular capacity or for a required duration.

It can therefore be argued that neoliberal imperatives are not necessarily equivalent to capitalist ones, as they also reflect an individualistic and entrepreneurial subjectivity applicable to other contexts. The provision of an urban commons can be understood to satisfy the ends of neoliberal governance, as it is consistent with responsibilisation as a government strategy for making individuals personally responsible for what was previously provided for by institutions (cf. Rose, 1999; Rose, O'Malley, & Valverde, 2012, p. 124), even though they may be only peripherally associated with capitalism through the pericapitalist conditions of their existence. Vintervikens trädgård provided a venue where a degree of resistance could be formulated and exercised by individuals and the collective, while at the same time conforming to the purpose and goals set out by municipal planners. Being 'made responsible' and 'taking responsibility' were thus not incomepatible, meaning that democratic citizenship could be practiced in the same instances where neoliberal governance conditioned a certain way behaving as political subjects. Each operated from a different ethos according to which individuals should be responsible for their living environment and quality of life.

As suggested earlier, however, this anti-obligation, 'loose' organisational model – considered central to the intended sense of place – was promoted by board members at the time of my fieldwork. It was the approach that prevailed after the board crisis, and although the board may have considered itself as resolved around the tension between association and foundation forms of organising (at least based on the discussions I was present for) the association beyond the board was not unanimously resolved. One former board member, Stefan, articulated an alternative perspective to that of the 'post-crisis' board when interviewed. As he framed it, there was a practical case to be made for having a foundation, but it was premised on what vision there was for the garden:

> Well, I think that one has to be very mindful, at least with this balance between the commercial and voluntary aspects and look at the mission of the association like this: "Is this here truly what we're doing? Do we need to change it? And how can one manage such a large organisation within the framework of a voluntary organisation?" It's highly doubtful that legally, economically and such with an organisation with a multi-million crown revenue. That's not the idea with a voluntary association as I understand it, you know? I've been a spokesperson for managing Vinterviken as a foundation, for example, to avoid structural problems in the future. (Stefan, interview, 10 March 2022; my translation)

Continuing, he recounted an event from the past to reinforce his concern:

> And you know about this, right? That there was an attempt… a hostile takeover of the association some years ago? You've heard about this, I'm sure. Yeah, well, I won't go into the history, but there was a group of men who had a contract to run the restaurant once upon a time and when they didn't get to continue, they weren't so happy, I suppose. And then they tried to take over the association. But someone figured out that this was going on and it's rather easy to take over an association like this. People just need to show up to the annual meeting normally. Say there's normally 15 attending and then 20 people come in with hostile intentions – vote out the board, create a new board, and decide what'll happen. And that's what they tried to do. But as luck would have it, someone learned about this and there was an appeal to all members […] and suddenly 75 people showed up at the annual meeting! That has never happened here. Not since either. Yeah, and so they were able to eliminate the threat. It was terrible though. But if you have a foundation something like that can't happen. (Stefan, interview, 10 March 2022; my translation)

In providing his interpretation of the disagreement that occurred during the 'crisis', Stefan told a story about another event to reinforce his own position on the matter. Doing so, he also conveyed a particular interpretation of the concept of sustainability and what Vinterviken should represent in relation to this, and through this underscored the contested nature of what it meant to be a volunteer. Raising concerns about the scale of the organisation, and the relative ease of taking it over should someone wish to try, Stefan understood this as sufficient motivation to move towards a foundation model.

While others expressed concern about sustaining the character of the garden's voluntary work model, his comments reflected a concern with sustaining the garden itself as a type of place, and only considered a foundation model to be advisable because of the significant revenue the association was generating.

Rather than compare an associational versus foundation model for operating Vintervikens trädgård, what is noteworthy here is that people can have an apparently similar projected rationality motivating their preferred course of action – ensuring the sustainability of the garden as a volunteer-based initiative – but with altogether different interpretations of how to materialise this norm in practice. Disagreements over the best legal form to sustain Vinterviken seemed to be a matter of whether one's guiding rationality was premised on ensuring structural security (sustaining the site as a garden) or protecting its ethos of voluntary work. The same projected rationality was premised on different interpretations of the intended sense of place people should associate with Vinterviken, resulting therefore in different beliefs about how to responsibly sustain the garden.

Considering Stefan's perspective in comparison to those apparently shared by the board at the time of my research, this calls attention to how the significance of the same events can be interpreted differently by those recalling them – the board crisis portrayed both as a crisis averted and as a reminder of a looming threat to the organisation's future. Whatever the position that informants took, each were operating from a concern for the garden's sustainability, but there were different discourses and interpretations of what this meant, who the primary beneficiaries were, and why it mattered to do so. The post-crisis board seemed to consider the sustainability and enjoyability of a particular type of voluntary approach to work a primary concern, while those who left were implied to have other ideals and values about work and associational life.

Recovering from Consumer Capitalist Working Life

It wasn't only how the organisational model was portrayed that seemed to matter for the position informants had on the direction taken by the board. Much like Vinterviken was characterised by remaining board members as not being like other organisations in the city, it was also associated by participants with a sense of recovery from normative ways of working that they portrayed as problematic. In addition to the legal relationship with the city and the board's interpretations of what the garden signified, personal experiences of working life, and how these experiences were understood to condition the behaviours and wellbeing of those I spoke with, thus also provided important context for understanding the relationship to voluntary work advocated among the collective.

"Setting Boundaries for Myself"

Speaking with Signe one day, a participant who had been involved at the garden for several months by the time I began my research, she described how Vinterviken represented balance for her, offering an opportunity for 'meditation' and deconditioning of behaviours she attributed to her upbringing and prior employment characterised by a constant pressure to "fix things now" for other people (Signe, personal communications, 7 April and 27 May 2018; my translation). This was a point she came back to repeatedly when working alongside her.

> When she was about to leave, Signe admonished me that it was important to set boundaries and leave myself free time in the day. She noted that it could be difficult to not feel bad conscience for leaving something unfinished, but that gardening is something that is ongoing – never finished. She offered that this was something she still struggled with, as she too was someone inclined to feel a sense of obligation. While continuing to feel somewhat of a bad conscience when she couldn't participate, she saw this as an area of personal growth, learning to let go of the feeling and appreciating that this pressure was not coming to her from the garden or the norms of its working culture. (fieldnotes, 21 April 2018)

> Signe emphasised to several of us, who were being perfectionists with the peat blocks we were replacing, that we needn't be worried about everything being perfect or complete, because it will never be so and can't be fully controlled for. We needed to let it be and not stress. Signe acknowledged that this was something she also struggled with. (fieldnotes, 13 May 2018)

> As she had many times before, Signe admonished us to rest and to not be too eager, reminding us to take care of ourselves and not just the garden. To not forget balance. (fieldnotes, 30 September 2018)

Reflecting on her various statements on the theme, I understood Signe to equate feelings of obligation or compulsion and perfectionist tendencies with unhealthy work practices, articulated each as threats to wellbeing and attributed them to workplace conditioning. This interpretation was based on the ways in which she would relate her personal experiences at Vinterviken, and what she observed myself and others doing there, to other aspects of her life and personal history.

The idea of efficiency she alluded to in speaking of feeling conditioned to "fix things now" for the clients she served, alongside concerns of balance and well-being could therefore be seen as critiques of a governmental rationality that, as Skålén et al. (2006) argue, involves a 'customer-oriented subjectivity' that "fosters people who believe, act and feel in accordance with customer requirements and who take for granted that this is the right way to be" (p. 14). Vinterviken represented, as I interpreted from Signe's emphasis on resisting such a subjectivity, a place for counter-conduct, somewhere where she could struggle against being conducted by external conditioning of this nature (cf. Foucault, 2007, p. 201). Understood thusly, her interest in sharing her experiences and counselling others to leave things unfinished – and thereby maintain a healthy relationship to their voluntary work – could be interpreted as strategies for reinforcing her own counter-normative ethos and for cultivating the same in others as an element of Vinterviken's sense of place.

Signe wasn't the only one who provided these reminders, but they did seem to be at the front of her mind. In a related vein, Ida discussed her involvement in terms of the need to recuperate from the stress of her work life:

> I started to garden because I worked a lot and needed to relax. […] I'd worked in healthcare and so I was burnt out. (Ida, interview, 10 March 2022; my translation)

She thus echoed the concerns Signe had expressed, with gardening providing a way to reorient herself from unhealthy psychological impacts of her prior work environment. Similarly, in speaking with a long-time volunteer, Göran, one autumn day, I mentioned my uncertainty about being involved the following spring, to which he replied that it was important that one does what one can, when one can, and to "not have a bad conscience" because of this (fieldnotes, 30 September 2018).

And while Kerstin didn't experience the challenge that Signe did in relation to Vinterviken, she reflected on being challenged with a similar sense of urgency and obligation in the past, not least at a *tillsammansodling* in another city where she used to be involved:

> Hmm, yeah, I know that it was tough for me to find a balance for myself with the association I was with before [in another city], where it was so clear that "okay, but if we don't dig and prepare that soil now and get it done, then it's

going to be a one more week before we can plant these things". So, it was truly like that back then. I work quite a lot and had trouble setting boundaries for myself. (Kerstin, interview, 30 October 2018; my translation)

Kerstin's reflections, like those of Signe, Ida, and Göran, implied a normative proclivity to work too hard in the pursuit of accomplishing as much as possible. The emphasis each placed on reconditioning themselves towards healthier relationships to work – and supporting others to do so as well – thus constituted Vintervikens trädgård as a place conducive to recovery or rehabilitation. Signe's comments, for example, suggest she was aware of how her background had conditioned her to behave as an efficient and effective employee, causing her to struggle with leaving work unfinished or issues unresolved. This internalised sense of obligation or responsibility was seen to affect her subjectivity, becoming one according to which balance and healthy boundaries were inconsistent. Performance obligations and expectations of efficiency were considered to transgress and decondition the ability for self-care and autonomy.

Like Signe, the experiences Kerstin and Ida reflected on could also be interpreted as implicit critiques of a customer-determined subjectivity in working life, to that extent that the lack of boundaries each described was consistent with "a 'service culture' characterised by constant striving to deliver 'superior' customer value" (Skålén, Fellesson, & Fougère, 2006, p. 12). Self-care was a challenge, as service-based working environments (all three worked in some form of public-facing public sector work) had the tendency to produce a "'customer-determined subject' whose thoughts, feelings and emotions are determined to varying degrees by customer requirements" (p. 14). Considering how informants made sense of Vinterviken's meaning for the community as a contrast to embodied behaviours and mindsets of obligation, concerns such as those expressed by Signe, Ida, and Kerstin suggest that this anti-obligation ethos should not be viewed in isolation from this subjectivity implied to be a result of workplace conditioning. The perfectionistic work ethic Signe had mentioned struggling with was something to be discouraged within the association, deemed contrary to the garden's intent much like the professional management tendencies that the board resisted in its operations.

This interpretation was reinforced, by others both in interviews and during working days. As Karl opined when I interviewed him, "people can't be passionate about something in the same way if it becomes an obligation" (Karl, personal communication, 21 March 2018; my translation). Speaking with Björn and I on Björn's first day as a new collaborator, Karl expanded on this thought:

> As the three of us were talking, Björn wondered about how often people help out and how long the working day tends to go. Karl talked about how everything is appreciated, and how it was a question of *"vad du känner for att göra, inte mer än vad du orkar"* [what you feel like doing, [and] not worrying about doing more than you have the energy for]. With an example I had heard a couple of times in different situations, and from different people, he said it was a matter of making an effort, not the type of effort or how much one could do – *"Det finns två äldre kvinnor, till exempel, som bara kommer förbi för att sköta rosorna...och vi är tacksamma för detta"* [there are two women, for example, who only come to take care of the roses, and we are thankful for that]. (fieldnotes, 17 November 2018).

Over a period of several months, I noted that there were also people who only chopped firewood, or only worked on construction and carpentry projects. It seemed this approach was highly valued by informants, as something that set Vinterviken apart from other places.

As Kerstin reflected when we spoke, there were several interwoven considerations that made the relaxed attitude meaningful and fulfilling in contrast to the *tillsammansodling* where she had volunteered prior to moving to Stockholm:

> It's totally open! I interpret it as being totally open. "Come and do what you want. You have good ideas? Come and let's do it!"
>
> [...]
>
> And then, for me, it becomes a type of peace of mind to get to be there and work in the sense that there isn't any need to be efficient or effective. You do something that doesn't need to be completed, it's nice if it gets finished, but...it's kind of meditative, meditative work that one gets to do in a group. That really gives me a positive energy.
>
> [...]
>
> I like that it's really just so *unpretentious* as well. It's...it's not this has got to be the world's best thing; rather it's like this: "now we're gonna throw together a jazz festival. Okay, done!" [she laughs].
>
> [...]

> I truly appreciate going there. It's truly like an oasis for me to get to come here, but I feel like I maybe don't necessarily *have* to participate in working and all those things. [...] There's not this bad conscience because I'm not there every weekend since I can't be there *every* weekend. (Kerstin, interview, 30 October 2018; her emphasis; my translation)

This relaxed, 'unpretentious' approach made it possible for a lot to get done while each person seemingly did very little, as Ida reflected when interviewed:

> Well, it can be like that, you know, it's about there being a bit of balance between everyone doing a little. Everyone does a little bit so that no one person is doing too much. Maybe that's what it is. So that one can give up control, that's how it is. That one gets to do what one feels like and wants to do. (Ida, interview, 10 March 2022; my translation)

In each case, a social value was being attributed to the garden for providing a place where people could enjoy working without the burdens normatively associated with work as placing performance demands on people. The articulation of the association with values of being easy-going, grateful, and appreciative any contribution – valuing involvement rather than level of ability or commitment – was thus presented as a departure from what might be expected elsewhere. Further, as Signe's reflections suggest, one could interpret the work environment at Vinterviken to facilitate an alternate ethos of self-care, characterised by boundaries and balance rather than efficiency and expediency.

Vinterviken was thus interpretable as a sanctuary or place of reprieve from normative work environments. Whatever happened, happened according to ability and willingness. As a demonstration garden, therefore, Vinterviken was associated with demonstrating more than gardening techniques; it was also associated with a particular ethos of voluntary responsibility, taking responsibility as an active and personally fulfilling choice. Vinterviken could therefore be understood as a place to foster various forms of counter-conduct, with informants and others I observed actively working to raise awareness of sedimented rationalities by which capitalist business practices were considered to have conditioned social life and individual behaviour in line with a consumer-centric rationality of social interaction. As a collective initiative, its success was realised through its continuity according to this approach.

Considering the unease expressed variously with foundations as a non-profit organisational model, the potential for statutory changes, or whether to leave work unfinished, each could be seen as expressions of underlying concerns with obligation. And as informant comments and observations at board meetings emphasised, it was through such concerns, and the grievances articulated in relation to them, that Vinterviken's significance was interpretable as a response to its broader social context. While there were implicit grievances with responsibilisation that could be seen to inform a particular relationship to voluntary work, there was also a notable porosity between what was often presented as a clear dichotomy between obligation and freedom. Resisting governmentality and obligation coincided with a practice of volunteer management reliant on responsibilisation to maintain the garden through voluntary labour, which thus implied some sense of obligation was nonetheless necessary for its continued care. Without explicit obligations to contribute, the association appealed to values of personal fulfilment and autonomy as articulated with wellbeing and quality of life (cf. Pyysiäinen, Halpin, & Guilfoyle, 2017). Doing so, the association and its volunteers fulfilled the municipality's neoliberal imperative of responsibilisation, with private citizens maintaining public land and providing community events and amenities as intended by municipal planners.

Concluding Discussion

Rather than a story of active resistance to urban development policies and other external factors – as observed at Prinzessinnengarten – much of what informants at Vinterviken described in their stories, reflections, and encouragements seemed to express a duality regarding responsibilisation. Responsibilisation was something to resist yet also fundamentally necessary for Vintervikens trädgård to exist. Exploring this duality, I came to find that concepts of obligation and freedom, which informants discussed in dichotomous terms, were often far more porous than their characterisations suggested. This complicated how the relationship between governmentality and counter-conduct can be understood in relation to conditioned versus autonomous expressions of responsibilisation. Being *made* or *made to feel* responsible was critiqued, while *taking* responsibility appeared necessary to struggle against the former. As interpretable from informant recollections of the board 'crisis', the association struggled with a sense of responsibility to protect the garden's character and how best to do so.

This tension was particularly present in governmentalising characterisations of normative working environments; however, the association's board nurtured their own version of this in their approach to voluntary work.

Informants tended to critique being made to act in a certain manner or feeling that their behaviour was out of their own control. Whether recounting struggles with internalised behaviours and habits, or their appreciation for the self-fulfilment offered by the garden's way of doing voluntary work, the social value of Vinterviken was interpretable as being a place for counter-conduct, exploring "how not to be governed like that, by that, in the name of those principles" (Foucault, 1997, p. 44). And yet, those on the board did hope that people would feel inspired to behave in a manner conducive to maintaining the garden. In the problems and significant events that inform-ants recalled, a recurrent issue was that of responsibility, and whether one assumed it as a free, autonomous choice made by responsible citizens or whether they felt compelled, coerced, or otherwise obligated to take res-ponsibility.

A dual relationship to responsibilisation – against being made responsible, but actively encouraging taking responsibility – was thus central to making sense of Vinterviken's significance as articulated by informants. It could be seen simultaneously as a case study of counter-conduct and of govern-mentality – the former through creating a place that could give rise to various forms of resistance at the individual and collective level (cf. Foucault, 1997, 2007), the latter because this was done while simultaneously conforming to the city government's desire for responsibilisation (cf. Rose, 1996, 1999). This complicates the view of the relationship between city and garden, as informants found value in the elements of freedom and fulfilment compatible with responsibilisation. Rather than inherently different or contradictory, *taking* responsibility and *being made* responsible – as operative rationalities among garden members and municipal planners – could both implicitly reflect interpretations of citizenship involving individual responsibility for the common good.

Because of this, I argue internal disagreements about the best way to sus-tain the garden were a matter of which aspects or characteristics of Vinter-vikens trädgård were considered imperative to protect when different inter-pretations of the association's responsibility conflicted. For people like Stefan, the tension over association versus foundation as an appropriate organisational model was related to his interpretation of the garden's precarity should it continue to grow; for board members who remained after the 'crisis', it was a sense of place of Vinterviken as constituted by its approach to voluntary work. As a rationality being associated by many informants with corporations, government, and non-profit foundations, professionalisation was considered to threaten a sense of joy and freedom associated with voluntary work. It was important that voluntary work continued to *feel* voluntary to those engaged in it, rather than an obligation that impinged upon their autonomy and pleasure in contributing to Vinterviken's care.

Feeling obligation or a sense of compulsion to do something was considered to go against the intent of the garden as a voluntary association, but at the same time, the freedom to take responsibility for the site and maintain the garden could also be seen as fulfilling neoliberal goals. In a time when choice and freedom are reflected in the normative ethos of neoliberal governance (see Rose 1996, 1999; Rose, O'Malley, & Valverde, 2012), informants could be understood to act as ideal neoliberal subjects while also critical of neoliberal organisational management and urban planning. The interest of Vinterviken's board to protect the integrity of the statutes as written can therefore be understood in terms of maintaining a precarious balance in how the association operated – between neoliberal imperatives and a counter-conduct ethos that was, in part, conducive to neoliberal governance. The concern with changes to the scope of work, manner of work, or organisational form could be interpreted in terms of a projected fear among board members about the risks of upsetting the current balance. Board members and volunteer gardeners alike appeared to value what was possible to do collectively and voluntarily, but growing sales income raised questions about the best interest of the garden versus the organisation.

Though not unanimous by any means, in portraying professionalisation as contrary to Vinterviken's intended sense of place, the board members who remained constituted the garden's significance in relationship to their interpretation of the status quo the garden operated within. Much like Polletta (2002) and Zackariasson (2006) argue in their respective research into the organisational models and meeting practices of social movement organisations, meetings can be important settings for developing and reinforcing alternative social relations and collective mindsets through active resistance to and questioning of sedimented deliberative and decision-making practices. Characterising its organisational model in relation to an anti-professional ethos, and the norm of professionalisation as a disruptive or threatening influence, informants could be understood to do so as a way of reinforcing Vinterviken as a place for non-capitalist or anti-capitalist practice.

Legally bound by a relationship of responsibilisation with the municipality, Vintervikens trädgård could be argued to fulfil the ends of neoliberal governance. Nonetheless, the desire for freedom and autonomy that helped to fulfil such ends were also consistent with a democratic interpretation of freedom. It is this duality, I contend, which made it simultaneously possible for Vintervikens trädgård to fulfil government interests while also maintaining the garden as a place for non-commercial social life and non-capitalist relationships to work that were themselves not necessarily consistent with the imperatives of neoliberal capitalism.

8. Conclusions: Collective Gardens as Sites of Critical and Rehabilitative Practice

As the aim of this study was to explore the political significance of collective gardens, this concluding chapter brings together the varied lines of enquiry followed in pursuit of this aim. Before doing so, I first return to the research questions that guided this investigation into the cultivation of alternative norms in connection with sites of urban agriculture:

> 1. What sense of place can be understood to be nurtured in relation to collective gardens, and what does this convey about citizenship and experiences of urban life in the context of neoliberal capitalism?

> 2. Looked at aesthetically, how does the material culture of collective gardens situate them in relation to their contemporary urban environments, and what can their aesthetic expression be interpreted to convey about alternative norms of urban life?

> 3. How do narratives about collective gardens constitute them in relation to the historical and contemporary socio-political contexts in which they were established and now operate, and what significance is associated or attributed to these gardens in doing so?

With regards to the first of these questions, the sense of place being nurtured in the two case studies investigated here arguably varied depending on the source of its description; but common among all expressions of the character of these gardens was their basis in struggle and resistance. Specifically, their relevance to the collectives internal to them could be interpreted as having been shaped and conditioned by active democratic struggle with the conditions of life in neoliberal capitalist cities.

Garden collectives and public officials each struggled, in their own ways and to their own ends, to make socially marginalised areas more liveable. The relevance of Prinzessinnengarten and Vintervikens trädgård alike was thus inextricable from grievances with normative social relationships, land use practices, and ways of working and consuming that had created the conditions that the gardens were meant to address. Much like allotment gardens and community gardens could be considered reflective of their times and contexts, I would argue similarly of my case studies, and by extension, other collective gardens like them. Discourses of autonomy and responsibility were characteristic of how individuals, garden collectives, and city governments related to and made sense of the role of collective gardens in the city.

While allotments were often promoted as solutions meant to condition people towards ideals desirable for the advancement of industrial society and modernist urban and social development (see e.g., Bellows, 2004; Bergquist, 1996; Liesemer, 2019; L'œuvre des jardins ouvriers, 1898), community gardens tended to develop with a mission to promote ideals of inter-personal relationships and place-based relationships considered weakened in the political and economic context of post-industrial cities (see Eizenberg, 2013; Rosol, 2010; Turner, Henryks, & Pearson, 2011). As a subset of community gardens, collective gardens could be argued to build on the former's solution orientation. As argued through analysis of both case studies, compelling arguments can be made for interpreting these gardens as places for enacting citizenship as a critical practice, premised on an ethos of personal responsibility. With Prinzessinnengarten, there was a clear emphasis on fostering global solidarity and critical consumers as part of this political subjectivity; at Vintervikens trädgård, informants emphasised autonomy and personal fulfilment as contrasts to an efficacy-oriented subjectivity that conditioned how people thought and behaved, threatening their wellbeing.

Before expanding further on these themes, however, it is informative to revisit the other two questions, reflecting on how aesthetics and narratives articulated the character of the collective gardens studied here. Returning to the primary research question once more, I then entertain the peripherality of collective gardens – operating on the margins of neoliberal capitalist urban norms in a variety of ways – and how this counter-normative positionality in the materials analysed presented its own duality in relation to citizenship and governance. Through conflicting yet mutually reinforcing relationships to responsibility and gentrification, neoliberal capitalist discourses were enmeshed in complex ways with non-capitalist and anti-capitalist ones, influencing one another in diffuse manners that were not always readily apparent.

Aesthetic Politics as Social Critique

Apparent in visiting *tillsammansodlingar* and *Gemeinschaftsgärten* was their contrast with normative urban design and spatial use practices. But to understand the political significance of this – specifically, what they represented about the organisation of social life – context needed to be provided through which to interpret the forms these gardens took in relation to the broader built environments in which they were established. Observations across gardens therefore facilitated my analysis and the translation of aesthetic experience into linguistic expression for the purposes of this text. Recurrent aesthetic vocabularies were observed through which prototypical aesthetic genres could be discerned and described alongside photographic representations. By developing the requisite background of aesthetic experience and context, it became possible to 'read' and thereby interpret the aesthetic expressions of each genre of collective gardens (cf. Dufrenne, 1983, p. 209). This aided not only in distinguishing equivalences and contrasts in the aesthetic vocabularies of *tillsammansodlingar* and *Gemeinschaftsgärten*, but also how they referenced or diverged from other types of places in the cities where they were located.

The aesthetic genre of *Gemeinschaftsgärten* became interpretable in discourse with its immediate environment through apparent contrasts with their urban settings characterised by property development, consumerism, and commodification. In juxtaposition with these trends, *Gemeinschaftsgärten* could be made sense of as places that explored alternatives norms, promoting DIY and salvage practices that rearticulated relationships to materials typically treated as waste due to their perceived lack of commercial value. In turning away from local aesthetics and rationalities of development, land, object relations, and social life, these gardens appeared to have been influenced by places far across the world (such as Cuba, in the case of Prinzessinnengarten) in concept, material form, and their politics of anti-capitalist solidarity.

Vintervikens trädgård and similar *tillsammansodlingar* elsewhere in Sweden did not seem, at first glance, to manifest a similarly explicit aesthetic reaction to their immediate environment. As I would suggest, this may have something to do with the character of modernist urban planning in Sweden, which alongside its focus on density and concentration of housing and services has been notable for its integration of green spaces and green corridors. Similarly, the persistence of allotment gardens near most gardens gave the impression that urban agriculture remained a part of living heritage and was thus a familiar use of space to encounter. Discerning the particular character of *tillsammansodlingar* thus required more detailed attention to spatial design and ways of using space – rather than the materials used to construct them – as a way to make sense of their relationship to urban space as a phenomenon distinct from allotment gardens and cultural heritage sites.

Although all three could be found in the same cities, and they shared certain commonalities in their aesthetic vocabularies, *tillsammansodlingar* differed from the latter two in their collective and non-commercial character and anti-modernist layout and design.

Despite observable differences between *tillsammansodlingar* and *Gemeinschaftsgärten*, and Prinzessinnengarten and Vintervikens trädgård especially, I found there to be more in common between the two than a cursory aesthetic analysis may have suggested. On the one hand, the material cultures of these gardens reflected different visions of urban life and relationships to objects and resources. At the same time, both aesthetic genres of collective gardening connoted a distancing from contemporary aesthetic norms of urban design and urban spatial planning. While both forms provided for non-capitalist social and economic life to occur, German gardens most often took form through the repurposing of commercial waste whereas Swedish ones appeared to reject modern methods and materials in favour of vernacular design and traditional techniques. In both cases, this was done despite the availability of new techniques and ready-made solutions. As such, they could each be argued to reflect "an anti-elitist foundation whereby anyone could make [one], both as a matter of production costs and technical skills" (Gunnarsson Payne, 2006, p. 158; my translation). Although quite different aesthetically speaking, the material repertoires and construction characteristic of each genre manifested more sustainable practices than disposal or new construction through similarly anti-professional DIY political aesthetics, only using dissimilar aesthetic vocabularies.

Not unlike the allotment gardens in Bergquist's (1996) study, collective gardens observed and analysed could be argued to reflect utopian discourses to the extent that their design and use of materials emphasised a recognition of the future as open to possibilities. As a time that is 'not yet' is 'yet to be determined', the future is open to being shaped and imagined (cf. Muñoz, 2009; Ricœur, 1997), and experimentation and development of alternative aesthetic norms can be seen as one element of a prefigurative politics attempting to bring about other possible futures for how people inhabit urban space (cf. Boggs, 1977; Yates, 2015). Unlike Gothenburg's allotment gardens and those elsewhere which emerged under the same period however, their aesthetics were visibly rejecting normative, modernist conceptions of urban space whereby land was privatised and social life compartmentalised.

Solving Problems through Storytelling

Unlike aesthetics, through which objects and places are often interpretable through the ability of the observer to discern relationship to other objects and places external to those in question (see Dufrenne, 1953, 1983), the context for interpreting narratives tends to be already present within stories. Their 'terms of evaluation' are available through the configuration of people and events, word choices, and various other verbal and nonverbal rhetorical devices (cf. Polletta, DoCarmo, Ward, & Callahan, 2021, p. 71; Koskinen-Koivisto, 2016). While a broad exploration of material culture provided a foundation for analysing collective gardens, engagement with written and oral narratives of Prinzessinnengarten and Vintervikens trädgård contextualised how different people and different interests made sense of the relevance of these two prototypical case studies. Narratives internal to their respective collectives were reflective of citizenship, collective action, and autonomously taking responsibility; external, government, and commercial narratives, for their part, reinscribed the gardens within their own realities, co-opting these practices and conditioning citizens to take responsibility for them within government-defined constraints in service of city branding and urban redevelopment.

As was the case with analysing collective garden aesthetics, understanding the meanings or significance communicated in narratives was premised on the ability of the audience to make sense of cues. This meant following the terms of evaluation provided by narrators through linear progressions of causality and resolution, characterisations of people and events, references, as well as appeals to emotion. Through the combination of these and other rhetorical devices, it was possible to interpret how individual informants, garden collectives, and public officials conveyed and reinforced a sense of place for these gardens to their audiences. As argued here, they did so by formulating social problems that they also presented as being solved in some degree by the presence of these gardens. Narratives were therefore as much about mediating and cultivating how people related to their environment as they were about informing the course of action deemed necessary to protect these gardens as specific places worth defending and preserving. The histories (and pre-histories) of gardens such as Vinterviken and Prinzessinnengarten shaped not only how they were valued, but also the practices by which people involved with them worked to preserve a sense of place through which these locations were characterisable as socially, and thus politically, significant.

If, as Basso (1996b) states, "with any sense of place, the pivotal question is not where it comes from, or even how it gets formed, but what, so to speak, it is made with" (p. 84), it can thus be argued that the sense of place of collective gardens recounted in collective and individual narratives was built upon a rejection of key conditions of contemporary urban life. At both Vinterviken and Prinzessinnengarten, concerns were expressed about consumer behaviours and how they were portrayed to condition social life in Stockholm and Berlin, respectively. Representing social life in Berlin and Stockholm as conditioning people to behave in accordance with economic interests, internal narratives constituted both gardens as places to escape customer and consumer-determined subjectivities in favour of autonomy, critical reflection, and self-realisation. A sense of place for both gardens could therefore be understood as constituted in counterbalance to governmentality, fostering counter-conduct against normative, sedimented behaviours believed to condition people to behave in service of neoliberal capitalist objectives (cf. Foucault, 1997). Both gardens were attributed meaning by those who operated or volunteered in them as places to break out of normalised habits of social and working life.

In the official messaging of both case studies, as with narratives recounted by informants at Vinterviken, the preference for anti-capitalist practice couldn't be divorced from how narratives portrayed Kreuzberg and Aspudden as (once or currently) uninviting places. Both areas were characterised by multiple forms of social precarity and development patterns that conditioned consumer capitalist subjectivities. Accordingly, these gardens made sense and had value to people as places where critical political practice was able to be nurtured. Portrayed in internal narratives as representative of collective refusals to accept normative conditions of work, land rights, or social life, it suggested they were relevant as sites of democratic citizenship, premised on an implicit engagement with political life and collective interests (cf. Mouffe, 2018).

Similar contrasts were evident in the juxtaposition between collective and individual narratives and those found in local government documents. While internal narratives emphasised autonomy and self-realisation, external ones from government institutions, bureaucrats, and local politicians emphasised marketability, compliance, and control. Also, while the former portrayed the surrounding cityscape as overly commercialised and increasingly dense, the latter seemed to subsume collective gardens within their own narratives – of tourism and marketing, ecosystem services, social planning, and land development. For government institutions and public officials, they were presented as something supported, initiated, or otherwise made possible as strategic investments in the welfare and prosperity of the city.

Despite being internally portrayed as places apart from their urban milieux, Prinzessinnengarten and Vintervikens trädgård were economically and politically enmeshed with them. External actors were invested in the existence of these gardens; public officials and institutions enabled and influenced them, constituting elements of what they became through strategic planning and lease conditions. They also co-opted the phenomenon, displacing the political ethos associated with collective gardens to represent them as being in alignment with city branding and neoliberal governmentality (cf. LaForge, Anderson, & McLachlan, 2017; McRobbie, 2009; Trumpy, 2008).

As places situated within wider social contexts, these gardens existed because the social circumstances in Berlin and Stockholm provided their constitutive outside. They were possible because neglected and abandoned land was available for their use and encouraged by local governments. They came about through collective reactions to 'wastelands' and 'dumping grounds', benefiting from their status as such because these were otherwise undesirable areas. Although the rationalities by which the sense of place of these gardens was constituted and their significance articulated may have differed, individual, collective, and government narratives did evidence some degree of intersection. Certain meanings associated with collective gardens operated as floating signifiers, values that were ambiguous enough in meaning to be associable with political projects that were otherwise ideologically at odds with one another (cf. Laclau, 2005, p. 133; Moraes, 2014, p. 30). Common ground could thus be found through complementary elements, such as when public officials praised these gardens in terms of their benefit for the environment, the desirability of a neighbourhood, or as contributions to local social life. While these values were being articulated with neoliberal capitalist rationalities within city planning, tourism, and economic development discourses, the values themselves were not inherently antithetical to those ascribed to collective gardens from within their collectives.

Pericapitalism, Gentrification, and Responsibilisation

As both case studies illustrated, relationships with local government involved an aspect of precarity. Social, economic, and political norms were articulated as threats to the sense of place of collective gardens by their collectives. This precarity, it could be argued, had to do with the normative privilege given to the exchange or monetary value of land over alternative value propositions such as those fostered by garden collectives and informants. Along these lines, participation and engagement in the work of *tillsammansodlingar* and *Gemeinschaftsgärten* could be made sense of as a productive resistance to elements of urban living – particularly its privatised and commercialised elements, and the subjectivities associated with contemporary workplaces – being associated with a lack of autonomy and barriers to personal fulfilment. Involvement in these gardens could not be separated from such a sense of place thus ascribed them, constituted as it was in relation to relationships of critique and resistance to other places, rationalities, and experiences taking place beyond these sites. They were as much defined by the values characterising their sense of place as they were by those being actively excluded.

Interpreting collective gardens in pericapitalist terms, they cultivated non-capitalist or salvage capitalist economies in circumstances that were nonetheless conditioned by neoliberal capitalist rationalities of privatisation with implications for land use and urban planning policies. This duality, much like the duality of responsibilisation, was helpful for *making sense* of the economic plurality of collective gardens in a constructive manner, although not for *explaining* it. Acknowledging the plurality of forms of responsibilisation expands understanding of this concept beyond its typical association with actors being 'made responsible' for the public good on matters that were previously in the domain of government institutions (cf. Rose, 1999).

Consistent with the position of Pyysiäinen et al. (2017) that "the stickiness of neoliberal rule may be best explained by a combination of more than just one mechanism of responsibilisation" (p. 230) – in their case appeals to freedom, the fear of loss of personal control, a welfarist orientation, and psychological reactance – I submit that responsibilisation, like pericapitalism, is best understood in the example of collective gardens as a relationships of *both/and*. As collective gardens advance non-capitalist practices alongside their enmeshment in capitalist economies, they involve both forms of economic practice and cannot therefore be reduced to either. Following a similar line of reasoning, responsibilisation can be interpreted as *both* a governmentalising rationality of institutions *and* an expression of individual and collective autonomy and self-fulfilment beyond institutional conditioning. In other words, the responsibilisation observable in collective gardens such as Prinzessinnengarten and Vintervikens trädgård was both a product of municipal governments limiting their responsibility and of collectives who recognised the limitations of reliance on institutions to provide for every need due to their proclivity to prioritise some causes over others.

While government reports and lease and use agreements reflected collectives being *made responsible,* informant and collective narratives articulated a desire to *take responsibility* for aspects of social life that governments could not (or should not) be expected to provide for or satisfy due to their very nature (at least as characterised in the empirical materials collected and analysed here.

My argument here is that this duality, by which gardens *both* fulfil *and* reject neoliberal capitalist economic and governance practices, demonstrates that autonomy and governmentality are not inherently mutually exclusive means through which people think, act, feel, or behave. Both rationalities operate from similar – or at least partially complementary – premises of individual responsibility in interpretating how liberty should manifest in the organisation of social life, hence the ability for their alignment through processes of responsibilisation (cf. Pyysiäinen, Halpin, & Guilfoyle, 2017; Rose, 1999). The proclivity within neoliberal modes of governance towards the retrenchment of institutional provision of many services favours individual responsibility and liberty to choose, premised on certain economic assumptions and projected social rationalities by which improved services and reduced costs are argued to be in the interest of society (see Glynos, Speed, & West, 2014).

Conversely, the autonomous impulses within urban commons, community and collective gardens, and similar social movements, reflect critiques of government action on matters of social organisation and urban space, among other things. They also reflect an active desire among activists and others who become 'civically engaged' to have a sense of freedom over the constitution and conditions of their social lives – in this case, through the responsibility over the place where it occurs and the openness such a place affords in environments characterised (in my empirical materials) as privatised, compartmentalised, and commercialised. The motivations and rationalities of institutions and collective gardeners (and similarly inclined groups and individuals) find common ground in these places, however transactional and tenuous those relationships may be – and however fraught that the meeting of representative and radical democratic conceptualisations of responsibilisation may become when confronted with matters of regulatory compliance and competing social, economic, and environmental interests.

This was especially apparent where gentrification was concerned. Improvements to local communities as recounted in relation to Prinzessinnengarten and Vinterviken were not meant to be contained within the boundaries of each garden. They were portrayed by collectives and municipal governments alike as part of broader processes of social change and community improvement for which gentrification was, at best an 'unintentional' by-product (see Nomadisch Grün, 2019) and at worst an intentional strategy of socio-economic displacement (cf. Freeman, 2006). Rather than suggest the prefigurative politics of such gardens was for naught however, I argue this tension illustrates that although people and governments can affect and impact their environment and conditions of life, they do not fully control the results or outcomes of their actions. Collective gardens may not operate 'independent' from neoliberal capitalist economics, processes of gentryfication, or rationalities of governance by responsibilisation and commodefication, but this doesn't invalidate the significance of what is done within them to articulate alternatives to normative rationales of social organisation and economic behaviour. The 'unintentional coordination' between seemingly unrelated economies enables them to influence each other, making mutual transformation possible (cf. Tsing, 2015, pp. 22-23).

To refer to collective gardens as pericapitalist thus acknowledges how such places come to represent a shift towards the periphery of neoliberal capitalism by fostering alternative rationalities for social organisation. Pericapitalism could be likened to the borderland of these gardens, the fences, and gates where capitalist rationalities and alternatives to them necessarily came in contact, and where certain ideas, aesthetics, and practices came and went (floating) freely, with others being held at bay or contained within. Whereas local government rationales for permitting, planning, and encouraging *Gemeinschaftsgärten* and *tillsammansodlingar*, in both Berlin and Stockholm, found ways to articulate them within narratives of improved quality of life via land and economic development, narratives from within existing garden collectives held (what they saw as) threats at a distance while also benefiting from them, however precariously.

Both garden collectives and public officials found ways to work within their own spheres of interest, with the former able to actively resist or find ways to negotiate the conditions and rationalities under which they were permitted to operate. Much like consumer capitalism and property speculation in some ways provided the grounds and material for many *Gemeinschaftsgarten* to establish themselves, I posit that neoliberal governance could be seen to create the conditions for its own resistance through the responsibilisation of citizens by which *tillsammansodlingar* were both institutionally encouraged and collectively brought into being. The interest within municipal governments to reduce service costs did not compel gardeners to take over responsibility for public land; rather, they sought out the possibility to garden according to their own needs and interests in ways those locations did not already fulfil. The municipal governments, and their budgets, benefited from the willingness to come to some agreement, through income from interim leases and the contributions made to city branding.

Of course, this was not without issue, as both case studies illustrated – Vinterviken with its bee pavilion, Prinzessinnengarten with the antagonism between the senators for finance and urban development, and the future of *Gemeinschaftsgärten* as envisioned in the Berlin Senate's Charter for Urban Greenery. By relinquishing or devolving responsibility for public amenities and public land, responsibilisation could be seen to encourage the enactment of democratic citizenship, with people at Prinzessinnengarten and Vinterviken mobilising around and negotiating conflicting visions of social organisation, thereby nurturing political subjectivities through engagement in inherently political matters. At both gardens, it can be said that citizenship was practiced through a shared ethos of critical engagement and taking responsibility for the common good. Whether this came to expression through global solidarity or advocating the best interests of bees, the actions and positions of garden collectives were premised on more than personal interest.

Counter-Conduct and Rearticulated Relationships

It was through these and other such points of tension that the significance of collective gardens and the nature of threats collectives and informants discussed could be most succinctly interpreted. Whether the threat of relocation, threats to the organisational model of a garden, or the threat of redefining the conditions under which *Gemeinschaftsgärten* fit into the cityscape, each represented a threat to the conditions under which gardens existed and operated, and thus their sense of place as urban commons. A new physical location, corporate co-optation, governmental co-optation, or changes from a voluntary association to a foundation each involved rearticulating what collective gardens meant to those directly involved with them. Each scenario reflected a projected future in which the current relationships individuals and garden collectives had to these spaces became acutely uncertain.

This was especially apparent when the threat was to the organisational form or to the nature of gardens as salvaged places (rather than part of private development plans). Both appeared to represent the cessation of collective gardens as urban commons, to the extent that such changes would represent a shift away from pericapitalism towards the governmentality that collectives and individuals critiqued. *Gemeinschaftsgärten*, in line with the Berlin Senate's Charter for Urban Greenery, would be developed as amenities of new development, and thus be commodities; Vinterviken, if operating as a foundation with a professional, paid board, was feared to result in an organisation steered by and beholden to deliverables rather than one responsive to the interests and willingness of those who volunteered.

Such distancing from perceived threats is relatable if collective gardens are understood as serving a rehabilitative function. As agricultural engineer and environmental educator Pablo Llobera Serra (2014) contends, the cultural practices of *huertos urbanos comunitarios* [urban communal gardens][44] are interpretable by viewing them as places that signify "a discomfort with the dominant model of the city and the lifestyles it induces. [Collective gardens] articulate locally a plurality of sensibilities, demands and claims (environmental, neighbourhood, political, relational...)" (p. 120; my translation). Considered in these terms, the results of this study suggest that part of the potential of these gardens lies in their role as places meant to disrupt sedimented rhythms, aesthetics, and narratives about urban life and the direction of urban development into the future. They provide examples that people can adapt urban space to address unmet needs, and that even alternatives to a social order must negotiate the systems and values they seek to transform. The prefigurative politics taking place at these sites signified rejections and rearticulations of normative relationships to food cultivation, social life, and urban space, what Llobera Serra speaks of in terms of 'relational rehabilitation' (ibid.). It is this rehabilitative element – 'making able once again' – through which they offer people the potential to relate and interact in ways that are deemed healthier for environment, community, and self in comparison to those conditioned by normative work and (consumer) social environments.

At *tillsammansodlingar*, such a rehabilitative aspect could be observed in their stereotypically rural aesthetic, or how informants at Vintervikens trädgård described the garden in terms of relaxation, balance, and letting go of control and responsibility. As far as Vinterviken was concerned, such a perspective made it possible to understand the garden's significance in terms of its alternative, anti-corporate relationships to responsibility, voluntary work, and associational life. In *Gemeinschaftsgärten*, this could be seen in the rearticulation of material relationships and both local and global solidarity as

---

[44] One of several names used in Spain to refer to approaches consistent with collective gardens.

central to their political significance. At Prinzessinnengarten more specifically, it was observable in the relationships to expertise and experimentation – which its founders framed by rehabilitating the concept of dilettantism from its typically pejorative connotations – expressed as important to the vision of the site's approach to collective work and collaborative learning. Through the people caring for them and presenting them to the public, these gardens reflected motivations to change relationships – to oneself, others, and one's environment – away from those conditioned by neoliberal capitalist rationalities towards other possibilities.

Consequently, the rehabilitative character of the prefigurative politics taking place in collective gardens can be viewed in terms of counter-conduct. Collectives and individuals associated the gardens where they were involved as meaning something in terms of deconditioning, whether it had to do with how people interacted with urban space and what they expected of it, how they worked together, or how they related to themselves beyond identities as professionals, experts, or service providers. This was not unlike the "struggle[s] against the processes implemented for conducting others" that Foucault (2007) speaks of in describing the relationship of counter-conduct to governmentality (p. 201). Informants and others involved at collective gardens could – at least in part – be understood to reject normative conceptions of subjectivity conditioned by contemporary capitalism. This was a clear departure from many allotment movements, initiated with intentions to condition certain groups or sections of society in a manner that served contemporaneous or then emergent ideals of urbanity, progress, and citizenship (see e.g., Baratay, 1997; Bellows, 2004; Bergquist, 1996; Schäfer-Biermann, Westermann, Vahle, & Pott, 2016).

Concluding Reflections

In both case studies, as with the aesthetics of *tillsammansodlingar* and *Gemeinschaftsgärten* in general, the significance of collective gardens could be made sense of in terms of the alternate norms of city life they fostered. They rearticulated the physical form of urban space as well as how to live and work within it. The aesthetics, stories, and organisational models of the collective gardens studied here turned back in time and looked elsewhere to articulate a sense of place and thereby interpret their relationships to physical, social, and political environments. They conveyed equivalences with some things and antagonisms or resistance to others, disarticulating and rearticulating objects, relationships, and concepts to give them new or radically different meanings and significance. If there is any generalisable sense of place that could be attributed to collective gardens such as my case studies or others visited, it was how they meant something to people as places for critical reflection, critical practice, and relational rehabilitation. Achieving the latter by means of the former two, they represented places to transform relationships to self, society, and urban space through discussions and practices that rearticulated how they interacted with themselves as well as human and non-human others.

That these critical and rehabilitative practices could be read, heard, and observed to occur at Prinzessinnengarten and Vinterviken provided implicit and explicit evidence that urban life and urban space could be reimagined, and that those who were involved with these gardens desired such a reimageining. Dissatisfied with a status quo that continues to shape urban centres, they were rehabilitating what had been damaged and distanced through neoliberal capitalist rationalities that commercialised and compartmentalised *intra*personal, *inter*personal, as well as inter*species* relationships. Cityscapes were not meeting human or environmental needs, and institutional solutions were insufficient as they remained fixed in neoliberal rationalities of governance, serving short-term capitalist economic goals. Other approaches and other visions of urban life and urban space were needed and thus explored and negotiated. The presence of collective gardens can be interpreted to manifest a desire for non-commercial social life, and to be able to step out of everyday rhythms to look back and reflect on urban life and one's sense of self within it.

Because of this, I argue that collective gardens cultivated a type of political subjectivity vital to democratic practice and any hope of shifting towards more environmentally sustainable and equitable ways of living, working, and consuming. To the extent places like Vintervikens trädgård and Prinzessinnengarten operated as urban commons, they did so by achieving, on some scale, to inspire people to work towards and protect alternatives to the status quo of urban life as their collectives characterised this. This was done by providing environments outside of the norm where critical subjectivity could be fostered, enabling people to be more mindful of how their environment conditioned them – in positive and harmful ways. Doing so provided a reference point from which to reshape their environment and reorient themselves accordingly.

A particular contribution of this study was thus in demonstrating how a political subjectivity is cultivated in multitudinous ways – aesthetically and narratively, as I focus on here. The type of subjectivity being nurtured in collective gardens, through their collective and non-capitalist practices, privileged a democratic conceptualisation of citizenship that involves thinking critically and taking responsibility – individually and collectively – for local and global circumstances. It also provided observable evidence that prefigurative politics, while seeking to move beyond the status quo for which alternatives are sought, does not occur independent from the circumstances and grievances which motivate collective action. The collectives operating these gardens pushed the boundaries of established relationships to political institutions and economic practices, while also working in concert with them, resisting and cooperating simultaneously. Democratic citizenship involves critiquing and contradicting social and political institutions with the intent that they do better by the people they serve and represent. Rather than rejecting them altogether, they are neither taken for granted nor taken as given.

Studying collective gardens consequently provided more insight into the making of commons as a perpetual project, and the roles of narratives and aesthetics in sustaining them through meaning making and value propositions in relationship to wider social environments and normative values they critique. Furthermore, case studies elucidated various means by which people navigated physical and ideological precarity by looking outward or inward – outward through developing an ethos of solidarity with global social movements, inward by reflecting on and struggling with the norms fostered within a collective. Precarity needed not always involve being subject to violence, only exposure to threat. Whether or not precarity was chosen through the decision to agree to an interim lease (as was the case with most *Gemeinschaftsgärten*, as well as many *tillsammansodlingar* in Stockholm), or to resist organisational norms (as were especially apparent in interviews with informants at Vintervikens trädgård), such choices involved existential risks, reinforcing the necessity of narratives to sustain internal coherence and material culture to articulate gardens as part of something beyond themselves.

These places were possible for the same reasons that their futures were precarious. As such, they offered practical evidence of the porosity of economic models (cf. Tsing, 2012), visible in the contaminated diversity that manifested between gardens and other places in their cityscapes. The proximity and confluence of capitalist, salvage, and other economic forms both in and beyond these gardens demonstrated a complex interplay, observable in instances of co-optation and gentrification, as well as the legal and financial relationships between collectives and local governments. The interplay and interdependencies by which capitalist and non-capitalist economies, or governmentalising and grassroots forms of responsibilisation, unintentionally cooperate are necessary preconditions to rearticulate urban life and its economic, environmental, and social premises. This can be sobering as it requires and encourages a different way to approach social change in pursuit of alternatives to conditions that cause threat, harm, or suffering. In the cases studied here, this suggests the potential of alternative ways of conceptualising citizenship in which responsibility is not an obligation or duty, but a desire that individuals and garden collectives take upon themselves. Responsibilisation may in part be conditioned by institutions seeking to retrench their obligations to the public, but it also begs the question, at least in terms of urban commons and public spaces, whether or not public institutions can or should be the appropriate level at which such social organisation occurs – or whether their role is more appropriate in ensuring such places can exist for communities amidst other interests or rationalities exerting normative influence on urban space and society.

On a final note, this study demonstrates that there are many strategies by which people can find meaning amidst, and ways to explore alternatives to, social circumstances perceived as problematic or constraining. This is so even when those circumstances – in this case, neoliberal capitalism – do not seem to suggest the possibility of alternatives. Although the work occurring in *Gemeinschaftsgärten* and *tillsammansodlingar* may have in some ways served capitalist and neoliberal goals that garden collectives simultaneously could be observed to critique – by being commodifiable, contributing to gentrification, or through successful responsibilisation – it did not mean that they lacked the autonomy to also work at odds with those systems to create alternatives. Rather, the examples of Vintervikens trädgård and Prinzessinnengarten show that alternatives may come from within the systems they seek to change. By pushing at the periphery of capitalism or neoliberal 'governance-by-responsibilisation', the potential exists to rearticulate and thus re-centre social, political, and economic systems. Much like the gardens themselves, such a democratic project is a continual one that must be cared for and cultivated.

References

Unpublished Materials
Interviews & Personal Communications

Annabelle	Personal communication, 31 July 2018
Annika	Personal communication, 27 February 2018
Björn	Personal communication, 17 November 2018
Denise	Personal communication, 31 July 2018
Ernesto	Personal communication, 14 September 2018
Eva	Interview, 30 October 2018
Ida	Interview, 10 March 2022
Jenny	Personal communication, 17 March 2018
Karl	Personal communication, 21 March 2018
Kerstin	Interview, 30 October 2018
Lars	Personal communication, 7 December 2018
Signe	Personal communications, 7 April & 27 May 2018
Stefan	Interview, 10 March 2022

Observations

Fieldnotes from participant observation and interviews.

Photography from site visits and participant observation.

Charters and Manifestos

Le Jardin dans Tous Ses États. (2012). *Chartre du Jardin dans Tous Ses États: La terre en partage*. Retrieved from Le Jardin dans Tous Ses États: http://jardins-partages. org/IMG/pdf/JTSE-leger.pdf

Senatsverwaltung für Umwelt, Verkehr und Klimaschutz. (2020). *Charta für das Berliner Stadtgrün: Eine Selbstverpflichtung des Landes Berlin*. Berlin: Senatsverwaltung für Umwelt, Verkehr und Klimaschutz.

Urban Gardening Manifest. (2014). *Urban Gardening Manifest*. Retrieved September 03, 2021, from Urban Gardening Manifest: https://urbangardeningmanifest.de/

Legal Documents

Commission Implementing Decision 2021/914. *Commission Implementing Decision (EU) 2021/914 of 4 June 2021 on standard contractual clauses for the transfer of personal data to third countries pursuant to Regulation (EU) 2016/679 of the European Parliament and of the Council.* https://eur-lex.europa.eu/eli/dec/2021/914/oj

Regulation 2016/679. *Regulation (EU) 2016/679 of the European Parliament and of the Council of 27 April 2016 on the protection of natural persons with regard to the processing of personal data and on the free movement of such data, and repealing Directive 95/46/EC (General Data Protection Regulation).* https://eur-lex.europa.eu/eli/reg/2016/679/oj

Hägersten-Liljeholmens stadsdelsförvaltning. (2020). *Brukaravtal/Stadsodling.* Retrieved May 15, 2022, from https://edokmeetings.stockholm.se/welcome-sv/namnder-styrelser/hagersten-alvsjo-stadsdelsnamnd/mote-2020-09-24/protocol/brukaravtalstadsodling-pdf-1?downloadMode=download

Skärholmens stadsdelsförvaltning. (2014, March 31). *Brukaravtal – tillfällig stadsodling på parkmark i Skärholmens stadsdelsnämndsområde.* Retrieved May 15, 2022, from https://insynsverige.se/documentHandler.ashx?did=1754247

Skärholmens stadsdelsförvaltning. (2019). *Brukarskötselavtal.* Retrieved May 15, 2022 from https://edokmeetings.stockholm.se/welcome-sv/namnder-styrelser/skarholmens-stadsdelsnamnd/mote-2020-08-27/agenda/brukaravtal-kulturforeningen-varvsarbetarhusetpdf?downloadMode=open

Södermalms stadsdelsförvaltning. (2016). Avtal om brukarmedverkan. Retrieved May 15, 2022, from https://www.odlaihop.se/föreningen/brukaravtal-44303455

News Articles

Cornell, P. (2012, March 9). *Gammalt tågspår blir "Lilla Berlin".* Retrieved from Mitt i Södermalm: https://www.mitti.se/nyheter/gammalt-tagspar-blir-lilla-berlin/Ldelci!CBh13HFgFEAPnddfmbDEw/

Cowie, S. (2019, October 3). *Jair Bolsonaro pictured with second accused in Marielle Franco murder case.* Retrieved from The Guardian: https://www.theguardian.com/world/2019/oct/03/jair-bolsonaro-photo-marielle-franco-murder-accused

Der Tagesspiegel. (2011, August 16). Berliner Immobilien: So funktioniert der Liegenschaftsfonds. *Der Tagesspiegel.*

Die Welt. (2012, October 15). Prinzessinnengarten könnten weiter bestehen. *Die Welt.* Retrieved from https://www.welt.de/regionales/berlin/article109855225/Prinzessinnengaerten-koennten-weiter-bestehen.html

Heier, E. (2012, October 30). Franz Schulz über Entwicklungen in Friedrichshain-Kreuzberg. *tipBerlin.* Retrieved April 14, 2021, from https://www.tip-berlin.de/stadtleben/franz-schulz-uber-projekte-friedrichshain-kreuzberg/?q=%2Fkultur-undfreizeit-stadtleben-und-leute%2Ffranz-schulz-uber-projekte-friedrichshain-kreuzberg

Kaiser, T. (2017, December 24). Google: Kreuzberger Bürger wollen Start-up Campus verhindern. *Die Welt.* Retrieved February 6, 2023, from https://www.welt.de/wirtschaft/article171884997/Google-Kreuzberger-Buerger-wollen-Start-up-Campus-verhindern.html

Kerinec, M. (30 April 2018). Les gendarmes ont déversé une quantité record de grenades sur la Zad de Notre-Dame-des-Landes. *Reporterre.* Retrieved May 4, 2019, from https://reporterre.net/Les-gendarmes-ont-deverse-une-quantite-record-de-grenades-sur-la-Zad-de-Notre

Knight, B. (2018, October 25). Google leaves Berlin campus after demos.*Deutsche Welle.* Retrieved February 6, 2023, from https://www.dw.com/en/google-leaves-berlin-campus-after-anti-gentrification-demos/a-46045271

Lautenschläger, R. (2011, May 18). 10 Jahre Liegenschaftsfonds: Alles musste raus. *Die Tageszeitung.* Retrieved January 12, 2022, from https://taz.de/10-Jahre-Liegenschaftsfonds/!5120416/

Lodding, M. (2018, July 3). *Gerillaodlare intar Hästa gård.* Retrieved from SVT Nyheter: https://www.svt.se/nyheter/lokalt/stockholm/ gerillaodlare-intar-hasta-gard

Martens, D. (2012, May 19). Urbane Laborsituation. *Der Tagesspiegel.* Retrieved October 20, 2021, from https://www.tagesspiegel.de/berlin/serie-leserdiskussion-urbane-laborsituation/6649478.html

Sjöström, M. (2012, June 18). Odling lockar till nya möten. *Svenska Dagbladet.*

Stresing, L. (2012, April 29). Der Prinzessinnengarten in Kreuzberg. *Der Tagesspeigel.*

Svensson, M. (2018, February 22). *Trädgården på spåret byggs upp på ny plats.* Retrieved from Mitt i Södermalm: https://www.mitti.se/nyheter/ tradgarden-pa-sparet-byggs-upp-pa-ny-plats/reprbv!U7J8rwB1PFbl G9oiq2xWw/

Söderpalm, H. (2016, November 10). *Digging in the city - urban Swedes get back to their roots.* Retrieved from Reuters: https://www.reuters.com/article/us-sweden-urbanfarms-idUSKBN1351O9

Taylor, S. (2010, August). News report: Prinzessinnengarten. *Monocle.*

UN News. (2020, January 14). *Colombia: 'Staggering number' of human rights defenders killed in 2019.* Retrieved from United Nations News: https://news.un.org/en/story/2020/01/1055272

Willsher, K. (9 April 2018). French police fire teargas to expel anti-capitalist squatters. *Guardian.* Retrieved May 4, 2019, from https://www.theguardian.com/world/2018/apr/09/france-notre-dame-des-landes-police-anti-airport-activists-teargas

Reports

BIM Berliner Immobilienmanagement GmbH. (2021). *Digitale Landesbibliothek Berlin.* Retrieved from Zentral- und Landesbibliothek Berlin: https://digital.zlb.de/viewer/

api/v1/records/34411643_2020/files/images/BIM_Kennzahlenreport_2020.pdf/full.p
df

Bundesministerium für Umwelt, Naturschutz, Bau und Reaktorsicherheit (BMUB). (2015, July). *Gemeinschaftsgärten im Quartier: Handlungsleitfaden für Kommunen.* Retrieved from Bundesministerium für Umwelt, Naturschutz, Bau und Reaktorsicherheit: https://www.bmi.bund.de/SharedDocs/downloads/DE/publikationen/themen/bauen/wohnen/soziale-stadt-gemeinschaftsgaerten.pdf?__blob=publicationFile&v=3

Gatu- och fastighetskontoret Stockholms stad. (2001). *Kulturpark Liljeholmen. Slutredovisning.*

Kommunstyrelsen Stockholms stad. (2004, November 25). Prövning av det fortsatta ansvaret för Kulturpark Liljeholmen. Retrieved November 15, 2021, from https://insynsverige.se/documentHandler.ashx?did=48385

L'œuvre des jardins ouvriers. (1898). *Compte rendu du premier congrès de l'œuvre des jardins ouvriers tenu à Nancy le 25 septembre 1898.* Nancy: Gérardin, Nicolle.

OECD. (2020). *OECD Regions and Cities at a Glance 2020.* Paris: OECD Publishing. doi:https://doi.org/10.1787/959d5ba0-en

Vintervikens trädgård. (2017). *Verksamhetsberättelse för verksamhetsåret 2016-01-01–2016-12-31.* Stockholm: Vintervikens trädgård — ideell förening.

The World Bank. (2022a). Population, rural. *World Development Indicators.* Retrieved February 14, 2023, from https://datacatalog.worldbank.org/search/dataset/0037712/World-Development-Indicators

The World Bank. (2022b). Population, urban. *World Development Indicators.* Retrieved February 14, 2023, from https://datacatalog.worldbank.org/search/dataset/0037712/World-Development-Indicators

Websites, Webpages and Other Digital Materials

anstiftung. (2018). *Gärten im Überblick.* Retrieved July 15, 2018, from anstiftung: https://anstiftung.de/

anstiftung. (2022). *Die urbanen Gemeinschaftsgärten in Deutschland.* Retrieved April 29, 2022, from Urbane Gemeinschaftsgärten: https://urbane-gaerten.de/urbane-gaerten/gaerten-im-ueberblick

Basta Erwerbsloseninitiative. (2022). *Über uns.* Retrieved from Basta Berlin: https://bastaberlin.de/ueber

Berlin Tourismus & Kongress GmbH. (n.d.). *Urban gardening in Berlin.* Retrieved from visitBerlin: https://www.visitberlin.de/en/urban-gardening-berlin

Edible Cities Network. (2018). Retrieved from Edible Cities Network: https://www.edicitnet.com/

Göteborgs stad. (n.d.). *Stadsnära odling.* Retrieved September 15, 2022, from https://stadsnaraodling.goteborg.se/

HosieWulff. (2013). *History of space, Prinzessinnengarten*. Licensed under CC BY-SA 3.0. Retirieved February 11, 2019 from https://hosiewulff.wordpress.com/2013/11/07/history-of-space-prinzessinnengarten/

Nomadisch Grün. (2019). *Prinzessinnengarten dauerhaft als Gemeingut sichern*. Retrieved from Prinzessinnengarten: https://prinzessinnengarten.net/gemeingut-prinzessinnen garten/

Norrmalmsodlarna. (n.d.). *Om oss*. Retrieved February 17, 2020, from Bellevue Farm: https://www.bellevuefarm.se/om-oss/

Parker och natur, Stockholms stad. (2021, September 09). *Odla i stan*. Retrieved from Stockholms stad: https://parker.stockholm/odla-i-stan/

Partageons les Jardins. (2017). *Jardins collectifs. Retrieved from:*. Retrieved November 20, 2017, from Partageons les Jardins: http://partageonslesjardins.fr/jardins-collectifs/

Prinzessinnengarten. (2012). *About Prinzessinnengarten*. Retrieved from Prinzessinnengarten: https://prinzessinnengarten.net/about/

Prinzessinnengarten. (2012). *Über die Prinzessinnengärten*. Retrieved October 17, 2019, from https://prinzessinnengarten.net/wir/

Prinzessinnengarten. (2019). *Programm Prinzessinnengarten Kreuzberg 2019*. Retrieved from Prinzessinnengarten: https://prinzessinnengarten.net/programm-prinzess innengarten-kreuzberg-2019/

Prinzessinnengarten Kreuzberg. (2015, July 18). Retrieved November 13, 2018, from Facebook: https://www.facebook.com/prinzessinnengarten.kreuzberg/posts/1152217551460177

Prinzessinnengarten Kreuzberg. (2020, July 7). Retrieved February 17, 2021, from Facebook: https://www.facebook.com/prinzessinnengarten.kreuzberg/posts/36795784287 24064

Senatsverwaltung für Umwelt, Mobilität, Verbraucher- und Klimaschutz. (n.d.). *Plattform Produktives Stadtgrün*. Retrieved from Berlin.de: Das offizielle Hauptstadtportal: https://www.berlin.de/gemeinschaftsgaertnern/

Senatsverwaltung für Umwelt, Mobilität, Verbraucher- und Klimaschutz. (2021). *Berliner Gemeinschaftsgarten-Programm*. Retrieved from Berlin.de: Das offizielle Hauptstadtportal: https://mein.berlin.de/projekte/berliner-gemeinschaftsgarten-programm/

Stadsodling Malmö. (n.d.). *Stadsodlingar i Malmö*. Retrieved September 15, 2022, from https://stadsodlingmalmo.se/odla/

Stadsodling Stockholm. (n.d.). *Stadsodling Stockholm*. Retrieved from Facebook: https://www.facebook.com/stadsodlingstockholm/

Teatr Powszechny. (2016). *Stwórz z nami Ogród Powszechny! [Create a common garden with us!]*. Retrieved from Teatr Powszechny: https://www.powszechny.com/aktualnosci/stworz-z-nami-ogrod-powszechny.html?ref_page=controller,index,action,szukaj,szukaj,ogrody,lang,pl

Vintervikens trädgård. (n.d.). *Vintervikens trädgård - ideell förening*. Retrieved from Vintervikens trädgård - ideell förening: http://vinterviken.com

Vintervikens trädgård. (2017). *Om oss.* Retrieved February 12, 2017, from Vintervikens trädgård: http://vinterviken.com/om-oss/

Literature

Acker, P. (1907). Œuvres sociales de femmes, dernière partie. *Revue des deux Mondes, 42*(2), pp. 403–424.

Agnidakis, P. (2013). *Rätten till platsen: Tillhörighet och samhörighet i två lokala industrisamhällen under omvandling.* Höör: Brutus Östlings Bokförlag Symposion.

Ahmed, S. (2018, March 9). Complaint as diversity work. *Lecture at the Centre for Research in the Arts, Social Sciences and Humanities, University of Cambridge.* Retrieved February 3, 2020, from https://www.youtube.com/watch?v=JQ_1kFwkfVE

Appel, I., Grebe, C., & Spitthöver, M. (2011). *Aktuelle Garteninitiativen: Kleingärten und neue Gärten in deutschen Großstädten.* Kassel: kassel university press.

Arcudi, G. (2006). La sécurité entre permanence et changement. *Relations internationales* (125), 97–109.

Argaillot, J. (2014). Émergence et impacts de l'agriculture urbaine à Cuba. *Espaces et sociétés, 158,* 101–116.

Armstrong, D. (2000). A survey of community gardens in upstate New York: Implications for health promotions and community development. *Health and Place, 6*(4), 319–327.

Arrhenius, T. (2010). The vernacular on display: Skansen Open-Air Museum in 1930s Stockholm. In Helena Mattsson & Sven-Olov Wallenstein (Eds.), *Swedish modernism: Architecture, consumption and the welfare state.* London: Black Dog Publishing, pp. 134–49.

Bacchi, C. (2009). *Analysing policy: What's the problem represented to be?* Frenchs Forest, NSW: Pearson Education.

Bacchi, C. (2012). Introducing the 'What's the problem represented to be?' approach. In A. Bletsas, & C. Beasley (Eds.), *Engaging with Carol Bacchi: Strategic interventions and exchanges* (pp. 21–24). Adelaide: University of Adelaide Press.

Baker, J. M. (2022). Boreal plants that enchant: A lively ethnography of Sakâwiyiniwak (Northern Bush Cree) multispecies kinship obligations. *Environmental Humanities, 14*(2), 385–400.

Bamberg, M. (1997). Positioning between structure and performance. *Journal of Narrative and Life History, 7*(1–4), 335–342.

Bamberg, M., & Georgakopoulou, A. (2008). Small stories as a new perspective in narrative and identity analysis. *Text & Talk, 28*(3), 377–396.

Baratay, É. (1997). *Le Père Joseph Rey, serviteur de l'enfance défavorisée – Une expérience d'insertion au XIXe siècle.* Paris: Beauchesne.

Barrett, M., & Zani, B. (Eds.). (2015). *Political and civic engagement: Multidisciplinary perspectives.* Routledge.

Barron, J. (2017) Community gardening: Cultivating subjectivities, space, and justice. *Local Environment, 22*(9), 1142–1158.

Basso, K. H. (1996a). *Wisdom sits in places: Landscape and language among the Western Apache.* Albuquerque: University of New Mexico Press.

Basso, K. H. (1996b). Wisdom sites in places: Notes on a Western Apache landscape. In S. Feld, & K. H. Basso (Eds.), *Senses of Place* (pp. 53–90). Santa Fe: School for Advanced Research Press.

Beilin, R., & Hunter, A. (2011). Co-constructing the sustainable city: How indicators help us "grow" more than just food in community gardens. *Local Environment, 16*(6), 523–538.

Bellows, A. C. (2004). One hundred years of allotment gardens in Poland. *Food and Foodways, 12*(4), 247–276.

Berger, P., & Luckmann, T. (1966). *The social construction of reality: A treatise in the sociology of knowledge.* New York: Penguin Books.

Bergquist, M. (1996). *En utopi i verkligheten. Kolonirörelsen och det nya samhället.* Göteborg: Etnologiska föreningen i Västsverige.

Blehr, B. (1999). Ett krigsjubileum och en hemsida: Om NS-barn i den norska offentligheten. *Kulturella perspektiv, 8*, 22–31.

Blehr, B. (2001). Inledning. In B. Blehr (Ed.), *Kritisk etnologi: Artiklar till Åke Daun* (pp. 9–14). Falun: Prisma.

Boggs, C. (1977). Marxism, prefigurative communism, and the problem of workers' control. *Radical America, 11*(6), 99–122.

Bolin, G. (2012). Introduction: Cultural technologies in cultures of technology. In *Cultural technologies: The shaping of culture in media and society* (pp. 1–15). Taylor & Francis.

Bonow, M., & Normark, M. (2016). Urban community gardens' contribution to the new rurality: An example from Stockholm (Sweden). In P. Rytkönen, & U. Hård (Ed.), *Challenges for the new rurality in a changing world: Proceedings from the 7th International Conference on Localized Agri-Food Systems: 8–10 May 2016, Södertörn University, Stockholm, Sweden.* (pp. 37–38). Huddinge: Södertörns högskola.

Bonow, M., & Normark, M. (2018). Community gardening in Stockholm: Participation, driving forces and the role of the municipality. *Renewable Agriculture and Food Systems, 33*(6), 503–517.

Boulianne, M. (2001). L'agriculture urbaine au sein des jardins collectifs quebecois: Empowerment des femmes ou <<domestication de l'espace publique>>. *Anthropologie et Sociétés, 25*(1), 63–80.

Brüggemann, M., & Rödder, S. (Eds.). (2020). *Global warming in local discourses: How communities around the world make sense of climate change.* Cambridge: OpenBook Publishers.

Buchan, W. (1769). *Domestic medicine or, The family physician : being an attempt to render the medical art more generally useful, by shewing people what is in their own power both with respect to the prevention and cure of diseases.* Edinburgh: Balfour, Auld, and Smellie.

Casey, E. S. (1996). How to get from space to place in a fairly short stretch of time: Phenomenological prolegomena. In S. Feld, & K. H. Basso (Eds.), *Senses of place* (pp. 13–52). Santa Fe: School for Advanced Research Press.

Cashman, R. (2006). Critical nostalgia and material culture in Northern Ireland. *Journal of American Folklore, 119*(472), 137–160.

Certomà, C., & Tornaghi, C. (Eds.). (2015). Special issue on political gardening. *Local Environment: The International Journal of Justice and Sustainability, 20*(10).

Chaplin, E. (1994). *Sociology and visual representation.* London: Routledge.

Chatterton, P., & Pickerill, J. (2010). Everyday activism and transitions towards post-capitalist worlds. *Transactions of the Institute of British Geographers, 35*(4), 475–490.

Clark, E. (2005). The order and simplicity of gentrification – a political challenge. In R. Atkinson, & G. Bridge (Eds.), *Gentrification in a global context. The new urban colonialism.* New York: Routledge, pp. 256–265.

Clifford, J. (2001). Indigenous articulations. *Contemporary Pacific, 13*(2), pp. 468–490.

Clifford, J. (2005). Rearticulating anthropology. In D. Segal, & S. Yanagisako (Eds.), *Unwrapping the sacred bundle: Reflections on the disciplining of anthropology* (pp. 24–48). New York: Duke University Press.

Colding, J., & Barthel, S. (2013). The potential of 'urban green commons' in the resilience building of cities. *Ecological Economics, 86,* 156–166.

Collier, J., & Collier, M. (1986). *Visual anthropology: Photography as a research method.* Albuquerque: University of New Mexico Press.

Cosgrove, S. (1998). Community gardening in major Canadian cities: Toronto, Montreal and Vancouver compared. *Urban agriculture policy in Southern Africa: Productive Open Space Management Conference, 3–5 March 1998.* Pretoria, South Africa.

Cumbers, A., Shaw, D., Crossan, J., & McMaster, R. (2017). The work of community gardens: Reclaiming place for community in the city. *Work, Employment and Society, 32*(1), 133–149.

D'Andréa, N., & Tozzi , P. (2014). Jardins collectifs et écoquartiers bordelais: De l'espace cultivé à un habiter durable? *Norois, 231,* pp. 61–74.

Damsholt, T. (2008). The sound of citizenship. *Ethnologia Europaea, 38*(1), 56–65.

Davies, C. A. (2008). *Reflexive ethnography.* New York: Routledge.

Day, S., & Goddard, V. (2010). New beginnings between public and private: Arendt and ethnographies of activism. *Cultural Dynamics, 22*(2), 137–154.

de Moor, J., Marien, S., & Hooghe, M. (2017). Why only some lifestyle activists avoid state-oriented politics: a case study in the Belgian environmental movement. *Mobilization: An International Quarterly, 22*(2), 245–264.

del Viso, N., Fernández Casadevante, J., & Morán, N. (2017). Cultivando relaciones sociales. Lo común y lo "comunitario" a través de la experiencia de dos huertos urbanos de Madrid. *Revista de Antropología Social, 26*(2), pp. 449–472.

della Porta, D., & Diani, M. (1999). *Social movements: An introduction.* Oxford: Blackwell Publishers.

Dellenbaugh, M., Kip, M., Bieniok, M., Müller, A. K., & Schwegmann, M. (2015). Seizing the (every)day: Welcome to the urban commons! In M. Dellenbaugh, M. Kip, M. Bieniok, A. K. Müller, & M. Schwegmann (Eds.), *Urban commons: Moving beyond state and market* (pp. 9–25). Basel: Birkhaüser Verlag GmbH.

DelSesto, M. (2015). Cities, gardening, and urban citizenship: Transforming vacant acres into community resources. *Cities and the Environment, 8*(2).

Demailly, K.-E. (2014). Les jardins partagés franciliens, scènes de participation citoyenne? *EchoGéo, 27*, 1–18.

Desai, S., & Smith, H. (2018). Kinship across species: Learning to care for nonhuman others, *Feminist Review, 118*, 41–60.

Dobernig, K., & Stagl, S. (2015). Growing a lifestyle movement? Exploring identity-work and lifestyle politics in urban food cultivation. *International Journal of Consumer Studies, 39*, 452–458.

Dufrenne, M. (1953). *Phénoménologie de l'expérience esthétique.* Paris: Presses Universitaires de France.

Dufrenne, M. (1973). *The phenomenology of aesthetic experience.* Evanston, IL: Northwestern University Press.

Dufrenne, M. (1983). Perception, meaning, and convention. *The Journal of Aesthetics and Art Criticism, 42*(2), 209–211.

Duncombe, S. (1997). *Notes from underground: Zines and the politics of alternative culture.* London: Verso.

Duncombe, S. (1999). DIY Nike Style. *Z Magazine.* Retrieved from https://znetwork. org/zmagazine/diy-nike-style-by-stephen-duncombe/

Ehn, B., & Löfgren, O. (2012). Pausens mikrodramatik: En essä om önskade och oönskade avbrott. *Sosiologi i dag, 42*(1), 15–36.

Eizenberg, E. (2012). Actually existing commons: Three moments of space of community gardens in New York City. *Antipode, 44*(3), 764–782.

Eizenberg, E. (2013). *From the ground up: Community gardens in New York City and the politics of spatial transformation.* New York: Routledge.

Ekström, S., & Kaijser, L. (2018). Djur – ett kulturvetenskapligt perspektiv. In S. Ekström & L. Kaijser (Eds.), *Djur: Berörande möten och kulturella smärtpunkter.* Göteborg: Makadam förlag, pp. 7–34.

Ellis, C. (2007). Telling secrets, revealing lives: relational ethics in research with intimate others. *Qualitative Inquiry, 13*(1), 3–29.

Eriksen, A. (2014). *From antiquities to heritage: transformations of cultural memory.* New York: Berghan Books.

Errejón, Í., & Mouffe, C. (2016). *Podemos: In the name of the people.* London: Lawrence & Wishart.

Escoffier Martínez, S. (2023). *Mobilizing at the urban margins: Citizenship and patronage politics in post-dictatorial Chile.* Cambridge University Press.

Feenstra, G., McGrew, S., & Campbell, D. (1999). *Entrepreneurial community gardens: Growing food, skills, jobs, and communities.* Oakland, CA: UC Division of Agricultural and Natural Resources.

Feld, S., & Basso, K. H. (1996). Introduction. In S. Feld, & K. H. Basso (Eds.), *Senses of place* (pp. 3–11). Santa Fe: School of American Research Press.

Finlay, T. (2022). Re-presenting the gender-queer figure: Western appropriations of inappropriate/d others in 'A third gender'. *New Sociology: Journal of Critical Praxis, 3*, 1–15.

Firth, C., Maye, D., & Pearson, D. (2011). Developing "community" in community gardens. *Local Environment, 16*(6), 555–568.

Flavell, N. (2003). Urban allotment gardens in the eighteenth century: The case of Sheffield. *The Agricultural History Review, 51*(1), 95–106.

Fleming, P. (2014). Review article: When 'life itself' goes to work: Reviewing shifts in organizational life through the lens of biopower. *Human Relations, 67*(7), 875–901.

Follmann, A., & Viehoff, V. (2015). A green garden on red clay: creating a new urban common as a form of political gardening in Cologne, Germany. *Local Environment: The International Journal of Justice and Sustainability, 20*(10), 1148–1174.

Fontana, B. (1993). *Hegemony and power: On the relation between Gramsci and Machiavelli.* Minneapolis, MN: University of Minnesota Press.

Foucault, M. (1969). *L'archéologie du savoir.* Paris: Gallimard.

Foucault, M. (1982). The subject and power. In *Michel Foucault: Beyond structuralism and hermeneutics*, H. Dreyfus, & P. Rabinow (Eds.). Chicago: University of Chicago Press, pp. 208–226.

Foucault, M. (1988). The concern for truth. In L. D. Kritzman (Ed.), *Michel Foucault: Politics, philosophy, culture. Interviews and other writings, 1977–1984* (A. Sheridan, Trans.). London: Routledge.

Foucault, M. (1991). Politics and the study of discourse. In G. Burchell, C. Gordon, & P. Miller (Eds.), *The Foucault efect: Studies in governmentality* (pp. 53–72). Chicago: University of Chicago Press.

Foucault, M. (1997). *The politics of truth.* Los Angeles: Semiotext(e).

Foucault, M. (2007). *Security, territory, population: Lectures at the Collège de France, 1977–1978.* Palgrave-Macmillan.

Foucault, M. (2008). *The birth of biopolitics: Lectures at the Collège de France, 1978–79.* London: Palgrave.

Freeman, Lance (2006). *There goes the 'hood. Views of gentrification from the ground up.* Philadelphia: Temple University Press.

Freire, P. (2017). *Pedagogy of the oppressed.* Penguin.

Frykman, J. (1988). *Dansbaneeländet: ungdomen, populärkulturen och opinionen.* Stockholm: Natur & Kultur.

Geertz, C. (1973). *The interpretation of cultures.* New York: Basic Books.

Georgakopoulou, A. (2015). Small stories research: Methods – analysis – outreach. In A. DeFina, & A. Georgakopoulou (Eds.), *The handbook of narrative analysis* (pp. 255–271).

Gerner, P. (1881). *Handbok i rationell biskötsel.* Lund: Håkan Ohlssons boktryckeri.

Glass, Ruth (1964). Introduction. In Centre for Urban Studies (ed.), *London: Aspects of Change.* London: McGibbon and Kee, pp. xiii–xlii.

Glynos, J., & Howarth, D. (2007). *Logics of critical explanation in social and political theory.* London: Routledge.

Glynos, J., Speed, E., & West, K. (2014). Logics of marginalisation in health and social care reform: Integration, choice, and provider blind provision. *Critical Social Policy, 35*(1), 45–68.

Goffman, E. (1959). *The presentation of self in everyday life.* New York: Doubleday.

Goldstein, P. (2017). Post-Yugoslav everyday activism(s): A different form of activist citizenship? *Europe-Asia Studies, 69*(9), 1455–1472.

Gómez Rodríguez, J. N. (2014). *Agricultura urbana en América Latina y Colombia: Perspectivas y elementos agronómicos diferenciadores.* Medellín: Universidad Nacional Abierta y a Distancia.

Grahn, P., & Stigsdotter, U. (2003). Landscape planning and stress. *Urban Forestry & Urban Greening, 2,* 1–8.

Gregory, M., Leslie, T., & Drinkwater, L. (2016). Agroecological and social characteristics of New York city community gardens: contributions to urban food security, ecosystem services, and environmental education. *Urban Ecosystems, 19,* pp. 763–794.

Griggs, S., & Howarth, D. (2004). A transformative political campaign? The new rhetoric of protest against airport expansion in the UK. *Journal of Political Ideologies, 9*(2), 167–187.

Griggs, S., & Howarth, D. (2008). Populism, localism and environmental politics: The logic and rhetoric of the Stop Stansted Expansion campaign. *Planning Theory, 7*(2), 123–144.

Gunnarsson Payne, J. (2006). *Systerskapets logiker. En etnologisk studie av feministiska fanzines.* Institutionen for kultur och medier, Umeå universitet .

Gunnarsson Payne, J. (2013). Moving images, transforming media: The mediating communitas of HallonTV and DYKE HARD. *International Journal of Cultural Studies, 16*(4), 367–382.

Hackney, F. (2013). Quiet activism and the new amateur. *Design and Culture, 5*(2), 169–193.

Hall, S. (1997). *Representation: Cultural representations and signifying practices.* London: SAGE Publications Ltd.

Hall, S. (1999). Encoding, decoding. In S. During (Ed.), *The cultural studies reader* (pp. 507–517). London: Routledge.

Hallberg, P. M. (1982). Ölkaféer i Stockholm. *Stadsvandringar – Stockholm, 1982*(5), pp. 30–39.

Hallqvist, J. (2022). *Människoliknande teknik och det möjligt mänskliga: En etnologisk studie av relationer mellan människor och teknik.* Umeå: Umeå universitet.

Halweil, B., & Nierenberg, D. (2006). Farming the cities. In L. Starke (Ed.), *State of the world 2007: Our urban future. A Wordwatch Insitute report on progress toward a sustainable society* (pp. 48–63). London: Earthscan.

Haraway, D. (1988). Situated knowledges: The science question in feminism and the privilege of partial perspective. *Feminist Studies, 14*(3), 575–599.

Harvey, D. (2005). *A brief history of neoliberalism.* Oxford: Oxford University Press.

Harvey, D. (2008). The right to the city. *New Left Review, 53*(Sept/Oct), 23–40.

Harvey, D. (2012). *Rebel cities: From the right to the city to the urban revolution.* London: Verso.

Head, L., Atchison, J., Phillips, C., & Buckingham, K. (2014). Vegetal politics: belonging, practices and places. *Social & Cultural Geography, 15*(8), 861–870.

Horton, J., & Kraftl, P. (2009). Small acts, kind words and "not too much fuss": Implicit activisms. *Emotion, Space and Society, 2*(1), 14–23.

Howarth, D. (2005). Applying discourse theory: The method of articulation. In D. Howarth, & J. Torfing (Eds.), *Discourse theory in European politics* (pp. 316–349). London: Palgrave Macmillan.

Högdahl, E. (2007). *På andra sidan trädgårdsgatan.* Näringslivs och Marknadsavdelningen, Helsingborgs stad.

Jacobsson, K., & Korolczuk, E. (2017). Introduction: Rethinking Polish civil society. In K. Jacobsson, & E. Korolczuk (Eds.), *Civil society revisited: Lessons from Poland.* (pp. 1–35). New York: Berghahn Books.

Jameson, F. (1991). *Postmodernism, or, The cultural logic of late capitalism.* Durham: Duke University Press.

Jenkins, K. (2017). Women anti-mining activists' narratives of everyday resistance in the Andes: staying put and carrying on in Peru and Ecuador. *Gender, Place & Culture, 24*(10), 1441–1459.

Jones, M. D., & Song, G. (2014). Making sense of climate change: How story frames shape cognition. *Political Psychology, 35*(4), 447–476.

Kanosvamhira, T. P., & Tevera, D. (2023). Urban community gardens in Cape Town, South Africa: navigating land access and land tenure security. *GeoJournal, 88*(3), 3105–3120.

Kaplan, R., & Kaplan, S. (2005). Preference, restoration, and meaningful action in the context of nearby nature. In P. F. Barlett (Ed.), *Urban place. Reconnecting with the natural world* (pp. 271–298). Cambridge, MA: The MIT Press.

Keshavarz, M., & Bell, S. (2016). A history of urban gardens in Europe. In S. Bell, R. Fox-Kämper, M. Keshavarz, M. Benson, S. Caputo, S. Noori, & A. Voigt (Eds.), *Urban Allotment Gardens in Europe* (pp. 8–32). Routledge.

Kimmerer, R. W. (2003). *Gathering moss: A natural and cultural history of mosses.* Corvallis: Oregon State University Press.

Kimmerer, R. W. (2013). *Braiding Sweetgrass: Indigenous wisdom, scientific knowledge and the teachings of plants.* Minneapolis: Milkweed Editions.

Kingsley, J., & Townsend, M. (2006). 'Dig in' to social capital: Community gardens as mechanisms for growing urban social connectedness. *Urban Policy and Research, 24*(4), 525–537.

Klein, B. (2001). Knätofsforskning och hemsk slöjd: Om etnologin, hemslöjdsrörelsen och moraliska gemenskaper i Sverige. In B. Blehr (Ed.), *Kritisk etnologi:* (pp. 109–135). Falun: Prisma.

Koc, M., MacRae, R., Mougeot, L. J., & Welsh, J. (Eds.). (1999). *For hunger-proof cities: Sustainable urban food systems.* Ottowa: IDRC.

Kohne, S. (2020). *Gentrifiseringens flertydighet: En kulturvitenskapelig studie av endringer i to byområder i Berlin og Oslo.* Bergen: Universitetet i Bergen.

Koskinen-Koivisto, E. (2016). *Her own worth: Negotiations of subjectivity in the life narrative.* Helsinki: SKS.

Kristeva, J. (1986). Word, dialogue and novel. In J. Kristeva, & T. Moi (Ed.), *The Kristeva reader* (A. Jardine, T. Gora, & L. Roudiez, Trans., pp. 34–61). New York: Columbia University Press.

Kusenbach, M. (2003). Street phenomenology: the go along as ethnographic research tool. *Ethnography, 4*(3), 455–485.

Labaree, R. V. (2002). The risk of 'going observationalist': negotiating the hidden dilemmas of being an insider participant observer. *Qualitative Research, 2*(1), 97–122.

Laclau, E. (1990). *New reflections on the revolution of our time.* London: Verso.

Laclau, E. (1996a). Deconstruction, pragmatism, hegemony. In C. Mouffe (Ed.), *Deconstruction and pragmatism* (pp. 49–70). London: Routledge.

Laclau, E. (1996b). *Empancipation(s).* London: Verso.

Laclau, E. (2005). *On populist reason.* London: Verso.

Laclau, E. (2006a). Ideology and post-Marxism. *Journal of Political Ideologies, 11*(2), 103–114.

Laclau, E. (2006b). Why constructing a people is the main task of radical politics. *Critical Inquiry, 32,* 646–680.

Laclau, E., & Mouffe, C. (1985). *Hegemony and socialist strategy: Towards a radical democratic politics.* London: Verso.

Laclau, E., & Mouffe, C. (1987). Post-Marxism without apologies. *New Left Review, 166,* 79–106.

LaForge, J., Anderson, C., & McLachlan, S. (2017). Governments, grassroots, and the struggle for local food systems: Containing, coopting, contesting and collaborating. *Agriculture and Human Values, 34,* 663–681.

Lancry, G. (1899). *Le Terrianisme: La petite propriété insaisissable et assurée à tous.* Dunkerque: A. Delville.

Lave, J., & Wenger, É. (1991). *Situated learning: Legitimate peripheral participation.* Cambridge University Press.

Lawson, L. J. (2005). *City bountiful: A century of community gardening in America.* Berkeley: University of California.

Lefebvre, H. (1968). *Le droit à la ville.* Paris: Anthropos.

Lemke, T. (2001). The birth of bio-politics: Michael Foucault's lectures at the College de France on neo-liberal governmentality. *Economy and Society, 30*(2), 190–207.

Liesemer, D. (2019). Dr. Schreber und die Gärten: Vielerorts enstanden nun Klein-gartenanlagen – eine Idee mit vielen Vätern. Dans E.-M. Schnurr, & J. Mohr (Éd.), *Die Gründerzeit: Wie die Industrialisierung Deutschland veränderte* (pp. 171–177). München: Deutsche Verlags-Anstalt.

Linde, C. (1993). *Life stories: The creation of coherence.* Oxford: Oxford University Press.

Linn, K. (1999). Reclaiming the sacred commons. *New Village Journal, 1,* 42–49.

Llobera Serra, P. (2014). Horticultura urbana: La Red de Huertos Urbanos de Madrid. *Ambienta, 107,* 120–128.

Lorenz, C. (1999). Comparative historiography: problems and perspectives. *History & Theory: Studies in the Philosophy of History, 38*(1), 25–39.

Lothane, Z. (1992). *In defense of Schreber: Soul murder and psychiatry.* Taylor & Francis.

Lööw, J. (2010). *Odla i staden för välbefinnande: Om Sevedsbornas upplevelser av Barn i stans odlingsprojekt.* Alnarp: Sveriges lantbruksuniversitet.

Marcus, G. (1995). Ethnography in/of the world system: The emergence of multi-sited ethnography. *Annual Review of Anthropology, 24,* 95–117.

Marshall, M. (2016). *Hållbarhet till middag: en etnologisk studie om hur miljövänligt ätande praktiseras i vardagslivet.* Höör: Brutus Östlings Bokförlag Symposion.

Martinsson, L. (2012). Globala klasser. *Fronesis, 40–41,* 198–207.

Marx, K., & Engels, F. (1968). *L'idéologie allemande.* Paris: Éditions sociales.

Massey, D. (1991). A global sense of place. *Marxism Today, 38,* 24–29

Massey, D. (2005). *For space.* London, UK: SAGE Publications Ltd.

McNamara, T. (2016). *Crisis of urban agriculture: Case studies in Cuba.* New Haven, CT: Hixon Center for Urban Ecology at Yale University.

McRobbie, A. (2009). *The aftermath of feminism: Gender, culture and social change.* London: SAGE Publications Ltd.

Melucci, A. (1996). *Challenging codes. Collective action in the information age.* Cambridge University Press.

Miller, D. (2001). *The dialectics of shopping.* Chicago: The University of Chicago Press.

Monroe-Santos, S. (1998). Recent national survey shows status of community gardens in the U.S. . *Community Greening Review, 8,* 12–15.

Moore, L. J., & Kosut, M. (2014). Among the colony: Ethnographic fieldwork, urban bees and intra-species mindfulness. *Ethnography, 15*(4), 516–539.

Moraes, S. (2014). Global citizenship as a floating signifier. *International Journal of Development Education and Global Learning, 6*(2), 27–42.

Mouffe, C. (1988/2013). Hegemony and new political subjects. In J. Martin (Ed.), *Chantal Mouffe: Hegemony, radical democracy and the political* (pp. 45–57). London: Routledge.

Mouffe, C. (1991). Democratic citizenship and the political community. In M. T. Collective (Ed.), *Community at loose ends* (pp. 70–82). University of Minnesota Press.

Mouffe, C. (1992a). Democratic politics today. In C. Mouffe (Ed.), *Dimensions of radical democracy: Pluralism, citizenship, community* (pp. 1–14). London: Verso.

Mouffe, C. (1992b). Citizenship and political identity. *October, 61,* 28–32.

Mouffe, C. (2000). *The democratic paradox.* London: Verso.

Mouffe, C. (2005). *On the political.* Routledge.

Mouffe, C. (2018). *For a left populism.* London: Verso.

Mougeot, L. J. (2005). Neglected issues on form and substance of research on urban agriculture. In L. J. Mougeot (Ed.), *Agropolis: The social, political and environmental dimensions of urban agriculture* (pp. 267–280). Ottawa: Earthscan and IDRC.

Mousselin, G., & Scheromm, P. (2015). Vers une mise en politique des jardins collectifs urbains. Approche comparée de deux trajectoires municipales à Montpellier et à Lisbonne. *Articulo – Journal of Urban Research*(Special Issue 6), 1–17.

Muñoz, J. E. (2009). *Cruising utopia: The then and there of queer futurity.* New York: NYU Press.

Müller, C. (2012). Reiche Ernte in Gemeinschaftsgärten. Beim Urban Gardening findet Homo oeconomicus sein Korrektiv. In S. Helfrich, & Heinrich-Böll Stiftung (Eds.), *Commons. Für eine neue Politik jenseits von Markt und Staat* (pp. 267–272). Bielefeld: Transcript Verlag.

Nettle, C. (2010). *Community gardening as social action. The Australian community gardening movement and repertoires for change.* Adelaide: School of History and Politics, University of Adelaide.

Nieto López, J. (2010). Resistir obedeciendo. Para una etnografía de la resistencia civil no armada en Medellín. *Espacio Abierto, 19*(2), 219–251.

Nilsen, M. (2014). *The working man's green space: Allotment gardens in England, France, and Germany, 1870–1919.* Charlottesville, VA: University of Virginia Press.

Nilsson, F. (2000). *I rörelse: politisk handling under 1800-talets första hälft.* Nordic Academic Press.

Nomadisch Grün. (2012). *Prinzessinnengärten. Anders gärtnern in der Stadt.* Köln: DuMont.

Nystrand von Unge, E. (2019). *Samla samtid: Insamlingspraktiker och temporalitet på kulturhistoriska museer i Sverige.* Stockholm: Vulkan.

Ochs, E., & Capps, L. (2001). *Living narrative: Creating lives in everyday storytelling.* Cambridge, MA: Harvard University Press.

Passeron, J.-C., & Revel, J. (2005). *Penser par cas.* Paris: Éditions de l'école des hautes études en sciences sociales.

Petrova, T., & Tarrow, S. (2007). Transactional and participatory activism in the emerging European polity: The puzzle of East-Central Europe. *Comparative Political Studies, 40*(1), 74–94.

Pickerill, J., & Chatterton, P. (2006). Notes towards autonomous geographies: Creation, resistance and self-management as survival tactics. *Progress in Human Geography, 30*(6), 730–746.

Pink, S. (2008). Mobilising visual ethnography: Making routes, making place and making images. *Forum Qualitative Sozialforschung, 9*(3).

Pink, S. (2009). *Doing sensory ethnography.* London: SAGE Publications Ltd.

Pink, S. (2013). *Doing visual ethnography.* London: SAGE Publications Ltd.

Pink, S., Horst, H., Postill, J., Hjorth, L., Lewis, T., & Tacchi, J. (2016). *Digital ethnography: Principles and practice.* London: SAGE Publications Ltd.

Piotrowski, G., & Polanska, D. (2016). Radical urban movements in Poland – the case of squatting. *Miscellanea Anthropologica et Sociologica, 17*(1), 53–69.

Poe, M. R., LeCompte, J., McLain, R., & Hurley, P. (2014). Urban foraging and the relational ecologies of belonging, *Social & Cultural Geography, 15*(8), 901–919.

Polanska, D. V. (2018). Going against institutionalization: New forms of urban activism in Poland. *Journal of Urban Affairs*, 1–12.

Polanska, D. V., & Piotrowski, G. (2015). The transformative power of cooperation between social movements: Squatting and tenants' movements in Poland. *City: Analysis of Urban Trends, Culture, Theory, Policy, Action, 19*, 274–296.

Polletta, F. (1998a). "It was like a fever..." Narrative and identity in social protest. *Social Problems, 45*(2), pp. 137–159.

Polletta, F. (1998b). Contending stories: Narrative in social movements. *Qualitative Sociology, 21*(4), 419–446.

Polletta, F. (2002). *Freedom is an endless meeting: Democracy in American social movements.* The University of Chicago Press.

Polletta, F. (2006). *It was like a fever: Storytelling in protest and politics.* Chicago: University of Chicago Press.

Polletta, F., DoCarmo, T., Ward, K., & Callahan, J. (2021). Personal storytelling in professionalized social movements. *Mobilization: An International Quarterly, 26*(1), 65–86.

Postill, J., & Pink, S. (2012). Social media ethnography: The digital researcher in a messy web. *Media International Australia, 145,* 123–134.

Purcell, M., & Tyman, S. K. (2015). Cultivating food as a right to the city. *Local Environment: The International Journal of Justice and Sustainability, 20*(10), 1132–1147.

Pyysiäinen, J., Halpin, D., & Guilfoyle, A. (2017). Neoliberal governance and 'responsibilization' of agents: Reassessing the mechanisms of responsibility-shift in neoliberal discursive environments. *Distinktion: Journal of Social Theory, 18*(2), 215–235.

Reksten-Kapstad, C. (2001). *Når handling tar plass: ein kulturstudie av Fellesaksjonen mot Gasskraftverk.* Universitetet i Bergen.

Renouf, J. S. (2021). Making sense of climate change—the lived experience of experts. *Climatic Change, 164*(1), 1–18.

Rentzhog, S. (2007). *Friluftsmuseerna: en skandinavisk idé erövrar världen.* Stockholm: Carlssons bokförlag.

Ricœur, P. (1997). *L'idéologie et l'utopie.* Paris: Éditions du Seuil.

Rivera, D., Obón de Castro, C., Verdejo Alonso, E., Fajardo Rodríguez, J., Alcaraz Ariza, F. J., Carreño Sánchez, E., . . . Laguna Lumbreras, E. (2014). El huerto familiar, repositorio de cultura y recursos genéticos, tradición e innovación. *Ambienta, 107,* 20–39.

Rose, D. B., van Dooren, T., Chrulew, M., Cooke, S., Kearnes, M., & O'Gorman, E. (2012). Thinking through the environment, unsettling the humanities. *Environmental Humanities, 1*(1), 1–5.

Rose, N. (1996). Governing 'advanced' liberal democracies. In A. Barry, T. Osborne, & N. Rose (Eds.), *Foucault and political reason* (pp. 37–64). Chicago: Chicago University Press.

Rose, N. (1999). *Powers of freedom: Reframing political thought.* Cambridge: Cambridge University Press.

Rose, N., O'Malley, P., & Valverde, M. (2012). Gubernamentalidad. *Astrolabio, Nueva Época, 8,* 113–152.

Rosol, M. (2006). *Gemeinschaftsgärten in Berlin: eine qualitative Untersuchung zu Potenzialen und Risiken bürgerschaftlichen Engagements im Grünflächenbereich vor dem Hintergrund des Wandels von Staat und Planung.* Berlin: Humboldt-Universität zu Berlin.

Rosol, M. (2010). Gemeinschaftsgärten – Politische Konflikte um die Nutzung innerstädtischer Räume. In B. Reimers (Ed.), *Gärten und Politik* (pp. 208–217). München.

Rosol, M. (2012). Community volunteering as neoliberal strategy? Green space production in Berlin. *Antipode, 44*(1), 239–257.

Ruck, A., & Mannion, G. (2021). Stewardship and beyond? Young people's lived experience of conservation activities in school grounds. *Environmental education research, 27* (10), 1502–1516.

Ryghaug, M., Sørensen, K. H., & Næss, R. (2011). Making sense of global warming: Norwegians appropriating knowledge of anthropogenic climate change. *Public Understanding of Science, 20*(6), 778–795.

Sallaberger, W. (2007). From urban culture to nomadism: A history of Upper Mesopotamia in the late third millennium. *Sociétés humaines et changement climatique à la fin du troisième millénaire: une crise a-t-elle eu lieu en Haute Mésopotamie? Actes du Colloque de Lyon, 5–8 décembre 2005 (Varia Anatolica, 19)* (pp. 417–456). Istanbul: Institut Français d'Études Anatoliennes-Georges Dumézil.

Saltzman, K., Sjöholm, C., & Gunnarsson, A. (2016). Önskat eller oönskat? Trädgårdens växter mellan natur och kultur. *RIG: Kulturhistorisk tidskrift, 99*(1), 14–34.

Sassen, S. (1991). *The global city. New York, London, Tokyo.* Princeton: Princeton University Press.

Sassen, S. (2000). The global city: Strategic site/new frontier. *American Studies, 41*(2/3), 79–95.

Schäfer-Biermann, B., Westermann, A., Vahle, M., & Pott, V. (2016). *Foucaults Heterotopien als Forschungsinstrument: Eine Anwendung am Beispiel Kleingarten.* Wiesbaden: Springer.

Sepp, H. R., & Embree, L. (2010). Introduction. In H. R. Sepp, & L. Embree (Eds.), *Handbook of phenomenological aesthetics* (pp. xv–xxx). Dordrecht: Springer.

Sharzer, G. (2012). A critique of localist political economy and urban agriculture. *Historical Materialism, 20*(4), 75–114.

Sherfey, P. (2011). *Managing otherness: Segregation, sociality, and the planning of a sustainable Helsingborg.* Lund University Publications.

Sherfey, P. (2020). Odla tillsammans: Att rädda världen och skapa ett 'bi-tydelsefullt' vi. *Budkavlen: tidskrift för etnologi och folkloristik, 99,* 144–169. doi:https://doi.org/10.37447/bk.99539

Silomon-Pflug, F., & Heeg, S. (2013). Neoliberale Neuordnung städtischer Verwaltungen am Beispiel des Liegenschaftsfonds Berlin. *Geographische Zeitschrift, 101*(3/4), 184–200.

Simpson, L. B. (2014). Land as pedagogy: Nishnaabeg intelligence and rebellious transformation. *Decolonization: Indigeneity, Education & Society, 3*(3), 1–25.

Skålén, P., Fellesson, M., & Fougère, M. (2006). The governmentality of marketing discourse. *Scandinavian Journal of Management, 22*(4), 275–291.

Smit, J., Ratta, A., & Nasr, J. (1996). *Urban agriculture: Food, jobs, and sustainable cities.* New York: UNDP.

Stahre, U. (1999). *Den alternativa staden: Stockholms stadsomvandling och byalags-rörelsen.* Stockholm: Stockholmia.

Standing, G. (2015). The precariat and class struggle. *Revista Crítica de Ciências Sociais Annual Review, 7*, 3–16.

Stephenson-Abetz, J. (2012). Everyday activism as a dialogic practice: Narratives of feminist daughters. *Women's Studies in Communication, 35*(1), 96–117.

Sumner, S., Law, G., & Cini, A. (2018). Why we love bees and hate wasps. *Ecological Entomology, 43*, 836–845.

Sunderland, P. L., & Denny, R. M. (2007). *Doing anthropology in consumer research.* Routledge.

Sundgren, G. (2002). Folkbildning och folkbildningsforskning. *Utbildning & Demokrati, 11*(2), pp. 5–14.

Tjora, A. H. (2006). Writing small discoveries: An exploration of fresh observers' observations. *Qualitative Research, 6*(4), 429–451.

Tocqueville, A., & Beaumont, G. (1833). *Du système pénitentiaire aux États-Unis et de son application en France.* Paris: Imprimerie de H. Fournier et Cie.

Tornaghi, C., & Van Dyck, B. (2015). Research-informed gardening activism: Steering the public food and land agenda. *Local Environment: The International Journal of Justice and Sustainability, 20*(10), 1247–1264.

Trumpy, A. (2008). Subject to negotiation: The mechanisms behind co-optation and corporate reform. *Social Problems, 55*(4), 480–500.

Tsing, A. L. (2012). Contaminated diversity in 'slow disturbance': Potential collaborators for a liveable Earth. *RCC Perspectives, 9*, 95–97.

Tsing, A. L. (2015). *The mushroom at the end of the world: On the possibility of life in capitalist ruins.* Princeton, NJ: Princeton University Press.

Turner, B., Henryks, J., & Pearson, D. (Eds.). (2011). Special Issue on community gardens. *Local Environment: The International Journal of Justice and Sustainability, 16*(6).

Vallström, M. (2014). Berättelser om plats, platsen som berättelse. In M. Vallström (Ed.), *När verkligheten inte stämmer med kartan: Lokala förutsättningar för hållbar utveckling* (pp. 57–98). Lund: Nordic Academic Press.

van Veenhuizen, R. (Ed.). (2006). *Cities farming for the future: Urban agriculture for green and productive cities.* Ottawa: RUAF Foundation, IDRC, IIRR.

Varela, F., Thompson, E., & Rosch, E. (2016). *The embodied mind: cognitive science and human experience.* Cambridge, MA: MIT Press.

Villace, B., Labajos, L., Aceituno-Mata, L., Morales, R., & Pardo de Santayana, M. (2014). La naturaleza cercana. Huertos urbanos colectivos madrileños. *Ambienta, 107*, 54–73.

Vivienne, S., & Burgess, J. (2012). The digital storyteller's stage: Queer everyday activists negotiating privacy and publicness. *Journal of Broadcasting & Electronic Media, 56*(3), 362–377.

Wakefield, S., Yeudall, F., Taron, C., Reynolds, J., & Skinner, A. (2007). Growing urban health: Community gardening in South-East Toronto. *Health Promotion International, 22*(2), 92–101.

Wenger, É. (1998). *Communities of practice: Learning, meaning, and identity.* Cambridge University Press.

Wenger, É., McDermott, R., & Snyder, W. M. (2002). *Cultivating communities of practice.* Harvard Business Press.

Yates, L. (2015). Everyday politics, social practices and movement networks: Daily life in Barcelona's social centres. *British Journal of Sociology, 66*(2), 236–258.

Yúdice, G. (2003). *The expediency of culture: Uses of culture in the global era.* Durham, N.C.: Duke University Press.

Zackariasson, M. (2006). *Viljan att förändra världen: Politiskt engagemang hos unga i den globala rättviserörelsen.* Umeå: Boréa bokförlag.

Zembylas, M. (2013). Mobilizing 'implicit activisms' in schools through practices of critical emotional reflexivity. *Teaching Education, 24*(1), 84–96.

Zwanzig, A. (2012). *Gemeinschaftsgärtnern mit Dementen: Potenziale für eine innovative Altenpolitik in Berlin.* München: GRIN Verlag.

Södertörn Doctoral Dissertations

1. Jolanta Aidukaite, *The Emergence of the Post-Socialist Welfare State: The case of the Baltic States: Estonia, Latvia and Lithuania*, 2004

2. Xavier Fraudet, *Politique étrangère française en mer Baltique (1871–1914): de l'exclusion à l'affirmation*, 2005

3. Piotr Wawrzeniuk, *Confessional Civilising in Ukraine: The Bishop Iosyf Shumliansky and the Introduction of Reforms in the Diocese of Lviv 1668–1708*, 2005

4. Andrej Kotljarchuk, *In the Shadows of Poland and Russia: The Grand Duchy of Lithuania and Sweden in the European Crisis of the mid-17th Century*, 2006

5. Håkan Blomqvist, *Nation, ras och civilisation i svensk arbetarrörelse före nazismen*, 2006

6. Karin S Lindelöf, *Om vi nu ska bli som Europa: Könsskapande och normalitet bland unga kvinnor i transitionens Polen*, 2006

7. Andrew Stickley. *On Interpersonal Violence in Russia in the Present and the Past: A Sociological Study*, 2006

8. Arne Ek, *Att konstruera en uppslutning kring den enda vägen: Om folkrörelsers modernisering i skuggan av det Östeuropeiska systemskiftet*, 2006

9. Agnes Ers, *I mänsklighetens namn: En etnologisk studie av ett svenskt biståndsprojekt i Rumänien*, 2006

10. Johnny Rodin, *Rethinking Russian Federalism: The Politics of Intergovernmental Relations and Federal Reforms at the Turn of the Millennium*, 2006

11. Kristian Petrov, *Tillbaka till framtiden: Modernitet, postmodernitet och generationsidentitet i Gorbačevs glasnost' och perestrojka*, 2006

12. Sophie Söderholm Werkö, *Patient patients? Achieving Patient Empowerment through Active Participation, Increased Knowledge and Organisation*, 2008

13. Peter Bötker, *Leviatan i arkipelagen: Staten, förvaltningen och samhället. Fallet Estland*, 2007

14. Matilda Dahl, *States under scrutiny: International organizations, transformation and the construction of progress*, 2007

15. Margrethe B. Søvik, *Support, resistance and pragmatism: An examination of motivation in language policy in Kharkiv*, Ukraine, 2007

16. Yulia Gradskova, *Soviet People with female Bodies: Performing beauty and maternity in Soviet Russia in the mid 1930–1960s*, 2007

17. Renata Ingbrant, *From Her Point of View: Woman's Anti-World in the Poetry of Anna Świrszczyńska*, 2007

18. Johan Eellend, *Cultivating the Rural Citizen: Modernity, Agrarianism and Citizenship in Late Tsarist Estonia*, 2007

19. Petra Garberding, *Musik och politik i skuggan av nazismen: Kurt Atterberg och de svensk-tyska musikrelationerna*, 2007

20. Aleksei Semenenko, *Hamlet the Sign: Russian Translations of Hamlet and Literary Canon Formation*, 2007

21. Vytautas Petronis, *Constructing Lithuania: Ethnic Mapping in the Tsarist Russia, ca. 1800–1914*, 2007

22. Akvile Motiejunaite, *Female employment, gender roles, and attitudes: The Baltic countries in a broader context*, 2008

23. Tove Lindén, *Explaining Civil Society Core Activism in Post-Soviet Latvia*, 2008

24. Pelle Åberg, *Translating Popular Education: Civil Society Cooperation between Sweden and Estonia*, 2008

25. Anders Nordström, *The Interactive Dynamics of Regulation: Exploring the Council of Europe's monitoring of Ukraine*, 2008

26. Fredrik Doeser, *In Search of Security After the Collapse of the Soviet Union: Foreign Policy Change in Denmark, Finland and Sweden, 1988–1993*, 2008

27. Zhanna Kravchenko. *Family (versus) Policy: Combining Work and Care in Russia and Sweden*, 2008

28. Rein Jüriado, *Learning within and between public-private partnerships*, 2008

29. Elin Boalt, *Ecology and evolution of tolerance in two cruciferous species*, 2008

30. Lars Forsberg, *Genetic Aspects of Sexual Selection and Mate Choice in Salmonids*, 2008

31. Eglė Rindzevičiūtė, *Constructing Soviet Cultural Policy: Cybernetics and Governance in Lithuania after World War II*, 2008

32. Joakim Philipson, *The Purpose of Evolution: 'struggle for existence' in the Russian-Jewish press 1860–1900*, 2008

33. Sofie Bedford, *Islamic activism in Azerbaijan: Repression and mobilization in a post-Soviet context*, 2009

34. Tommy Larsson Segerlind, *Team Entrepreneurship: A process analysis of the venture team and the venture team roles in relation to the innovation process*, 2009

35. Jenny Svensson, *The Regulation of Rule-Following: Imitation and Soft Regulation in the European Union*, 2009

36. Stefan Hallgren, *Brain Aromatase in the guppy, Poecilia reticulate: Distribution, control and role in behavior*, 2009

37. Karin Ellencrona, *Functional characterization of interactions between the flavivirus NS5 protein and PDZ proteins of the mammalian host*, 2009

38. Makiko Kanematsu, *Saga och verklighet: Barnboksproduktion i det postsovjetiska Lettland*, 2009

39. Daniel Lindvall, *The Limits of the European Vision in Bosnia and Herzegovina: An Analysis of the Police Reform Negotiations*, 2009

40. Charlotta Hillerdal, *People in Between – Ethnicity and Material Identity: A New Approach to Deconstructed Concepts*, 2009

41. Jonna Bornemark, *Kunskapens gräns – gränsens vetande*, 2009

42. Adolphine G. Kateka, *Co-Management Challenges in the Lake Victoria Fisheries: A Context Approach*, 2010

43. René León Rosales, *Vid framtidens hitersta gräns: Om pojkar och elevpositioner i en multietnisk skola*, 2010

44. Simon Larsson, *Intelligensaristokrater och arkivmartyrer: Normerna för vetenskaplig skicklighet i svensk historieforskning 1900–1945*, 2010

45. Håkan Lättman, *Studies on spatial and temporal distributions of epiphytic lichens*, 2010

46. Alia Jaensson, *Pheromonal mediated behaviour and endocrine response in salmonids: The impact of cypermethrin, copper, and glyphosate*, 2010

47. Michael Wigerius, *Roles of mammalian Scribble in polarity signaling, virus offense and cell-fate determination*, 2010

48. Anna Hedtjärn Wester, *Män i kostym: Prinsar, konstnärer och tegelbärare vid sekelskiftet 1900*, 2010

49. Magnus Linnarsson, *Postgång på växlande villkor: Det svenska postväsendets organisation under stormaktstiden*, 2010

50. Barbara Kunz, *Kind words, cruise missiles and everything in between: A neoclassical realist study of the use of power resources in U.S. policies towards Poland, Ukraine and Belarus 1989–2008*, 2010

51. Anders Bartonek, *Philosophie im Konjunktiv: Nichtidentität als Ort der Möglichkeit des Utopischen in der negativen Dialektik Theodor W. Adornos*, 2010

52. Carl Cederberg, *Resaying the Human: Levinas Beyond Humanism and Antihumanism*, 2010

53. Johanna Ringarp, *Professionens problematik: Lärarkårens kommunalisering och välfärdsstatens förvandling*, 2011

54. Sofi Gerber, *Öst är Väst men Väst är bäst: Östtysk identitetsformering i det förenade Tyskland*, 2011

55. Susanna Sjödin Lindenskoug, *Manlighetens bortre gräns: Tidelagsrättegångar i Livland åren 1685–1709*, 2011

56. Dominika Polanska, *The emergence of enclaves of wealth and poverty: A sociological study of residential differentiation in post-communist Poland*, 2011

57. Christina Douglas, *Kärlek per korrespondens: Två förlovade par under andra hälften av 1800-talet*, 2011

58. Fred Saunders, *The Politics of People – Not just Mangroves and Monkeys: A study of the theory and practice of community-based management of natural resources in Zanzibar*, 2011

59. Anna Rosengren, *Åldrandet och språket: En språkhistorisk analys av hög ålder och åldrande i Sverige cirka 1875–1975*, 2011

60. Emelie Lilliefeldt, *European Party Politics and Gender: Configuring Gender-Balanced Parliamentary Presence*, 2011

61. Ola Svenonius, *Sensitising Urban Transport Security: Surveillance and Policing in Berlin, Stockholm, and Warsaw*, 2011

62. Andreas Johansson, *Dissenting Democrats: Nation and Democracy in the Republic of Moldova*, 2011

63. Wessam Melik, *Molecular characterization of the Tick-borne encephalitis virus: Environments and replication*, 2012

64. Steffen Werther, *SS-Vision und Grenzland-Realität: Vom Umgang dänischer und „volksdeutscher" Nationalsozialisten in Sønderjylland mit der „großgermanischen" Ideologie der SS*, 2012

65. Peter Jakobsson, *Öppenhetsindustrin*, 2012

66. Kristin Ilves, *Seaward Landward: Investigations on the archaeological source value of the landing site category in the Baltic Sea region*, 2012

67. Anne Kaun, *Civic Experiences and Public Connection: Media and Young People in Estonia*, 2012

68. Anna Tessmann, *On the Good Faith: A Fourfold Discursive Construction of Zoroastripanism in Contemporary Russia*, 2012

69. Jonas Lindström, *Drömmen om den nya staden: Stadsförnyelse i det postsovjetisk Riga*, 2012

70. Maria Wolrath Söderberg, *Topos som meningsskapare: Retorikens topiska perspektiv på tänkande och lärande genom argumentation*, 2012

71. Linus Andersson, *Alternativ television: Former av kritik i konstnärlig TV-produktion*, 2012

72. Håkan Lättman, *Studies on spatial and temporal distributions of epiphytic lichens*, 2012

73. Fredrik Stiernstedt, Mediearbete i mediehuset: Produktion i förändring på MTG-radio, 2013

74. Jessica Moberg, *Piety, Intimacy and Mobility: A Case Study of Charismatic Christianity in Present-day Stockholm*, 2013

75. Elisabeth Hemby, *Historiemåleri och bilder av vardag: Tatjana Nazarenkos konstnärskap i 1970-talets Sovjet*, 2013

76. Tanya Jukkala, *Suicide in Russia: A macro-sociological study*, 2013

77. Maria Nyman, *Resandets gränser: Svenska resenärers skildringar av Ryssland under 1700-talet*, 2013

78. Beate Feldmann Eellend, *Visionära planer och vardagliga praktiker: Postmilitära landskap i Östersjöområdet*, 2013

79. Emma Lind, *Genetic response to pollution in sticklebacks: Natural selection in the wild*, 2013

80. Anne Ross Solberg, *The Mahdi wears Armani: An analysis of the Harun Yahya enterprise*, 2013

81. Nikolay Zakharov, *Attaining Whiteness: A Sociological Study of Race and Racialization in Russia*, 2013

82. Anna Kharkina, *From Kinship to Global Brand: The Discourse on Culture in Nordic Cooperation after World War II*, 2013

83. Florence Fröhlig, *A painful legacy of World War II: Nazi forced enlistment: Alsatian/ Mosellan Prisoners of war and the Soviet Prison Camp of Tambov*, 2013

84. Oskar Henriksson, *Genetic connectivity of fish in the Western Indian Ocean*, 2013

85. Hans Geir Aasmundsen, *Pentecostalism, Globalisation and Society in Contemporary Argentina*, 2013

86. Anna McWilliams, *An Archaeology of the Iron Curtain: Material and Metaphor*, 2013

87. Anna Danielsson, *On the power of informal economies and the informal economies of power: Rethinking informality, resilience and violence in Kosovo*, 2014

88. Carina Guyard, *Kommunikationsarbete på distans*, 2014

89. Sofia Norling, *Mot "väst": Om vetenskap, politik och transformation i Polen 1989– 2011*, 2014

90. Markus Huss, *Motståndets akustik: Språk och (o)ljud hos Peter Weiss 1946–1960*, 2014

91. Ann-Christin Randahl, *Strategiska skribenter: Skrivprocesser i fysik och svenska*, 2014

92. Péter Balogh, *Perpetual borders: German-Polish cross-border contacts in the Szczecin area*, 2014

93. Erika Lundell, *Förkroppsligad fiktion och fiktionaliserade kroppar: Levande rollspel i Östersjöregionen*, 2014

94. Henriette Cederlöf, *Alien Places in Late Soviet Science Fiction: The "Unexpected Encounters" of Arkady and Boris Strugatsky as Novels and Films*, 2014

95. Niklas Eriksson, *Urbanism Under Sail: An archaeology of fluit ships in early modern everyday life*, 2014

96. Signe Opermann, *Generational Use of News Media in Estonia: Media Access, Spatial Orientations and Discursive Characteristics of the News Media*, 2014

97. Liudmila Voronova, *Gendering in political journalism: A comparative study of Russia and Sweden*, 2014

98. Ekaterina Kalinina, *Mediated Post-Soviet Nostalgia*, 2014

99. Anders E. B. Blomqvist, *Economic Natonalizing in the Ethnic Borderlands of Hungary and Romania: Inclusion, Exclusion and Annihilation in Szatmár/Satu-Mare, 1867– 1944*, 2014

100. Ann-Judith Rabenschlag, *Völkerfreundschaft nach Bedarf: Ausländische Arbeitskräfte in der Wahrnehmung von Staat und Bevölkerung der DDR*, 2014

101. Yuliya Yurchuck, *Ukrainian Nationalists and the Ukrainian Insurgent Army in Post-Soviet Ukraine*, 2014

102. Hanna Sofia Rehnberg, *Organisationer berättar: Narrativitet som resurs i strategisk kommunikation*, 2014

103. Jaakko Turunen, *Semiotics of Politics: Dialogicality of Parliamentary Talk*, 2015

104. Iveta Jurkane-Hobein, *I Imagine You Here Now: Relationship Maintenance Strategies in Long-Distance Intimate Relationships*, 2015

105. Katharina Wesolowski, *Maybe baby? Reproductive behaviour, fertility intentions, and family policies in post-communist countries, with a special focus on Ukraine*, 2015

106. Ann af Burén, *Living Simultaneity: On religion among semi-secular Swedes*, 2015

107. Larissa Mickwitz, *En reformerad lärare: Konstruktionen av en professionell och betygssättande lärare i skolpolitik och skolpraktik*, 2015

108. Daniel Wojahn, *Språkaktivism: Diskussioner om feministiska språkförändringar i Sverige från 1960-talet till 2015*, 2015

109. Hélène Edberg, *Kreativt skrivande för kritiskt tänkande: En fallstudie av studenters arbete med kritisk metareflektion*, 2015

110. Kristina Volkova, *Fishy Behavior: Persistent effects of early-life exposure to 17α-ethinylestradiol*, 2015

111. Björn Sjöstrand, *Att tänka det tekniska: En studie i Derridas teknikfilosofi*, 2015

112. Håkan Forsberg, *Kampen om eleverna: Gymnasiefältet och skolmarknadens framväxt i Stockholm, 1987–2011*, 2015

113. Johan Stake, *Essays on quality evaluation and bidding behavior in public procurement auctions*, 2015

114. Martin Gunnarson, *Please Be Patient: A Cultural Phenomenological Study of Haemodialysis and Kidney Transplantation Care*, 2016

115. Nasim Reyhanian Caspillo, *Studies of alterations in behavior and fertility in ethinyl estradiol-exposed zebrafish and search for related biomarkers*, 2016

116. Pernilla Andersson, *The Responsible Business Person: Studies of Business Education for Sustainability*, 2016

117. Kim Silow Kallenberg, *Gränsland: Svensk ungdomsvård mellan vård och straff*, 2016

118. Sari Vuorenpää, *Literacitet genom interaction*, 2016

119. Francesco Zavatti, *Writing History in a Propaganda Institute: Political Power and Network Dynamics in Communist Romania*, 2016

120. Cecilia Annell, *Begärets politiska potential: Feministiska motståndsstrategier i Elin Wägners 'Pennskaftet', Gabriele Reuters 'Aus guter Familie', Hilma Angered-Strandbergs 'Lydia Vik' och Grete Meisel-Hess 'Die Intellektuellen'*, 2016

121. Marco Nase, *Academics and Politics: Northern European Area Studies at Greifswald University, 1917–1992*, 2016

122. Jenni Rinne, *Searching for Authentic Living Through Native Faith – The Maausk movement in Estonia*, 2016

123. Petra Werner, *Ett medialt museum: Lärandets estetik i svensk television 1956–1969*, 2016

124. Ramona Rat, *Un-common Sociality: Thinking sociality with Levinas*, 2016

125. Petter Thureborn, *Microbial ecosystem functions along the steep oxygen gradient of the Landsort Deep, Baltic Sea*, 2016

126. Kajsa-Stina Benulic, *A Beef with Meat Media and audience framings of environmentally unsustainable production and consumption*, 2016

127. Naveed Asghar, *Ticks and Tick-borne Encephalitis Virus – From nature to infection*, 2016

128. Linn Rabe, *Participation and legitimacy: Actor involvement for nature conservation*, 2017

129. Maryam Adjam, *Minnesspår: Hågkomstens rum och rörelse i skuggan av en flykt*, 2017

130. Kim West, *The Exhibitionary Complex: Exhibition, Apparatus and Media from Kulturhuset to the Centre Pompidou, 1963–1977*, 2017

131. Ekaterina Tarasova, *Anti-nuclear Movements in Discursive and Political Contexts: Between expert voices and local protests*, 2017

132. Sanja Obrenović Johansson, *Från kombifeminism till rörelse: Kvinnlig serbisk organisering i förändring*, 2017

133. Michał Salamonik, *In Their Majesties' Service: The Career of Francesco De Gratta (1613–1676) as a Royal Servant and Trader in Gdańsk*, 2017

134. Jenny Ingridsdotter, *The Promises of the Free World: Postsocialist Experience in Argentina and the Making of Migrants, Race, and Coloniality*, 2017

135. Julia Malitska, *Negotiating Imperial Rule: Colonists and Marriage in the Nineteenth century Black Sea Steppe*, 2017

136. Natalya Yakusheva, *Parks, Policies and People: Nature Conservation Governance in Post-Socialist EU Countries*, 2017

137. Martin Kellner, *Selective Serotonin Re-uptake Inhibitors in the Environment: Effects of Citalopram on Fish Behaviour*, 2017

138. Krystof Kasprzak, *Vara – Framträdande – Värld: Fenomenets negativitet hos Martin Heidegger, Jan Patočka och Eugen Fink*, 2017

139. Alberto Frigo, *Life-stowing from a Digital Media Perspective: Past, Present and Future*, 2017

140. Maarja Saar, *The Answers You Seek Will Never Be Found at Home: Reflexivity, biographical narratives and lifestyle migration among highly-skilled Estonians*, 2017

141. Anh Mai, *Organizing for Efficiency: Essay on merger policies, independence of authorities, and technology diffusion*, 2017

142. Gustav Strandberg, *Politikens omskakning: Negativitet, samexistens och frihet i Jan Patočkas tänkande*, 2017

143. Lovisa Andén, *Litteratur och erfarenhet i Merleau-Pontys läsning av Proust, Valéry och Stendhal*, 2017

144. Fredrik Bertilsson, *Frihetstida policyskapande: Uppfostringskommissionen och de akademiska konstitutionerna 1738–1766*, 2017

145. Börjeson, Natasja, *Toxic Textiles – towards responsibility in complex supply chains*, 2017

146. Julia Velkova, *Media Technologies in the Making – User-Driven Software and Infrastructures for computer Graphics Production*, 2017

147. Karin Jonsson, *Fångna i begreppen? Revolution, tid och politik i svensk socialistisk press 1917–1924*, 2017

148. Josefine Larsson, *Genetic Aspects of Environmental Disturbances in Marine Ecosystems – Studies of the Blue Mussel in the Baltic Sea*, 2017

149. Roman Horbyk, *Mediated Europes – Discourse and Power in Ukraine, Russia and Poland during Euromaidan*, 2017

150. Nadezda Petrusenko, *Creating the Revolutionary Heroines: The Case of Female Terrorists of the PSR (Russia, Beginning of the 20th Century)*, 2017

151. Rahel Kuflu, *Bröder emellan: Identitetsformering i det koloniserade Eritrea*, 2018

152. Karin Edberg, *Energilandskap i förändring: Inramningar av kontroversiella lokaliseringar på norra Gotland*, 2018

153. Rebecka Thor, *Beyond the Witness: Holocaust Representation and the Testimony of Images – Three films by Yael Hersonski, Harun Farocki, and Eyal Sivan*, 2018

154. Maria Lönn, *Bruten vithet: Om den ryska femininitetens sinnliga och temporala villkor*, 2018

155. Tove Porseryd, *Endocrine Disruption in Fish: Effects of 17α-ethinylestradiol exposure on non-reproductive behavior, fertility and brain and testis transcriptome*, 2018

156. Marcel Mangold, *Securing the working democracy: Inventive arrangements to guarantee circulation and the emergence of democracy policy*, 2018

157. Matilda Tudor, *Desire Lines: Towards a Queer Digital Media Phenomenology*, 2018

158. Martin Andersson, *Migration i 1600-talets Sverige: Älvsborgs lösen 1613–1618*, 2018

159. Johanna Pettersson, *What's in a Line? Making Sovereignty through Border Policy*, 2018

160. Irina Seits, *Architectures of Life-Building in the Twentieth Century: Russia, Germany, Sweden*, 2018

161. Alexander Stagnell, *The Ambassador's Letter: On the Less Than Nothing of Diplomacy*, 2019

162. Mari Zetterqvist Blokhuis, *Interaction Between Rider, Horse and Equestrian Trainer – A Challenging Puzzle*, 2019

163. Robin Samuelsson, *Play, Culture and Learning: Studies of Second-Language and Conceptual Development in Swedish Preschools*, 2019

164. Ralph Tafon, *Analyzing the "Dark Side" of Marine Spatial Planning – A study of domination, empowerment and freedom (or power* in, of *and* on *planning) through theories of discourse and power*, 2019

165. Ingela Visuri, *Varieties of Supernatural Experience: The case of high-functioning autism*, 2019

166. Mathilde Rehnlund, *Getting the transport right – for what? What transport policy can tell us about the construction of sustainability*, 2019

167. Oscar Törnqvist, *Röster från ingenmansland: En identitetsarkeologi i ett maritimt mellanrum*, 2019

168. Elise Remling, *Adaptation, now? Exploring the Politics of Climate Adaptation through Post-structuralist Discourse Theory*, 2019

169. Eva Karlberg, *Organizing the Voice of Women: A study of the Polish and Swedish women's movements' adaptation to international structures*, 2019

170. Maria Pröckl, *Tyngd, sväng och empatisk timing – förskollärares kroppsliga kunskaper*, 2020

171. Adrià Alcoverro, *The University and the Demand for Knowledge-based Growth The hegemonic struggle for the future of Higher Education Institutions in Finland and Estonia*, 2020

172. Ingrid Forsler, *Enabling Media: Infrastructures, imaginaries and cultural techniques in Swedish and Estonian visual arts education*, 2020

173. Johan Sehlberg, *Of Affliction: The Experience of Thought in Gilles Deleuze by way of Marcel Proust*, 2020

174. Renat Bekkin, *People of reliable loyalty…: Muftiates and the State in Modern Russia*, 2020

175. Olena Podolian, *The Challenge of 'Stateness' in Estonia and Ukraine: The international dimension a quarter of a century into independence*, 2020

176. Patrick Seniuk, *Encountering Depression In-Depth: An existential-phenomenological approach to selfhood, depression, and psychiatric practice*, 2020

177. Vasileios Petrogiannis, *European Mobility and Spatial Belongings: Greek and Latvian migrants in Sweden*, 2020

178. Lena Norbäck Ivarsson, *Tracing environmental change and human impact as recorded in sediments from coastal areas of the northwestern Baltic Proper*, 2020

179. Sara Persson, *Corporate Hegemony through Sustainability – A study of sustainability standards and CSR practices as tools to demobilise community resistance in the Albanian oil industry*, 2020

180. Juliana Porsani, *Livelihood Implications of Large-Scale Land Concessions in Mozambique: A case of family farmers' endurance*, 2020

181. Anders Backlund, *Isolating the Radical Right – Coalition Formation and Policy Adaptation in Sweden*, 2020

182. Nina Carlsson, *One Nation, One Language? National minority and Indigenous recognition in the politics of immigrant integration*, 2021

183. Erik Gråd, *Nudges, Prosocial Preferences & Behavior: Essays in Behavioral Economics*, 2021

184. Anna Enström, *Sinnesstämning, skratt och hypokondri: Om estetisk erfarenhet i Kants tredje Kritik*, 2021

185. Michelle Rydback, *Healthcare Service Marketing in Medical Tourism – An Emerging Market Study*, 2021

186. Fredrik Jahnke, *Toleransens altare och undvikandets hänsynsfullhet – Religion och meningsskapande bland svenska grundskoleelever*, 2021

187. Benny Berggren Newton, *Business Basics – A Grounded Theory for Managing Ethical Behavior in Sales Organizations*, 2021

188. Gabriel Itkes-Sznap, *Nollpunkten. Precisionens betydelse hos Witold Gombrowicz, Inger Christensen och Herta Müller*, 2021

189. Oscar Svanelid Medina, *Att forma tillvaron: Konstruktivism som konstnärligt yrkesarbete hos Geraldo de Barros, Lygia Pape och Lygia Clark*, 2021

190. Anna-Karin Selberg, *Politics and Truth: Heidegger, Arendt and The Modern Political Lie*, 2021

191. Camilla Larsson, *Framträdanden: Performativitetsteoretiska tolkningar av Tadeusz Kantors konstnärskap*, 2021

192. Raili Uibo, *"And I don't know who we really are to each other": Queers doing close relationships in Estonia*, 2021

193. Ignė Stalmokaitė, *New Tides in Shipping: Studying incumbent firms in maritime energy transitions*, 2021

194. Mani Shutzberg, *Tricks of the Medical Trade: Cunning in the Age of Bureaucratic Austerity*, 2021

195. Patrik Höglund, *Skeppssamhället: Rang, roller och status på örlogsskepp under 1600-talet*, 2021

196. Philipp Seuferling, *Media and the refugee camp: The historical making of space, time, and politics in the modern refugee regime*, 2021

197. Johan Sandén, *Närbyråkrater och digitaliseringar: Hur lärares arbete formas av tids-strukturer*, 2021

198. Ulrika Nemeth, *Det kritiska uppdraget: Diskurser och praktiker i gymnasieskolans svenskundervisning*, 2021

199. Helena Löfgren, *Det legitima ägandet: Politiska konstruktioner av allmännyttans privatisering i Stockholms stad 1990–2015*, 2021

200. Vasileios Kitsos, *Urban policies for a contemporary periphery: Insights from eastern Russia*, 2022

201. Jenny Gustafsson, *Drömmen om en gränslös fred: Världsmedborgarrörelsens reaktopi, 1949–1968*, 2022

202. Oscar von Seth, *Outsiders and Others: Queer Friendships in Novels by Hermann Hesse*, 2022

203. Kristin Halverson, *Tools of the Trade: Medical Devices and Practice in Sweden and Denmark, 1855–1897*, 2022

204. Henrik Ohlsson, *Facing Nature: Cultivating Experience in the Nature Connection Movement*, 2022

205. Mirey Gorgis, *Allt är våld: En undersökning av det moderna våldsbegreppet*, 2022

206. Mats Dahllöv, *Det absoluta och det gemensamma: Benjamin Höijers konstfilosofi*, 2022

207. Anton Poikolainen Rosén, *Noticing Nature: Exploring More Than Human-Centred Design in Urban Farming*, 2022

208. Sophie Landwehr Sydow, *Makers, Materials and Machines: Understanding Experience and Situated Embodied Practice at the Makerspace*, 2022

209. Simon Magnusson, *Boosting young citizens' deontic status: Interactional allocation of rights-to-decide in participatory democracy meetings*, 2022

210. Marie Jonsson, *Vad vilja vegetarianerna? En undersökning av den svenska vegetarismen 1900–1935*, 2022

211. Birgitta Ekblom, *Härskarhyllning och påverkan: Panegyriken kring tronskiftet 1697 i det svenska Östersjöväldet*, 2022

212. Joanna Mellquist, *Policy Professionals in Civil Society Organizations: Struggling for Influence*, 2022

213. David Birksjö, *Innovative Security Business – Innovation, Standardization and ndustry Dynamics in the Swedish Security Sector, 1992–2012*, 2023

214. Roman Privalov, *After space utopia: Post-Soviet Russia and futures in space*, 2023

215. Martin Johansson, *De nordiska lekarna: Grannlandsrelationen i pressen under olympiska vinterspel*, 2023

216. Anna Bark Persson, *Steel as the Answer? Viking Bodies, Power, and Masculinity in Anglophone Fantasy Literature 2006–2016*, 2023

217. Josefin Hägglund, *Demokratins stridslinjer: Carl Lindhagen och politikens omvandling, 1896–1923*, 2023

218. Lovisa Olsson, *I vinst och förlust: Köpmäns nätverk i 1500-talets Östersjöstäder*, 2023

219. Kateryna Zorya, *The Government Used to Hide the Truth, But Now We Can Speak: Contemporary Esotericism in Ukraine 1986–2014*, 2023

220. Tony Blomqvist Mickelsson, *A Nordic sport social work in the context of refugee reception*, 2023

221. Ola Luthman, *Searching for sustainable aquaculture governance: A focus on ambitions and experience*, 2023

222. Emma Kihl, *Äventyrliga utföranden: En läsning av Agneta Enckells dikter med Isabelle Stengers kosmopolitik*, 2023

223. Cagla Demirel, *Analyzing Competitive Victimhood: Narratives of recognition and non-recognition in the pursuit of reconciliation*, 2023

224. Joel Odebrant, *Spår, kropp, tid: En undersökning av den måleriska gestens materialitet 1952–1965*, 2024

225. Li Xiaoying, *Energy Efficiency in Buildings in the Baltic States and the Nordic Countries*, 2024

226. Thérèse Janzén, *Ticks – Ecology, New Hazards, and Relevance for Public Health*, 2024

227. Paul Sherfey, *Cultivating Responsible Citizenship: Collective Gardens at the Periphery of Neoliberal Urban Norms*, 2024

www.ingramcontent.com/pod-product-compliance
Lightning Source LLC
LaVergne TN
LVHW010816200726
843507LV00003B/615